GENESIS, A ROYAL EPIC

Genesis, A Royal Epic

Introduction, Translation, and Notes

Second Edition

LOREN R. FISHER

CASCADE *Books* • Eugene, Oregon

GENESIS, A ROYAL EPIC
Introduction, Translation, and Notes / Second Edition

Copyright © 2011 Loren R. Fisher. All rights reserved. Except for brief quotations in critical publications or reviews, no part of this book may be reproduced in any manner without prior written permission from the publisher. Write: Permissions, Wipf & Stock, 199 W. 8th Ave., Eugene, OR 97401.

Cascade Books
An Imprint of Wipf and Stock Publishers
199 W. 8th Ave., Suite 3
Eugene, OR 97401
www.wipfandstock.com

ISBN 13: 978-1-61097-301-4

Cataloging-in-Publication data:

Fisher, Loren R.
 Genesis, a royal epic : introduction, translation, and notes / Loren R. Fisher.

 Second Edition.

 xvi + 252 p. ; 23 cm. Includes bibliographical references and indexes.

 ISBN 13: 978-1-61097-301-4

 Note: First Edition 2001.

 1. Bible. O.T. Genesis—Criticism, interpretation, etc. 2. Bible. O.T. Genesis. English. I. Title.

BS1233 F57 2011

Manufactured in the U.S.A.

For
Cyrus H. Gordon

Contents

Acknowledgments · ix
Preface to the Second Edition · xi
Preface to the First Edition · xiii
Abbreviations · xv

Introduction · 1
The Final Form of Genesis · 31
Part I: Genesis 1:1—11:26 · 37
Part II: Genesis 11:27—25:18 · 69
Part III: Genesis 25:19—37:1 · 117
Part IV: Genesis 37:2—50:26 · 168

Appendix 1: You Can't Tell a Book by Its Cover · 211
Appendix 2: Let There Be Light: A Scientific Approach to Genesis · 221

Bibliography · 233
Index of Ancient Documents · 239
Index of Names · 250

Acknowledgments

THIS TRANSLATION IS DEDICATED to Cyrus H. Gordon, my teacher and my friend. I have never known another person like him. His classes were always exciting, and his store of knowledge was always there to help the discussion. He is a real pioneer in Mediterranean studies. Loren Eiseley explained Charles Darwin's importance to biological history in a way that also explains Gordon's importance to Mediterranean studies. Eiseley said:

> Almost every scientific generalization is a supreme act of creative synthesis. There comes a time when an accumulation of smaller discoveries and observations can be combined in some great and comprehensive view of nature. At this point the need is not so much for increased numbers of facts as for a mind of great insight capable of taking the assembled information and rendering it intelligible. Such a synthesis represents the scientific mind at its highest point of achievement.[1]

Gordon's comprehensive view of the Mediterranean World and his synthesis has created a new and an enlightened way of approaching our search for the foundations of our culture. It is a privilege to have worked with Cyrus H. Gordon.

Stan Rummel, who studied with me at Claremont and took over the Ras Shamra Parallels project when I left Claremont, has assisted me during the preparation of this translation. I want to thank him for his help. We have worked on many of the problems of Genesis during regular meetings that were scheduled for that purpose. He has put a lot of time into this project, and this work is much better because of his help.

---

1. Eiseley, "Charles Darwin."

Acknowledgments

I also thank the members of the Hebrew Bible Seminar of the Westar Institute (the late Robert W. Funk, director) for their comments and help on translation problems. From 1987 to 1991, we met twice a year. At each meeting, Genesis and its complexities took more than their share of the time.

I extend many thanks to Dr. K. C. Hanson, Editor-in-Chief at Wipf and Stock Publishers, for his help with this second edition. His editorial work was important as usual, and his scholarly intuition and assistance has been priceless. As always, I thank my wife, Jane Sheldon, for her editorial help.

I want to thank my son, Prof. Daniel C. Fisher—who is Claude W. Hibbard Collegiate Professor at the University of Michigan and Curator of Paleontology at the University of Michigan Museum—for all of his encouragement and help, especially with Appendix II, and my conversations with Judith P. Fisher concerning the cover have been extremely rewarding. I want to thank Betty Lou Whaley for the original front cover concept. The embossed background on the cover of the first edition is an image of a gastropod mollusc (*Murex trunculus*), one of the snails used by the Phoenicians to produce a precious purple dye. It was used to dye garments for the royalty. I have used it as a symbol for this very precious Royal Epic. The following terms are interesting in that they refer to both the Phoenicians and their purple dye:

Mycenaean Greek, *Po-ni-ke*

Ugaritic, *Pwn* and *Pwt*

Hebrew, *Pûnî*

Greek, *Phoinix* and *Phoinikes*

Latin, *Punicus*

Preface to the Second Edition

THERE ARE NOT MANY changes in this second edition. The format and structure of the translation has been changed, and it is now divided into four parts:

Part I	1:1—11:26
Part II	11:27—25:18
Part III	25:19—37:1
Part IV	37:2—50:26.

Part IV has been reset to represent the prose, as opposed to epic line, structure of that section. Furthermore, the bibliography has now all been gathered to the end, and an Index of Ancient Documents has been provided to track the references in the Introduction, notes, and appendices.

Genesis is a royal epic constructed from many sources by the scribes of Jerusalem, and I suggest that this could have happened during the reign of King David. In my novel, *The Jerusalem Academy*, I try to show how this happened. I am more convinced than ever about this event. One reason for my optimism is the discovery in Jerusalem—or to be more specific in the City of David, the oldest part of Jerusalem—of a cuneiform tablet. There is a good article on this by Eilat Mazar, Wayne Horowitz, Takayoshi Oshima, and Yuval Goren.[1] Actually the tablet is just a fragment (designated Jerusalem 1), and that means we cannot say much about the content. However, by analyzing the signs carefully, the authors who studied it have determined that the scribe, who wrote this tablet, had a better hand than the two scribes who wrote tablets 285-

---

1. Mazar et al., "A Cuneiform Tablet from the Ophel in Jerusalem."

291 of the Amarna letters. The Amarna letters were sent by the ruler of Jerusalem, Abdi-Heba, to the Egyptian Pharaoh.[2] So the authors say:

> In fact, it is our impression that the scribe of Jerusalem 1 shows greater expertise than the scribes of Abdi-Heba in EA 285–290. Our conclusion, then, is that the scribe of the Jerusalem fragment seems capable of producing high-quality international-standard scribal work, a conclusion that is also supported by the shape of the fragment, as indicated by the surviving piece of the left edge, which seems to us to be closer to the Mesopotamian ideal than most tablets from the cuneiform west.[3]

This new information may not prove my view that there was a scribal school in Jerusalem before and during the Davidic monarchy, but it certainly points to a great teacher and at least two other scribes. My view is based on the fact that great centers needed and had scribal schools. In my novel, Magon of Tyre was such a scribe and a great teacher of Babylonian cuneiform.

Genesis is a wonderful collection of stories arranged in a fascinating structure. It has been and remains a most important element in western culture. The scribes who produced it should be given all the credit. I tire of hearing that otherworldly agents accomplished the great achievements of the ancient Mediterranean world. These scribes were thoughtful and talented human beings who deserve more than a Pulitzer or Nobel Prize in Literature. They may have helped each other, but this just proves the point made in the Egyptian text, *The Instruction for King Meri-Ka-Re*: "Great is a great man when his great men are great."[4]

18 April 2011
Walnut Creek, CA
Loren R. Fisher

---

2. See Moran, ed. and trans., *The Amarna Letters*, 325–34.
3. Mazar et al., "A Cuneiform Tablet from the Ophel in Jerusalem," 11.
4. John Wilson's translation in *ANET*, 415; see also *COS* 1.35 (pp. 61–65).

Preface to the First Edition

I HAVE BEEN PUBLISHING essays on the book of Genesis since 1962. I did not start this translation, however, until 1985. I finished it in 1993, and at that time, I started my historical novel, *The Jerusalem Academy* (dealing with the scribes who put Genesis together). I have now finished this novel, and since I needed to use parts of this translation in the novel, I found out that this translation works well.

During the last six years other translations have appeared by Robert Alter and Everett Fox (see "Works Consulted"). At the end of my introduction, I make some comments on these translations in a long note that I have added (note 53 at the end of the Introduction), but I was not able to use them during the time that I was working on this translation. Also during the last six years, I have discovered that this translation speaks to some very important problems for which the Alter and Fox's translations are not very helpful. This is not something that I planned. I just made a very open translation, and it has turned out to be very useful. The first problem has to do with the study of Israel's ancient history. I have referred to this problem in note 9 in the Introduction. There is now a group of scholars (N. P. Lemche, P. R. Davies, T. L. Thompson, and others) who have argued that Saul, David, Solomon, and the entire Davidic Monarchy are all just parts of a literary fiction written in Persian and Hellenistic times. In my opinion, this is a misguided effort to do away with the history of ancient Israel. My new translation of Genesis is based on the presupposition that Genesis is *The Royal Epic* of the Davidic Monarchy, and I think that the Davidic Monarchy needed the book of Genesis in order to unify Israel and Judah and to entertain the people on great occasions. Also, stories of the patriarchs and the patriarchs themselves are not much older than the monarchy. I think these stories took their form at the tombs of the

Preface to the First Edition

patriarchs, and I have shown how they are much older than Lemche and others suggest (I have dealt with this problem in *Appendix I: You Can't Tell a Book by Its Cover*).

The second problem has reminded me that my work also stands at the focal point of a much larger problem. This larger problem just resurfaced in Kansas when its State Board of Education voted effectively to exclude references to evolution from the public school curricula. To whom does my work speak? Not to the creationists, because their dogma has already closed their ears to most of what I would say, and not really to evolutionary biologists, at least as they act in that capacity. It is directed instead at the onlookers to this debate—the 'third parties who are trying to make honest sense of this conflict. People who are interested in the education of their children are entitled to some help as they listen to the old debate between the creationists and the evolutionists. They can learn something of the growth of the Genesis traditions in my novel, *The Jerusalem Academy*; but these onlookers need a very clear translation of Genesis. In this translation you will not find the word "create" or "creation." The creationists, along with some other theologians, have maintained that the word creation means "creation out of nothing." They have brought this dogma to the story. So I have not used the "C" word. I use words such as "form" or "order" (I have another essay on this problem which appears here as *Appendix II: Let There Be Light: A Scientific Approach To Genesis*).

15 Oct 2000
Willits CA
Loren Fisher

Abbreviations

AAT	An American Translation
AB	Anchor Bible (see E. A. Speiser and Marvin H. Pope in Bibliography)
AML	Ancient Mediterranean Literature
ANET	Ancient Near Eastern Texts
Buber and Rosenzweig	Die Fünf Bücher der Weisung
BWL	Babylonian Wisdom Literature, W. G. Lambert
CAD	The Assyrian Dictionary: Of the Oriental Institute of the University of Chicago
Cassuto	A Commentary on the Book of Genesis
CBQ	Catholic Biblical Quarterly
COS	The Context of Scripture, 3 vols., edited by William W. Hallo
CRST	The Claremont Ras Shamra Tablets, edited by Loren R. Fisher
EA	El Amarna tablets
Gesenius	Gesenius' Hebrew Grammar, edited by E. Kautzsch and A. E. Cowley
Gen R	Genesis Rabba (A midrash on the book of Genesis)
HTR	Harvard Theological Review
JAOS	Journal of the American Oriental Society

Abbreviations

JBL	*Journal of Biblical Literature*
JCS	*Journal of Cuneiform Studies*
JNES	*Journal of Near Eastern Studies*
JSOTSup	Journal for the Study of the Old Testament Supplement Series
JSS	*Journal of Semitic Studies*
KAI	*Kanaanäische und Aramäische Inschriften*, edited by Herbert Donner and Wolfgang Röllig
KJ	King James Version
LCL	Loeb Classical Library
MT	Masoretic Text
NEB	New English Bible
NRSV	New Revised Standard Version
PRU III/ IV	*Le Palais royal d'Ugarit*, edited by Jean Nougayrol
RSP I/II/III	*Ras Shamra Parallels*, edited by Loren R. Fisher and Stan Rummel
RSV	Revised Standard Version
Sam	Samaritan Text
Tanakh	*The Holy Scriptures*
TC Genesis	*Genesis*, JPS Torah Commentary, Nahum Sarna
UF	*Ugarit-Forschungen*
Ug V/VI	*Ugaritica* V/ VI
UT	Ugaritic text
UT	*Ugaritic Textbook*, Cyrus H. Gordon
VAB	Vorderasiatische Bibliothek
ZAW	*Zeitschrift für die alttestamentliche Wissenschaft*
LXX	Septuagint
[ ]	contains words added by the translator

Introduction

THE TRANSLATOR ALWAYS STANDS between the reader and a text, and no translator proceeds apart from some view of how to determine the meaning of the text. The Hebrew text in which Genesis was written cannot "speak for itself" to those who do not read Hebrew. The translator must help the text find its voice, and to find ways to allow the text to speak to modern readers as it once spoke to ancient readers. From the determination of the meanings of individual words, to the syntax of phrases and sentences, to the sense of paragraphs and larger units of material, the translator must constantly endeavor to convey the significance of the text to the reader.

To illustrate the role of the translator, we might turn to Gen 5:22 and 24, where I have translated a Hebrew phrase in each verse as "Enoch walked with the gods." The reader is not likely to find "the gods" in other translations, which will read simply "God." How should we account for the two different interpretations of the phrase?

In the Bible, the title "God" is often expressed by the Hebrew word *'elohim*, which is the word used in Gen 5:22 and 24. This Hebrew word is not a singular noun! The *-im* ending is plural. *'Elohim* literally signifies "gods," and when the word appears in texts outside the Bible it is always translated as a plural. However, in the Bible *'elohim* usually denotes one god, and in these cases, this translation just leaves it as Elohim. When translators of Genesis see the word *'elohim*, how can they know whether it refers to one god or any number of gods?

They could use grammar as a basis. In Gen 5:22 and 24 *'elohim* is preceded by the definite article, so that it literally reads "the *'elohim*." The translation "the gods" better conveys the grammatical sense of the text than the translation "God." Why, then, do most translators use "God" for the phrase "the 'elohim"?

Gesenius' Hebrew Grammar, the reference grammar used by most students throughout the twentieth century, shows us the reason. According to Gesenius, we should translate the plural form *'elohim* as a singular unless the speaker of the passage can be understood as a "heathen!"[1] So according to Gesenius, Enoch could walk with only one God because Enoch was not a heathen. Gesenius's expectations about the meaning of the text are shaped by theology more than grammar.

Genesis 6:9 offers another example of a man, in this case Noah, walking with "the 'elohim."[2] I have translated: "With the gods, Noah walked," where other translators perceive Noah walking with "God." Again, the difference is between the translators, not the wording of the text. Not only do other translators ignore the definite article and the plural form of the noun, they also overlook the narrative fact that Noah in Genesis 6 and Enoch in Genesis 5 live before the Flood. In the traditions inherited by the Israelites, the Flood marks a major dividing-line in human affairs, and the pre-Flood heroes were not monotheistic theologians! The point is that the grammar of the texts and their ancient contexts lead me in one direction, while an anachronistic theological presupposition leads Gesenius in another direction.

The treatment of *'elohim* illustrates the need for translators to state their basic understandings of texts and the methods they use to translate the texts. In order to clarify my own understanding of the book of Genesis, I will first consider the question of the sources of the book as it now exists. Next I will describe the kind of literature we have in the book of Genesis, which I believe is "royal" literature. Then I will discuss the structure of Genesis, which offers additional evidence about the royal nature of the material. The cycle of "burial, blessing, and birth" has special significance in royal literature, and I will show how this cycle enlarges our understanding of Genesis. As the last part of this Introduction, I will state the main characteristics of this translation.

---

1. Gesenius, §145i, p. 463.

2. For another example, note Gen 6:11 in this translation: "The earth was found corrupt before the gods . . ." This is a court scene in the assembly of the gods.

Introduction

Sources of the Book of Genesis

Early Jewish tradition (Babylonian Talmud, *Baba bathra* 14b–15a) considered Moses as the author of Genesis and the rest of the Torah or the Pentateuch (the first "five books"). The early Christians followed this Jewish tradition. Later, there were early Church Fathers who questioned the Mosaic authorship, and Medieval Jewish authors also raised the question.³ In our day, the Mosaic authorship has become an impossible view, because there are too many indications that the author(s) lived in the land west of the Jordon at a later time.⁴ During the eighteenth and nineteenth centuries, literary criticism demonstrated that the Torah was a composite from several sources, and that it was put together long after the time of Moses. I do not intend to go into great detail here concerning the sources (you can read these details in any good commentary; see the Bibliography), but I do want to give a short sketch of the development of this criticism and describe the present state of such studies. Then we can look at some new suggestions.

Jean Astruc, a French physician, separated two major documents in Genesis by using the divine names of Yahweh and Elohim. In other words, one name was used in one document/source, and the other name was used in the second source. He published his work in 1753. He was followed by others and this became known as the Old Documentary Hypothesis. The next step was called the Fragment Hypothesis. This was developed by Alexander Geddes (1800), J. S. Vater (1802), and W. M. L. de Wette (1807). By using this theory the critics could see in a book like Genesis many fragments/sources but could not account for any continuity or plan in such a book. Still later, the Supplement Hypothesis was developed by Heinrich Ewald (1831). In this theory one basic document was proposed (providing the plan), and then to this document material was added from later traditions.

In 1853 H. Hupfeld played a major role in developing the New Documentary Hypothesis. This theory, after a few years and the contributions of others, came up with four sources for the Pentateuch and put them in chronological order: P (the Priestly source), E (the Elohist), J (the Yahwist), and D (Deuteronomy). Through the work of Reuss, Graf,

---

3. E.g., Porphyry and Celsus among the Church Fathers (see Origen, *Contra Celsum* IV, 42) and Abraham Ibn Ezra among Jewish authors.

4. See Gen 12:6; 36:31; and 50:10.

Kuenen, and Wellhausen these sources were given a new order because of new dates that were assigned to them: J (850 BCE), E (750 BCE), D (622 BCE), and P (450 BCE). All of this was "set in concrete" in Julius Wellhausen's great book, *Prolegomena to the History of Ancient Israel* (1878). Since then we speak of the Wellhausen Hypothesis.

Wellhausen arranged the sources of the Pentateuch in chronological order so that he could give us a history of the development of Israel and of the religion of Israel. Since the time of Wellhausen, however, there have been many new theories. Today the picture is very unclear. Many scholars have divided documents, added new documents, or have maintained that we do not have continuous documents but rather source strata. These strata have in them old and late materials. It is not a neat system today as it was for Wellhausen. In fact, the Uppsala School in Sweden maintains that these materials were oral for so many years that it would be impossible to separate such things as J and E. So it goes. For the past thirty years scholars have been saying that there is no consensus in all of this, but they usually move along in their work as if all is well.[5]

I have learned a great deal from the research of the past, but it is not going to help much to re-date J or P or invent new sources. Today we have more information than ever before. The archaeological information that we have could have made things a lot easier for the likes of Wellhausen. In fact, we have recovered entire libraries at sites such as Ugarit/Ras Shamra. When Wellhausen discussed the ritual calendars in the Hebrew Bible (e.g., Numbers 28 and 29), he said that these belong to P and they are late. Why? Because definite dates and details in ritual calendars can only be late. But at Ugarit (ca. 1400 BCE, certainly before the time of Israel), there are many ritual texts of various kinds. If we thought like nineteenth-century critics, we would take these ritual texts and put them in chronological order, the simple ones early and the more complex ones late. These texts do have dates for some of the rituals and even detailed instructions, but this does not make them late.

---

5. Some scholars who have given up on the traditional literary criticism have actually gone ahead to something new. This is the case with John Van Seters (see Van Seters, *Abraham in History and Tradition*). His "something new" is a supplement theory. For the Abraham traditions the sources are literary not oral. There are five stages in the development of this tradition, and each stage or source supplements the earlier source. He sets it up as follows: Pre-Yahwistic first stage, Pre-Yahwistic second stage, Yahwist (exilic), Priestly (post-exilic), and Post-Priestly.

Rather the different text types functioned in different ways within the cult.[6] Wellhausen had no way of knowing such things.

One thing is very clear. Genesis is made up of several sources, and these sources are put together with a plan and with great care. I would add that the sources are not continuous, and it is an important task to find out what these sources are saying in their present context. At times it may be possible to push beyond the present context, but we do not always know enough to do this. It is also clear that there are some late additions to this book, i.e., additions from a time after the main sources were put together in their present setting.[7] In the notes to this translation, I will inform the reader when I think that we are dealing with a separate source.[8] I will also note when such decisions are just too difficult. Everyone has the right to know that in Genesis there is one source that is used in Gen 1:1—2:3 and another in 2:4—3:24; there are then two accounts of the formation of all things. If we do not know such things, we can never ask the question, "Why?" The answer to this question is more important than trying to prove that the first one is P (and therefore late) and that the second one is J (and therefore early). If one compares Israel to the other literate states of the Mediterranean world, Israel is so late on the scene that they have ready at hand all types of ideas and literary forms. In one sense, all that Israel had was late; it was available, and Israel used it very well indeed.

So why is there no movement toward a consensus?[9] Perhaps, we continue to ask the wrong questions. Are we asking the impossible? In

---

6. We will have to deal with Num 28 and 29 in a new way. See Fisher, "A New Ritual Calendar From Ugarit."

7. For an example, see Gen 32:33.

8. Gen 46:8–27 is a separate source. Some say that it is P, but it is different from other sections that are said to be P. It is best to say that it is an unknown source.

9. One reason is that there is a movement, just now, away from consensus. I do not think that this movement will succeed, but there are several scholars who date most of the traditions in the Hebrew Bible to late Persian and early Hellenistic times (including the traditions about David). Also, they reinterpret Israel's material remains as pertaining to much later times. These people see David and his monarchy as fiction. There is a good article on this matter by Knoppers, "The Vanishing Solomon: The Disappearance of the United Monarchy from recent Histories of Ancient Israel." These scholars (Philip R. Davies, Thomas L. Thompson, Niels Peter Lemche, and others) would not agree with the position taken in this introduction. For them, Genesis could not be published during the Davidic monarchy if there was no Davidic Monarchy. But this group makes a lot of very basic mistakes. For example, they try to argue that there

order to answer our usual questions as to the nature of the sources, we would need to find a complete document which was very much like one of the ones which we have proposed. Plus we would need some evidence as to where and when it was used. I doubt if we find such things in the near future. If we do, I will change my ways. For now, I think it would be interesting for us to ask some different questions, and I hope we can learn something about Genesis in asking them. Also the readers of this translation need to know something about these "different questions" in order to appreciate the notes to this translation.

Genesis as Royal Epic

What kind of literature do we have in the Book of Genesis? This is an example of a different question. This does not mean it has never been asked, but it is certainly not the primary focus of most students of Genesis.[10] Some just assume that everyone knows the answer, but this is not very realistic. Some think this is historical literature. Some think it is myth. Others say it is legend. It is possible that it contains many of these things, but most of these answers are not big enough. I think the book of Genesis was produced during the Davidic monarchy, and it was "published" by the state.[11] What we have in Genesis is a good example of royal literature.

Royal literature is a very broad term. This has its advantages and disadvantages. In talking about Genesis, I sometimes narrow the terminology to "royal epic" (meaning: literature that unites and gives identity to a people and their king). But for many the word epic is a red flag; if you use the word epic, they want you to prove that there is Homeric epic poetry in Genesis. There is a lot of poetry in Genesis, but it is never enough. Others try to show that there was originally an epic poem underlying the Genesis narratives. This may be the case, but it is very

---

is "no evidence of a Jerusalem in the LB period," but in order to say this, they have to set aside the six Amarna letters (EA 285–290) from the king of Jerusalem at that time. See Lemche, "From Patronage Society to Patronage Society," 119 n. 32.

10. This is a form-critical question. Many ask about the kind/type/genre of small units and of oral tradition; but when one asks such a question of a book it is a much more difficult question.

11. At this point, it is important to ask the question, "Did private parties 'publish' books?"

difficult to look behind the text that we have. I would maintain that the narratives in Genesis contain many epic features, themes, and structures. After all, these stories are dealing with Israel's heroic age; they deal with the ancestors of Israel's kings. In fact, the literature that deals with the ancestors and the periods down through David and Solomon is just different from the later traditions (i.e., in social customs, religion, and laws). In the notes to this translation, I will point out many epic features of these stories.

The presupposition of this introduction and of this translation is that the book of Genesis was a significant part of the royal literature of the Davidic monarchy.[12] This book was a political document of the state, and its major function was to exalt David and his monarchy, not only with his own people but also among the other states of that world. The scribes of the monarchy used many sources for this work, and certainly the literary criticism of the past has helped us to isolate many of these sources. However, the view presented here is quite different from the older criticism in that the sources that were used in this work must date from before the exile. This is obvious, if the sources were used by the scribes of the Davidic monarchy.[13] None of this can be said with dogmatic zest, but we can at this point discuss some reasons why it seems possible to see Genesis in this way.

One reason Genesis is to be seen as royal literature is that the narratives point to the later kings. In Gen 17:3–8, not only will Elohim

12. This is based upon about thirty years of work on this material (e.g., see Fisher, "The Patriarchal Cycles"). Also, note the discussion of this material by Rummel in *RSP* III (285–95). Rummel suggests that I have a lot more work to do on this topic, and this introduction aims to get at the task once again.

13. I cannot prove that we are dealing with David's scribes. Perhaps Genesis was produced during the time of Solomon or even later. But I am prepared to argue that it was pre-exilic. I have at times argued that Genesis was put together during David's time, because I want to emphasize that this is a real possibility. Robert Alter, "Introduction to the Old Testament," 30, deals with this in a more general way. He says, "The golden age of Hebrew narrative was the First Commonwealth era, when the great sequence of works from Genesis to Kings was given its initial formulation . . . most of the new Hebrew narratives created after 586 BCE are distinctly the products of a postclassical age." Benjamin Mazar adds to this conversation ("The Historical Background of the Book of Genesis," 74) when he says, "It is within reason that Genesis was given its original written form during the time when the Davidic empire was being established, and that additional supplements of later authors were only intended to help bridge the time gap for contemporary readers, and had no decisive effect on its contents or overall character."

establish a covenant with Abraham and his descendants, giving them the land of Canaan as "an everlasting holding" (which is always the case in royal land grants),[14] but in v. 6c it also says, "Kings shall come forth from you." Later in v. 16, Elohim says of Sarah, "Kings of peoples shall issue from her." Abraham and Sarah will produce kings. Who is it that wants the people to know this? It is the kings; those who trace their lines back to Abraham and Sarah. It is the kings; the ones who want to show that they are the legitimate rulers.[15] This is not the only place where such a thing is said. In Gen 35:11 Elohim says to Jacob, "Kings shall come forth from your loins." The fathers and the mothers in the Genesis narratives were the fathers and mothers of kings.

A second reason for viewing Genesis as royal literature is that the content of Genesis is what we would expect in a political document of the monarchy. Our method in all of this is comparative, and we have centuries of AML before the time of the Hebrews. The Babylonian creation story, *Enuma elish*, according to Thorkild Jacobsen, celebrates "Babylon's and Marduk's rise to rulership over a united Babylon, but projected back to mythical times and made universal. It is also an account of how the universe is ruled; how monarchy evolved and gained acceptance as a unifier of the many divine wills in the universe. It is a story of world origins and world ordering."[16] Gordon and Rendsburg stress the political nature of *Enuma elish*.[17] In this world when a powerful king like David became ruler of both Judah and Israel, the other states of that world would expect a publication from Jerusalem dealing with "world origins" and "world ordering." Jerusalem was not really interested in dealing with "world origins" (e.g., the birth of the gods), but they were interested in dealing with "world ordering" (i.e., ordering chaos and the formation of this world). In addition, Jerusalem included the stories of the fathers and mothers as mentioned in reason number one (see above). These stories were made to point to David in several ways, with the insertion of Genesis 38 being the most explicit example (see below).

---

14. Kings gave their loyal officials land grants that were "forever," but that did not mean that the grants were unconditional. One had to remain loyal.

15. Van Seters in *Abraham in History and Tradition*, 153, makes no sense to me when he says, "Nothing in Genesis suggests a concern for royal legitimation of any kind."

16. Jacobsen, *The Treasures of Darkness*, 191.

17. Gordon and Rendsburg, *The Bible and the Ancient Near East*, 43–44.

Introduction

A third reason we look at Genesis as royal literature is that the stories of the ancestors in Genesis probably were formed at the tomb and used by the kings of Israel as a part of the rituals at the royal tombs of those ancestors. We know that such rituals were important for the kings for the purpose of receiving the blessings of their ancestors.[18] To receive the blessing of such a father or patriarch meant that the king would produce an heir, and that the dynastic line would continue.

Miriam Lichtheim has an interesting discussion of how in Egypt, "it was in the context of the private tomb that writing took its first steps toward literature." Here "the autobiography was born," and it "became a truly literary product."[19] Also in her introduction to "Prose Tales," she relates that the *Story of Sinuhe* "is told in the form of the autobiography composed for the tomb . . ."[20] I relate these comments for the purpose of pointing out that my suggestions concerning the growth of literature at the tomb are not new in our studies of ancient literature. But it certainly may be new for many to think about the growth of the patriarchal cycles at the tomb. Genesis 48:15–16 is a passage that can help us introduce this subject.

The context of the blessing in Gen 48:15–16 is as follows: 1) Jacob's instructions for his burial (47:28–31); 2) Jacob's adoption of Joseph's sons (48:1–7); and 3) Jacob's blessing of Joseph which includes the blessing of Joseph's sons (48:8–20) and Jacob's gift of Shechem to Joseph (48:21–22).

---

18. There is a growing bibliography on the cult of the dead. Note the following: Lewis, *Cults of the Dead in Ancient Israel and Ugarit*; also his article "The Ancestral Estate in 2 Samuel 14:16"; Bloch-Smith, *Judahite Burial Practices and Beliefs about the Dead*; also her review of Lewis' book, and her article "The Cult of the Dead in Judah: Interpreting the Material Remains"; Smith, "The Invocation of Deceased Ancestors in Psalm 49:12c"; and Murphy, "Ideologies, Rites and Rituals: A View of Prepalatial Minoan Tholoi." Schmidt, *Israel's Beneficent Dead*, presents a different view of the cult of the dead, at odds with these authors. For details on these and others see the Bibliography.

19. Lichtheim, *Ancient Egyptian Literature*, vol. 1, 3–4.

20. Ibid., 211.

Genesis, a Royal Epic

Genesis 48:15–16

15 He[21] blessed Joseph.[22]
He said:[23] "The God before whom my fathers, Abraham and Isaac, walked, the God who has been my shepherd from my birth until this day,[24] **16** the Messenger who has delivered me from all harm, may he bless these young men. My name and the names of my fathers, Abraham and Isaac, shall be called forth by them.[25] They will become a multitude in the land."

The most important part of this passage for us is v. 16b. I do not know of any translation that does it this way, and yet this is a very easy translation. These "young men" shall call forth the names of the fathers at the tomb. Then they will receive the blessing; they will become a multitude. But most just do not understand what it means "to call forth" (*qara'*) the names, and they do not understand the ritual setting. So they have suggested that it has to do with everything from "recalling" to "perpetuating" the name(s).[26] Note the following translations:

---

21. This is Jacob/Israel.

22. The LXX replaces "Joseph" with "them" referring to Joseph's sons. This seems to make more sense, but it is difficult to account for such a mistake in the MT. It is much easier to have Jacob doing two things: he is blessing Joseph by blessing his sons and by giving Joseph Shechem.

23. This is the blessing on the sons. Also note v. 20, which shows how all of this is continued.

24. The phrase "from my birth until this day" is literally "from my beginning to this day." This phrase also appears in Num 22:30.

25. Also see Gen 21:12. The names of the fathers are called forth or summoned during a ritual for the dead, and when this is done, one is blessed with heirs.

26. Theodore Lewis should really understand this ("The Ancestral Estate," 604); but in his article it seems that he is thinking more in terms of "perpetuating" and "preserving" "the memory of the family name" in Gen 21:12 and in 48:16. Also, Westermann does not understand this passage, and he sees it as a late addition (exilic or postexilic; *Genesis 37–50*, 189–90). He thinks that it has to do with the name of the fathers living on in the grandchildren, and thus the history of the fathers, "which was a history with God," will continue in the children. This gives the time of the fathers a meaning for the later history of Israel. But he does say something that is important, even though he does not really understand it: "This is the clearest and most important passage in the Old Testament where one can recognize the link between patriarchal tradition and the liturgy of Israel."

AB: "That in them be recalled my name, and the names of Abraham and Isaac, my fathers, . . ."

Tanakh: "In them may my name be recalled, And the names of my fathers Abraham and Isaac, . . ."

AAT: ". . . so that my name may be carried on through them, together with the names of my fathers, Abraham and Isaac; . . ."

NEB: ". . . they shall be called by my name, and by that of my forefathers, Abraham and Isaac; . . ."

NRSV: ". . . ; and in them let my name be perpetuated, and the name of my ancestors Abraham and Isaac; . . ."

None of these translations does justice to the Hebrew text, and they all miss the point.

The key for understanding this passage has not been available for very long. We now have a burial ritual from Ugarit in which the "fathers" and the recently departed kings are "called forth" (*qara'* = "call/invite/summon," the same word that we have in the Genesis text) in order for the new king to receive a blessing. In our passage Ephraim and Manasseh will "call forth" at the tomb the names of the fathers. It is important to see the Ugaritic text at this point:

An Ugaritic Liturgy RS 34.126

Translation

1. A document of a celebration of ancestors:
2. You have been summoned, O Rephaim of the netherworld;
3. You have been invited, O Assembly of the Didanites.
4. Ulkn, the Rapha, has been summoned.
5. Trmn, the Rapha, has been summoned.
6. Sdn-w-Rdn, [the Rapha], has been summoned.
7. Tr-'Illmn, [the Rapha], has been summoned.
8. The ancient Raphaim have been summoned.
9. You have been summoned, O Raphaim of the netherworld;
10. You have been invited, O Assembly of the Didanites.
11. King Ammishtamru has been summoned.
12. Also, King Niqmaddu has been summoned.

13. O throne of Niqmaddu, weep!

14. Let his footstool shed tears;

15. Before him, let the table of the king weep;

16. Let it swallow its tears!

17. Bereft, bereft, and bereft!

18. Be hot, O Shapshu!

Be hot, (19) O great luminary!

Above us, Shapshu shouts:

20. "After your lord, from the throne,

After (21) your lord,

To the netherworld descend!

To the netherworld (22) descend;

Go down low into the world of death.

Below (23) is Sdn-w-Rdn!

Below is Tr- (24) 'Illmn!

Below are the ancient Rephaim!

25. Below is King Ammishtamru!

26. Below is King Niqmaddu, as well!"

27. [Day] one and an offering,

[Day] two and an offering,

28. [Day] three and an offering,

[Day] four and an offering,

29. [Day] five and an offering,

[Day] six and an offering,

30. [Day] seven and an offering:

You shall present a bird.

31. Shalom!

Shalom, Ammurapi!

32. Shalom (to) his house, as well!

Shalom, Tharyelli!

33. Shalom (to) her house!

Shalom, Ugarit!

34. Shalom (to) her gates![27]

---

27. See Bordreuil and Pardee, "Le rituel funéraire ougaritique RS 34.126," for the best text which we have used, and Levine and Tarragon, "Dead Kings and Rephaim," for a good treatment of this text.

Introduction

This is a remarkable document. In lines 2–12 the departed ancestors and kings are "summoned/called" ten times and invited twice to participate in this ritual. The furniture of Niqmaddu's throne room weeps, the sun (Shapshu) must locate those who have been summoned, and offerings are presented in a seven-day ritual. The occasion for this ritual seems to be just after the death of Niqmaddu and during the succession or coronation rituals for the new king (Ammurapi) and his queen (Tharyelli). They seek the blessing of the departed ancestors and kings. They do this in order that their line may continue. I have compared this text on several occasions to the Babylonian *kispu* or mortuary offerings of food and drink for the dead kings who are invoked by name in a ritual. The *Genealogy of the Hammurapi Dynasty*, which contains a king list and other helpful comments, was written for such an occasion.[28] There is also a king list from Ugarit which was no doubt used in the same way, i.e., in the context of the Ugaritic funeral ritual.[29]

One of the most interesting facts that comes out of comparing these texts (including the *Assyrian King List*) is that the Did/tanites (see lines 3 and 10 in the funeral ritual) have been related to each group. The Babylonians and Assyrians both go back to the Didanites in their genealogies, and the Ugaritians witness to that same Amorite ancestry in their ritual and epic.[30] In the *Keret Epic* from Ugarit, we have the story of the patriarch Keret. The later kings of Ugarit looked back to him as their father, an ancient father from North Mesopotamia. He was related by story and ritual to Ugarit in the same way that Abraham (also from North Mesopotamia) was related to Jerusalem. In the *Keret Epic*,[31] Keret is blessed with these words:

> Be most exalted, O Keret,
> In the midst the Raphaim of the netherworld,
> In the gathering of the assembly of the Didanites. (UT 128:III:13–15)

In our funeral text, the "Raphaim of the netherworld" and "the assembly of the Didanites" are summoned for the ritual. At Ugarit the

---

28. For this see Finkelstein, "The Genealogy of the Hammurapi Dynasty."
29. See Kitchen, "The King List of Ugarit."
30. For a detailed treatment of this see Astour, "A North Mesopotamian Locale of the Keret Epic?"
31. We will give more details of the story later.

most important ancestor of that assembly would be Keret.[32] Therefore, I think that there is a real possibility that the *Keret Epic* was used on such occasions.

The sons of Joseph were to summon Jacob, Abraham, and Isaac at the tomb. By doing this they would be blessed; they would become a multitude. Now it is my guess that at some point in the observance of such rituals, the stories of the ancestors were told. I do not think that we can get back to the earliest forms of these stories, but the stories that we have may be based on such stories, and they were used by the kings of Israel.[33]

Genesis 48:16 is not the only place where the burial ritual is implied. In Gen 21:12b it says,

> Whatever Sarah demands of you,
> listen to her voice,
> because through Isaac,
> descendants will *call forth* to you.

In other words, Isaac's descendants will care for you at the tomb, and you will bless them. We will see other examples in Genesis when we discuss the structure of these stories of the ancestors. Outside of Genesis this sort of thing is mentioned in Ruth 4:14. Concerning Boaz (David's ancestor) it says, "May his name be called forth in Israel." Perhaps the most revealing passage is Isa 14:4-21. Here the king of Babylon is shown to be the most horrible of all the kings. All the great kings are glorified in their tombs, but this one has no grave, no place to lay his head! "You

---

32. See de Moor, "Rapi'uma—Rephaim," 335, where he comments on the Ugaritic funeral liturgy as follows (Kuritu = Keret): "Most important, however, is the first part of the ritual. It proves that the Ugaritic dynasty traced its origins back to the same ancestor Ditanu/Didanu as Kuritu. This finally explains why the Legend of Kuritu was handed down in Ugarit." Van Seters, *In Search of History*, 200–202, is clearly wrong when he says, "There is, therefore, at present no evidence to suggest that Keret was an ancestor or royal model for the people of Ugarit."

33. We do not know much about Jacob, Abraham, or Isaac from these stories, but when the scribes put together such stories and formed an epic in order to unite the people, they were not in a position to invent new names or write new stories. For entertainment, the people wanted their stories. The new historians who see such "hero-kings" as imaginary (i.e., "never living persons") are just not in touch. N. P. Lemche sees a parallel between "Kirta" and the later kings of Ugarit and David and the later kings of Judah. He could make a better case with a parallel between Kirta and Abraham. See Lemche, "From Patronage Society to Patronage Society," 120.

shall not be joined with them in burial, because you destroyed your land; you murdered your people. Let the descendants of evildoers nevermore be called forth" (v. 20). He will not receive proper burial and neither will his descendants. His line is finished. This reminds one of a passage from an Assyrian text, Assurbanipal's campaign against Elam, VI 70–76:[34]

> The sepulchres of their ancient [and] recent kings, who did not fear Ashur and Ishtar, my masters, who harassed the kings, my fathers, I ravaged, destroyed, and exposed to the sun.[35] I took their bones to Assyria. I made their shades insomniacs; I deprived them of funerary offerings[36] and libations of water."[37]

So the kings of Israel were certainly interested in genealogies and the stories of their ancestors, because they used these materials in rituals wherein they would receive a blessing and their line would endure. The book of Genesis contains royal literature.[38]

There are many other reasons for seeing in Genesis royal literature, and these items will be mentioned in the notes to the translation. But now, I want to turn to the structure of Genesis, and this will show some additional evidence as to the royal nature of the material.

The Structure of Genesis

At the end of this introduction there is an outline of Genesis titled "The Final Form of Genesis." This outline will be helpful, because in this section on structure and in the notes to the translation, I will refer to the section numbers of this outline.

Most studies of Genesis divide the book into the Primeval History/Events (as seen in Genesis 1–11) and the Patriarchal History (Genesis 12–50). This way of looking at the book is not very helpful, and it is the invention of modern times. In this translation, Genesis is viewed as

---

34. Streck, *Assurbanipal, II Teil: Texte*, 54–57. Also see IV 65–82, 38–39, for another example.

35. See *CAD*, Vol. 8, 523.

36. This is a translation of *kispu*.

37. In light of all this, it appears that David in 2 Sam 21:10–14 is not helping his cause in giving a proper burial to Saul and Jonathan, but more on this below.

38. The common people also had their rituals for the dead. These were usually held in the House of the *Marzeaḥ*. For a discussion of this see below.

Genesis, a Royal Epic

divided by the final editor. In other words, we take seriously the titles or division markers between the eleven segments (S 1–11 in the outline) of the book. If one wants to make another kind of division, it could be helpful in some situations, but it would probably have to do with pre-flood stories and post-flood stories. Even so, it is necessary to note that due to parallel literature, Genesis 1–10 should be seen as a unit.[39] It may be useful to briefly state the main content of Genesis 1:1—11:26, because I do want to deal in some detail with the structure of the following chapters. So note the following:

1. Elohim brought order out of Chaos (Gen 1:1—2:3).

2. All humans and the other animals are mortal. The humans have a special vocation and have obtained all knowledge. This made the development of civilization a reality (Gen 2:4—4:26).

3. Genesis has its pre-flood sages, and it has accounted for the heroes of old (Gen 5:1—6:4).

4. The Genesis story of the flood is very interesting, and its flood hero, Noah, has given the Hebrews all of the pre-flood knowledge. Thus David, their king, "has wisdom like the wisdom of a messenger of the gods to know all things that are on earth" (2 Sam 14:17, 20). This is a new beginning (Gen 6:5—9:29).

5. The scribes were aware of post-flood developments and the world situation of their day (i.e., David's day), and they were also interested in background materials for understanding the fathers of the kings of Israel (Gen 10:1—11:26).

In Genesis, there are three major cycles of tradition concerning the ancestors of the kings of Israel and Judah (see sections 6, 8, and 10 of chart one at the end of this Introduction).[40] But we need a closer look at the shape of these three documents:

---

39. Lambert, after discussing the new material, says, "The very considerable importance of this material is the proof it offers that the whole framework of the Hebrew traditions in Gen. i–x, and not just the episode of the flood, has its counterpart in Sumero-Babylonian legend" ("New Light on the Babylonian Flood," 116).

40. Between these three major sections, there is in each case a very short section dealing with the elder brother. Genesis 25:12–18, "These are the stories of Ishmael" and Gen 36:1–8 and 9–43 where there are two documents with two titles, "These are the stories of Esau."

Introduction

1) All three have similar titles:
   a) "These are the Stories of Terah," Gen 11:27—25:11.
      (Terah is the father of Abraham, but the stories are about Abraham.)
   b) "These are the Stories of Isaac," Gen 25:19—35:29.
      (Isaac is the father of Esau and Jacob, but most of the stories are about Jacob.)
   c) "These are the Stories of Jacob," Gen 37:2—50:26.
      (Jacob is the father of the twelve brothers, but most of the stories are about Joseph.)

   In this sequence we are missing a document between a) and b) that could be given the title "These are the Stories of Abraham." If we had such a document the stories would be about Isaac. Some material from such a document has survived and can be found in Genesis 24 and 26 (see chart two at the end of this Introduction).

2) All three cycles have structural and thematic parallels in the following order:
   a) All are interested in the birth of an heir, but great difficulties are always present (famine, seduction [Sarah, Rebekah, and Joseph], and infertility).
   b) There is always the point made that the "elder shall serve the younger" (Gen 25:19-34 and 37:2-36). This was not the normal custom, but royal literature is not normal (even David was the youngest).
   c) The hero either buys or receives land (e.g., the burial cave [Gen 23] and Shechem [Gen 33:18-20]).
   d) Similar conclusions containing three parts: a burial scene (Gen 23:1-20; 35:16-20; 50:1-14), additional material on the heir(s) (Gen 24:1—25:6; 35:21-26; 50:15-21), and a death scene (Gen 25:7-11; 35:27-29; 50:22-26).

This last section (d) of these stories is very important. From our earlier discussion, it is clear that proper burial was important for the blessing of the next "father." Without such a blessing there would not be another heir.

Now, the overall structure of these cycles is very useful in identifying fragments of such cycles. In Genesis 38, we have the first part of such a cycle (i.e., points 2.a and b). I have given this fragmented cycle the title of "These are the Stories of Judah" (with stories about Perez—see chart two). In Genesis 38, one can see that the scribe hurries by the early events, but soon we are aware of the danger: Judah's sons are being killed by Yahweh![41] How can his line continue? We could have predicted the seduction scene, and the birth of the twins is very much like the birth of Esau and Jacob. Yes, once again the elder will serve the younger. Now we have more questions: Why did the scribes need this Judah cycle? Why did they only use part of it?

In order to address these questions, it is important to think about David's situation when he became king. In 2 Sam 2:4 we read, "The men of Judah came, and there they anointed David king over the house of Judah." David ruled Judah in Hebron seven years and six months. During this time his royal scribes probably produced the document that we have called, "These are the Stories of Judah." This document would have contained stories about Perez, and it would have given us the line of David plus a story about the death and burial of Judah (probably at the cave near Hebron that was purchased by Abraham).[42] It would have been used by David to prove that he was the legitimate king of Judah. Since we do not have all of this document, we are forced to use the book of Ruth to complete the Story of Judah (Ruth 4:13–22 and also note Gen 46:12). In Ruth 4:18 we have another title, "These are the Stories of Perez," so we can suppose that they did have even more materials.

Later the elders of Israel came to David in Hebron, and they made him king over Israel. When David became king over both states, he moved to Jerusalem, and "he ruled over all Israel and Judah thirty-three years" (2 Sam 5:5). At this point the royal scribes had to integrate the stories of the two states and especially the stories of Joseph (from Israel) and Judah. David's scribes were very talented and they included a lot of very important things. They stressed the importance of Joseph, but they also made Judah very important in the main part of the Joseph story.

---

41. Here Yahweh punishes as he does in David's time (2 Sam 12:15).

42. Hebron was David's first royal residence (2 Sam 2:1–7), and it is also the location of the cave of the Machpelah, the ancestral tomb (Gen 23:1–20; 25:7–11; 35:29; 49:29–31; 50:13), as well as the location of Absalom's sacrifice and declaration of his kingship (2 Sam 15:7–12).

Introduction

These scribes also put in the Stories of Judah (Genesis 38) that pointed to David. So all of this material was put into its present form at the time of the Davidic monarchy. It was a royal document, and it not only made David the legitimate heir, but it helped to unify both Israel and Judah.

It is clear that Genesis 38 is very important for David's kingdom. The scribes had to include this material. Perhaps they thought that in a narrative concerning Joseph where Judah is also a main character, the readers should know more about Judah and the line of David. It still bothers me that they put it where they did, as it interrupts the Joseph story. However the inclusion of the Judah material was necessary, and at least they did it with political taste; they did not give too much of the Judah story, and they were not hostile as scribes were in later materials. Note Ps 78:67–68:

> He [God] rejected the clan of Joseph;
> the tribe of Ephraim he did not choose.
> He chose the tribe of Judah,
> Mount Zion, which he loved.

The royal scribes did not want to cause problems; they wanted to unite these states and show their world that the story points to David.

Burial, Blessing, and Birth

In the above discussion on the structure of these cycles, we were looking on the surface of these narratives and noting similar beginnings and conclusions. But within these similar elements, it is very interesting that there is a very real cycle of burial, blessing, and birth that keeps on turning. I say, "very real," because it appears that a storyteller could start at any point on this circle. The blessing can come first, then birth and burial, and it goes on for another round or two. First, I want to look at a story from Ugarit as an example of this cycle.

The Epic of Aqhat

This story begins with Danel[43] participating in a seven-day ritual. This ritual has usually been described as a "rite of incubation." T. H. Gaster

---

43. Danel is the father who is known for his wisdom. In fact, Ezekiel knew of him and listed him along with Noah and Job (see 14:13–20 or 28:3).

says, "The suppliant lodges for a few days in the precincts of the sanctuary in order to entreat the god and obtain the divine oracle in a dream or by some other manner."[44] However, I think that today we can be more specific; it is possible that this is a funeral ritual. The ritual is for seven days; Danel gives food and drink to the gods, which could be Danel's departed ancestors; the god Baal makes Danel's request for a son known to the god El. El blesses Danel so that he can have a perfect son. Danel's son, Aqhat, is born, and he is a fine son. But, later in the story, the goddess Anat has Aqhat killed. Now, Danel must find Aqhat's "fat and bone," because there has to be a proper burial. Danel does find Aqhat's "fat and bone," and so the cycle begins again. In this case, Aqhat must be buried "in the grave of the gods of the netherworld," i.e., the departed fathers and kings who are also called the rephaim. There are some Rephaim texts (UT 121–124) that show how these rephaim were invited to the funeral by Danel. They come first to the threshing floor and then to the palace. They come for the food and drink, but they also come to bless. We do not have all of the story, but I think that Danel is not only blessed again, but he also has another son. The cycle turns again.

Abraham

With the story of Aqhat in mind, we turn back to Genesis. The cycle that deals with Abraham is contained in Gen 11:27—25:11 ("These are the stories of Terah"). At the beginning of this material, we learn about the death of Abraham's father, Terah. Since it is not mentioned, we are left to assume that indeed there was a burial. We have the post-funeral blessing in Gen 12:1–3. In this story we have to wait a long time for the next element or the birth story. In chapter 21, we have the story of the birth of Isaac. Sarah, with the help of Yahweh, produces a son for Abraham to help him in his old age, and more importantly to be his heir. In Gen 21:12, we catch a glimpse of how the heir (and his heirs) will "call forth" to Abraham at his grave. As the cycle turns, there should be another burial. Genesis 23 tells us about the burial of Sarah. In the Genesis cycles (as discussed above), the last three sections of each cycle deal with 1) death and burial, 2) another word concerning the heirs,

---

44. Gaster, *Thespis*, 330.

Introduction

and 3) another death and burial. Following the burial of Sarah, the second section from the end (Gen 24:1—25:6) mentions how Yahweh has blessed Abraham in every way, how Abraham arranged for the "right" wife for Isaac, and gives us some information concerning Abraham's other children. The last section of the Abraham material is about his death. By this time, it should not surprise us to read in Gen 25:9 that "Isaac and Ishmael, his sons, buried him . . ." And the expected note in v. 11 reads, "It was after the death of Abraham that Elohim blessed Isaac, his son."

Jacob

The cycle that deals with Jacob is contained in Gen 25:19—35:29 (These are the stories of Isaac). Isaac has the "right" wife. He has already been blessed after the burial of his father (Gen 25:11), so that an heir will be in the picture. Therefore, the first element in this cycle is the birth of Jacob and Esau with the epic notation that "the older shall serve the younger." As we have noted in these epic cycles, the younger son always rules (and so it was with David). All of these cycles have their own individual ways of arriving at a similar end. In the Jacob material, Jacob obtains his father's blessing before his father's death, and he takes an epic journey in order to get away from Esau but also for the purpose of obtaining his rightful wife. This part of the story is very much like the story of Keret from Ugarit who also must go on such a journey to get his rightful wife.[45] Jacob gets his wives and finally his children are born. In Gen 35:16-21, we have the death and burial of Rachel. "Jacob set up a sacred pillar on her grave" (v. 20a). Next there is a list of Jacob's heirs, and finally there is the death and burial of Isaac (Gen 35:27-29). Esau and Jacob buried Isaac.

---

45. I have discussed this in great detail in several places, e.g., Fisher, "The Patriarchal Cycles"; and Fisher, "Literary Genres in the Ugaritic Texts." For an excellent discussion of all of this see Rummel, "Narrative Structures in the Ugaritic Texts." Perhaps we should add at this point that after Keret mourns the loss of his family, he is given instructions for his journey to obtain his bride who will produce for him children. This is similar to Abraham's burial of Sarah followed by the journey to obtain a wife for Isaac.

Genesis, a Royal Epic

Joseph

The Joseph material is contained in Gen 37:2—50:26 (These are the stories of Jacob). Here the heirs are already born, so the first thing to establish is that the younger will rule the elders. In fact, Joseph is really not the youngest, but he is next to the youngest and Jacob's favorite. In 37:2-36, the fact that Joseph will rule is driven home again and again even though at the end of the chapter one wonders, how will this be? But Joseph is very successful. In chapter 48, Joseph and his sons are blessed, and within these blessings we are able to discern that the real blessing and the continuation of that blessing will come from God and the fathers, who will bless them as they call forth the names of the fathers at the tomb. They will become a multitude. In Gen 49:29—50:14, the death and burial of Jacob is given in great detail. In the first part, Jacob is still alive, and he charges his sons to bury him with his ancestors in the cave "that Abraham purchased." After Jacob died, he was embalmed, and "the Egyptians wept for him seventy days." Then Joseph was granted permission to take his father's remains to Canaan. According to this story, Joseph left Egypt with a huge entourage made up of Egyptian officials, his brothers, other relatives, and a military guard. When this group was still east of the Jordan river, they arrived at the threshing floor of the Atad. There they lamented and mourned for seven days. As in the story of Aqhat, the funeral begins at the threshing floor; but in this story instead of moving to the palace (to complete the ritual), they continue their journey, moving to the cave that Abraham had purchased.[46] This is the way the story reads.[47] We really do not have

---

46. There is a very interesting text from Ugarit (*Ugaritica V*, 499–504). The instructions are written in Ugaritic, but the main part of the text is in Hurrian. It is "A celebration for Astarte" that begins in four sacred areas of the threshing floor and then moves to the temple for the main sacrifices. It is also interesting to note that at a much later time Marcus Terentius Varro (116–27 BCE) in his book *De Lingua Latina* relates the Latin *area* ("threshing floor") to *ara* ("funeral pyre/altar"); note Hebrew *'arah*, "altar-hearth." The threshing floor was a very interesting place.

47. It has been suggested in the past that here we have one story about Jacob's burial at Machpelah (Gen 49:29-33 and 50:12, 13 or P) and another story about Jacob's burial "beyond the Jordon" (Gen 50:1-11 and 14 or J), which of course does not comply with Jacob's request. It could be that we have material from more than one source, but the story is told in order to meet all of the requirements for such a story. The burial at Machpelah is important, and the journey to the threshing floor of Atad is also important. It is the first part of the funeral ritual. It lasted for seven days (see 1 Sam

to assume that Joseph and his brothers were blessed because of their efforts; it is clear that in Gen 50:15–21 Joseph will care for the brothers and their children. Finally, we have in Gen 50:22–26, the death and burial of Joseph with his request that his bones be brought up from Egypt.[48]

When we look at all of these stories and see the importance of burial, blessing, and birth to both the form and content of these stories, we see from a slightly different angle what we have said before: this material was shaped in part by funeral rituals and was used by the monarchy in the interest of the monarchy.

Proper Burial

The importance of proper burial can be seen in some of the materials that we have concerning David. In 2 Sam 21:10–14, David takes a chance. On the one hand, he can score some political points if he gives Saul and his sons proper burial rites in the tomb of Saul's father Kish. But on the other hand, by so doing, David could be sending the wrong signal to the house of Saul. After all, to give proper burial is one way of preserving a dynastic line. Up to this point, our discussion of proper burial has concentrated on the royal tomb, but we also know that proper burial was important to all members of society. We now know that the people formed funeral associations (a *marzeaḥ*) to take care of burial and mourning rites, and they usually had a place to meet (called "the House of the *Marzeaḥ*" or *Bet Marzeaḥ*).[49] In Jer 16:1–9, there is a gruesome picture of life or rather death in Judah. The word is do not marry, because your children will die and not be buried; "they shall be like dung on the surface of the ground." In v. 5 Yahweh says, "Do not enter the *Bet Marzeaḥ*, . . . for I have taken away my Shalom from this people." In other words, there is no point anymore in proper burial and "the care and feeding of the dead," because there will be no

---

31:13). After these seven days the party went on to Machpelah. It would be impossible to deal with the historical situation behind this story. We do not know the route nor the place. But, from what we do know of funerals and rituals, these two parts form a complete story.

48. See Exod 13:19 and Josh 24:32.

49. On this subject see Miller, "The Mrzh Text"; and Dahood, "Additional Notes on the Mrzh Text."

blessing, i.e., no Shalom to put it into the words of Jeremiah and of the royal tomb liturgy from Ugarit. So, there will be no burial, no blessing, and no children.

One thing that we do not know very much about has to do with when these funeral rituals were used. They must have been used at the time of burial, but also they may have been used in some kind of yearly ritual. Some people have thought that the reference in 1 Sam 20:6 by David to an annual sacrifice by his whole family may have had to do with "the care and feeding of the dead." It would also renew the blessings for such a family. I think that we really do not know much about this. However, I do think that the Ugaritic funeral ritual which we have been discussing was used in connection with the enthronement of the new king. Did enthronement take place at the tomb? We can say that David became king of both Judah and Israel in Hebron and that the scribes of the monarchy located the tomb of the fathers in Hebron. Here David could become king and receive the blessings of the ancestors. David's rebel son, Absalom, also became king in Hebron. Solomon became king in Jerusalem before the death of David, but since David was buried there, they both started a new tradition. I think that all of this means that the monarchy had a real need for Genesis.

Characteristics of This Translation

The Hebrew Bible is an amazing collection of ancient documents. These documents were gathered over many years, and they were preserved in several textual traditions. The discovery of the Dead Sea Scrolls has opened our eyes to the many textual traditions that were around in pre-Christian Palestine. Most translators of the Hebrew Bible start with a Masoretic text (MT) known as the Leningrad Codex B 19A.[50] This was copied in about 1009 CE. When these translators encounter problems, they may find a better reading in some other textual tradition, e.g., the Samaritan text (for the first five books) or perhaps in the Hebrew text that was behind the Septuagint (a Greek translation from the third century BCE). In this translation of Genesis, you will not find this kind of search for the best text; this translation is a translation of the Masoretic textual tradition. Other textual traditions are also important, but the translation of those traditions represents another project.

50. This is the text used for this translation of Genesis.

Introduction

This translation of Genesis tries to make use of recent discoveries. Throughout this introduction, it is clear that new discoveries have given us new information on burial customs. By the study of AML, we are constantly learning more about literary parallels and the meaning of words. Also, we have learned that the peoples of the ancient Mediterranean world formed a cosmopolitan whole. At least the urban centers were in constant contact with each other and shared their learning and traditions. The Mediterranean World had very few isolated communities. There was just too much shipping by sea and trading by land. Fernand Braudel says that one of the great truths that remains unchallenged in his work on the Mediterranean is "the unity and coherence of the Mediterranean region."[51] So, the key is to bring all new information to bear upon our text. We attempt to let the Hebrew text have its day. This is not a revision of the English tradition of Bible translations.

Another characteristic of this translation is that it is not bound by modern theological concerns. In the past, for example, some theologians have demanded that Gen 1:1 be translated, "In the beginning God created the heavens and the earth." But Genesis does not read that way. It does not deal with ultimate origins. In fact, the first two verses describe the circumstance when God first began to bring order out of chaos. The theological demands were designed to protect the doctrine of God from any kind of dualism or pantheism. It is clear that in Genesis God orders chaos. The Hebrew authors did not address the problem of where the matter came from. In this translation, I do not use the words "create" or "creation." The emphasis of many that "creation" means "creation out of nothing" is just wrong. I hate to give up on good words, but I have been compelled to use the more basic meanings of Hebrew words, in this case "to sculpt"/"to form." Thus, my own translation of Gen1:1a is "When Elohim first began to form the heavens and the earth . . ."

Other theological problems are not so well known. You will recall that at the start of the Introduction we discussed the plural "gods" in Gen 5:22 and 24 and 6:9. There is another example of this sort of thing in Gen 35:7. In this passage, Jacob "built there an altar; he called the sanctuary El-Bethel, for there the gods were revealed to him when he

---

51. Braudel, *The Mediterranean*, vol. 1, 14. And more recently, Gilmore, ed., *Honor and Shame and the Unity of the Mediterranean*; and Horden and Purcell, *The Corrupting Sea: A Study of the Mediterranean*.

Genesis, a Royal Epic

was fleeing from his brother." Here we have not only the definite article with *'elohim*, but even the verb ("were revealed") is plural! Genesis 35:7 refers back to 28:20–22 where Jacob deals with two gods, one designated "Elohim" and the other designated "Yahweh." This is a strong case for the use of the plural, but most translators avoid the issue.[52]

This translation places a premium on context. The context has a very important influence on the meaning of a word. In Gen 2:6, we are told that "the entire surface of the ground" was flooded. Given this context it becomes impossible to translate v. 7 in the traditional manner: "Yahweh-Elohim formed the human [from] the dust of the ground." In this context, there would be no "dust." The options have to do with either "mud" or "clay." At this point in the translation, there will be a detailed note concerning these options.

This may be the place for a word concerning inclusive language. I can understand that a translator should not import sexist language into the translation, but if such language is in the text, the translator should not remove it. Because of the fear of using sexist language, the New Revised Standard Version (and others) tries to avoid saying "father" or "son" at all costs. But this practice can lead to inconsistencies. In Gen 23:5, "sons of Heth" is translated "Hittites" in a context which suggests that the reference is to Hittite men. In fact, v. 10 contains a different term for "Hittite" that does not denote gender. In Gen 27:46, where the context makes it certain that the reference is to women, inconsistency is forced on the NRSV, which must translate the "daughters of Heth" not as "Hittites" but rather "Hittite women." Let the text have its day.[53]

There is a lot of poetry in the book of Genesis. Where it was possible, this translation has given the reader a poem in English. In this po-

---

52. If Genesis 28 is separated into the J and E sources and if "Yahweh" in 28:21b is seen as an addition, it is possible to see one God in the story, but that is not the way it stands in its present form. Also, for more examples of "gods," see Gen 20:13, 17, 18; and 31:53.

53. There are so many things that one could say about this translation, and most of them will be mentioned in the notes. For example, most scholars translate the Hebrew *waw* conversive as a conjunction, and they run a lot of short sentences together with "and," "then," "but since," and other interpretive words. I consider this to be possible, but it is misleading. This *waw* is a tense indicator, and in this translation it performs that function. Look at the difference between this translation and others in Gen 38:1–9. The other translations destroyed this fast moving narrative with its staccato statements. See Gordon, *UT*, §12.9, pp. 110 and 111.

Introduction

etry, I have sometimes added a word or repeated a word (in brackets)[54] to make the lines balanced in English. In addition to the poetry, there is "high prose" in Genesis, which is set in meaningful and rhythmic cola. In other places, the text takes the form of a play. I hope that this emphasis on format will be helpful in reminding the reader that this is royal epic.

After completing the first edition of this translation, two new translations have appeared. These are by Everett Fox and Robert Alter. Fox (*The Five Books of Moses*) has been interested in the Buber-Rosenzweig translation of the Hebrew Bible into German for many years. He says, "*The Five Books of Moses* is in many respects an offshoot of the Buber-Rosenzweig translation" (x). For Buber and Rosenzweig (and for Fox), it is important to remember that this was a book to be read aloud. I like the way Fox has given the text of this poetry and "high prose" in lines based on "spoken phrasing" (xv, and for Buber's comments on this see Buber and Rosenzweig, *Scripture and Tradition*, 179). If this is the case, then I must say that Fox confuses me. He usually gives a proper name like "*Perat*" in its Hebrew pronunciation and then follows it with a translation (in this case "Perat/Euphrates"). This does not help me to return to the spokenness of the text (Buber and Rosensweig, 179). Fox's translation is part of an edition of the Torah. He has translated what Genesis has become in a modern context. I have tried to translate a Royal Epic that had an important ancient context.

Robert Alter (in *Genesis*) has some of the same interests as Fox. He says, "the mesmerizing effect of these ancient stories will scarcely be conveyed if they are not rendered in cadenced English prose that at least in some ways corresponds to the powerful cadences of the Hebrew" (xxvi). The disappointing thing about Alter's book is that his publisher has reduced his "cadenced English prose" down to blocks of prose.[55] The cadence is buried. I consider this to be a major problem. (The publisher was also in a hurry. The headings in chapter 12 for the

---

54. Throughout the translation all additions to the text are put in brackets.

55. I have also used blocks of prose in the Joseph story, but I have done this to show that the Joseph story has been worked and reworked and is a refined story if we compare it to the earlier epic cycles. In chapters 18 and 39 in my novel, *The Jerusalem Academy*, I show how this material was edited by at least three persons. It is different from the earlier cycles, and it does not follow the Egyptian tradition of first person autobiographies but tells the story in the third person.

chapter and verses on each page all read 11 instead of 12; see 50–53.) The format takes away what Alter calls the "distinctive music" of biblical Hebrew (xxxix). Alter's emphasis reflects his literary interests, but at times, these interests seem to hide other important issues and problems.

Both of these translations are better than most translations of Genesis. Yet, neither translation makes any real headway on some of the most notorious problems (e.g., 4:8; 35:4; 37:7; or 37:36). The following examples illustrate some of the differences between all three translations:

1:1

Alter: "When God began to create heaven and earth..."

Fisher: "When Elohim first began to form the heavens and the earth..."

Fox: "At the beginning of God's creating of the heavens and the earth..."

Alter has translated this as "the heavens and the earth" on page xix of his introduction. The fact that he has left out "the" in 1:1 is serious, because on page xx, part of his argument for keeping every "and" is that they are not inaudible elements in the Hebrew text. In v. 1, "the" is not an inaudible element, but it is left out. He can't have it both ways.

2:4b

Alter: "On the day the Lord God made earth and heavens..."

Fisher: "On another day when Yahweh-Elohim was about to make earth and heaven..."

Fox: "At the time of YHWH, God's making of earth and heaven..."

I cannot understand Fox's "At the time of YHWH..."

28:20

Alter: "...If the Lord God be with me..."

Fisher: "If Elohim will be with me..."

Fox: "If God will be with me..."

Introduction

It is difficult to understand Alter's translation. There is no word for "Lord" in the Hebrew text. There is the verb "to be," which looks something like Yahweh, and Alter does translate Yahweh as "Lord." (The double name does not occur in this section of Genesis. Also see Alter's note to 35:3.)

35:7

Alter: ". . . for there God was revealed to him . . ."

Fisher: ". . . for there the gods were revealed to him . . ."

Fox: ". . . For there had the power-of-God been revealed to him . . ."

Fox understands that there is a problem because of the plural form of the verb, but he does not really deal with the problem.

48:16

Alter: ". . . let my name be called in them and the name of my fathers Abraham and Isaac . . ."

Fisher: ". . . My name and the names of my fathers, Abraham and Isaac, shall be called forth by them."

Fox: ". . . May my name continue to be called through them and the name of my fathers, Avraham and Yitzhak!"

I do not know what Alter's translation means. Fox's translation is better, but it is still lacking. My translation assumes a ritual context (see above). The names of the fathers are called forth, or in other words, the fathers are summoned during a ritual for the dead. It was in this context that the stories of the fathers were told, stories that were later incorporated into the Book of Genesis. This is a very important point to consider.

Chart One

Section Headings in the Final Form of Genesis

1. These are the stories of the heavens and the earth since their formation (Gen 2:4a).
2. This is the document of the stories of Adam (Gen 5:1a).
3. These are the stories of Noah (Gen 6:9a).
4. These are the stories of the sons of Noah (10:1a).
5. These are the stories of Shem (11:10a).
6. These are the stories of Terah (11:27a).*
7. These are the stories of Ishmael (25:12a).
8. These are the stories of Isaac (25:19a).*
9. These are the stories of Esau (36:1).
10. These are the stories of Jacob (37:2a).*

*Major cycles of the fathers (see Chart Two for details).

Chart Two

The Three Major Cycles of the Fathers plus Fragments

6. These are the stories of Terah (Gen 11:27—25:11).
   (Stories about Abraham)
   Missing: These are the stories of Abraham.
   (Stories about Isaac—the material in Genesis 24 and 26 could be from this missing cycle.)
8. These are the stories of Isaac (Gen 25:19—35:29).
   (Stories about Jacob)
10. These are the stories of Jacob (Gen 37:2—50:26).
    (Stories about Joseph)
    Plus: These are the stories of Judah (Genesis 38).
    (Stories about Perez—Genesis 38 is just the beginning of this cycle.)
    Plus: These are the stories of Perez (Ruth 4:18–22).

Introduction

The Final Form of Genesis

S1:G1–2[56] *The Seven Days, 1:1—2:3*

G1 The Formation of the Cosmos, 1:1–31

    G1.1 Let there be light, 1:1–5

    G1.2 Let there be a vault, 1:6–8

    G1.3 Let there be seas, land, and vegetation, 1:9–13

    G1.4 Let there be lights, 1:14–19

    G1.5 Let there be creatures of the sea and air, 1:20–23

    G1.6 Let there be creatures of the land and humans, 1:24–31

G2 The Seventh Day, 2:1–3

S2:G3–9 *These are the Stories of Heaven and Earth since their formation, 2:4—4:26*

    Title, 2:4a

G3 Yahweh-Elohim formed the human, 2:4b–7

G4 The garden and its keeper, 2:8–17

    G4.1 Yahweh-Elohim planted a garden, 2:8–9

    G4.2 The rivers, 2:10–14

    G4.3 The human becomes the keeper, 2:15–17

G5 Yahweh-Elohim forms others; the human is not alone, 2:18–24

G6 Wise but mortal humans, 2:25—3:24

    G6.1 Naked and knowing, 2:25—3:7

    G6.2 The naked and mortal are clothed, 3:8–21

    G6.3 Sent from the garden to till the ground, 3:22–24

G7 Cain and Abel, 4:1–16

G8 Cities and Culture, 4:17–24

G9 The birth of Seth, 4:25–26

S3:G10–13 *This is the Document of the Stories of Adam, 5:1—6:8*

    Title, 5:1a

G10 The making of human beings, 5:1b–2

---

56. S1:G1–2 = Segment 1: Genesis §1 and 2.

Genesis, a Royal Epic

    G11   From Adam to Noah, 5:3–32
    G12   The Sages, 6:1–4
    G13   The sorrow of Yahweh, 6:5–8

S4:G14-16 *These are the Stories of Noah*, 6:9—9:29
        Title, 6:9a
    G14   The Flood, 6:9b—8:22
    G15   Blessing and Covenant, 9:1–17
    G16   Noah planted a vineyard, 9:18–29

S5:G17-18 *These are the Stories of the sons of Noah*, 10:1—11:9
        Title, 10:1
    G17   Friends, enemies, and kin, 10:2–32
    G18   The tower of Babel, 11:1–9

S6:G19 *These are the Stories of Shem*, 11:10-26
        Title, 11:10a
    G19   From Shem to Terah, 11:10b–26

S7:G20-36 *These are the Stories of Terah*, 11:27—25:11
        Title, 11:27a
    G20   Introduction and Promise, 11:27b—12:4
    G21   The journey to Canaan, 12:5–9
    G22   The journey to Egypt, 12:10—13:1
    G23   The move to Hebron, 13:2–18
    G24   Abram and Melchizedek, 14:1–24
    G25   Yahweh makes a covenant with Abram, 15:1–21
    G26   The birth of Ishmael, 16:1–16
    G27   Another covenant and Sarah will bear, 17:1–27
    G28   Yahweh's visitation, 18:1—19:38
        G28.1   Sarah shall have a son, 18:1–16
        G28.2   Abraham intercedes for Sodom, 18:17–33

Introduction

      G28.3   The destruction of Sodom and Gemorrah, 19:1–29

      G28.4   Lot and his daughters, 19:30–38

G29   Abraham and Sarah in Gerar, 20:1–18

G30   The Birth of Isaac, 21:1–21

G31   Abraham in Beersheba, 21:22–34

G32   Abraham is put to the test, 22:1–19

G33   The Aramaic tribes, 22:20–24

G34   The death and burial of Sarah, 23:1–20

G35   Abraham's heirs, 24:1—25:6

      G35.1   Isaac and Rebekah, 24:1–67

      G35.2   Keturah, 25:1–6

G36   The death and burial of Abraham, 25:7–11

S8:G37 *These are the Stories of Ishmael*, 25:12–18

    Title, 25:12a

G37   The tribes of Ishmael, 25:12b–18

S9:G38–54 *These are the Stories of Isaac*, 25:19—35:29

    Title, 25:19a

G38   The elder shall serve the younger, 25:19b–34

G39   Isaac and Rebekah in Gerar, 26:1–33

G40   Jacob obtains the blessing, 26:34—27:45 (26:34–35?)

G41   Jacob is sent to the house of Bethuel, 27:46 and 28:1–9

G42   Jacob's departure and his vow at Bethel, 28:10–22

G43   Jacob married Leah and Rachel, 29:1–30

G44   Leah, Rachel, and their children, 29:31—30:24

G45   Jacob's success, 30:25–43

G46   Jacob's return to the land of his fathers, 31:1—32:1

G47   Jacob's fear of Esau, 32:2–21

G48   Jacob's ordeal, 32:22–32

G49   Jacob meets Esau, 33:1–17

G50   Jacob goes to Shechem, 33:18—34:31

Genesis, a Royal Epic

G51 Jacob returns to Bethel, 35:1–15
G52 The death and burial of Rachel, 35:16–20
G53 Jacob and his sons, 35:21–26
G54 The death and burial of Isaac, 35:27–29

S10:G54-55 *These are the Stories of Esau*, 36:1—37:1
    Title, 36:1
G54 Esau/Edom, 36:2—36:43
    G54.1 Esau in Canaan, 36:2–8
    G54.2 Another Title, 36:9
    G54.3 Esau in Seir, 36:10–43
G55 But Jacob was in Canaan, 37:1

S11:G56-72 *These are the Stories of Jacob*, 37:2—50:26
    Title, 37:2a
G56 The elders shall serve the younger, 37:2b–36
G57 An interruption from the Story of Judah (the elder will serve the younger), 38:1–30
G58 Joseph and his success, 39:1—41:57
    G58.1 Joseph and Potiphar's wife, 39:1–23
    G58.2 Joseph interprets dreams, 40:1–23
    G58.3 From prisoner to ruler, 41:1–57
G59 Joseph and his brothers, 42:1—45:28
    G59.1 Joseph's ten brothers went down to Egypt, 42:1–38
    G59.2 They return to Egypt with Benjamin, 43:1–34
    G59.3 Benjamin's sack, 44:1–34
    G59.4 Joseph makes himself known to his brothers, 45:1–28
G60 First stop on the journey to Egypt, 46:1–7
G61 "These are the names," 46:8–27
G62 Joseph meets his father, 46:28–34
G63 The brothers before the Pharaoh, 47:1–6
G64 Jacob blessed the Pharaoh, 47:7–12

G65 Give us bread, 47:13–26
G66 Joseph's oath, 47:27–31
G67 The elder shall serve the younger, 48:1–20
G68 The gift of Shechem, 48:21–22
G69 Jacob's words to the twelve tribes, 49:1–28
G70 The death and burial of Jacob, 49:29—50:14
G71 Joseph comforted his brothers, 50:15–21
G72 The death and embalming of Joseph, 50:22–26

PART I

Genesis 1:1—11:26

1:1	When Elohim first began to form[1] the heavens and the earth,
2	The earth was devastation and desolation,[2]
	Darkness was over [the] deep,[3]
	The wind of Elohim was storming over the waters,[4]
3	Elohim said:
	"Let there be light."
	There was light.
4	Elohim saw that the light was good.
	Elohim divided between the light and between the darkness.
5	Elohim called the light day.
	The darkness he called night.
	There was evening.
	There was morning:

1. The word "form" is used instead of the traditional "create," because the term "create" carries with it just too much baggage (e.g., "creation out of nothing"). The Hebrew root means "to form or fashion" by means of cutting; it means "to sculpt." Elohim, the sculptor, starts with less than ideal material.

2. The Hebrew phrase behind "devastation and desolation" is also used in Jer 4:23.

3. "Deep" is a good translation, but an argument can be made for leaving the Hebrew untranslated. It could be the proper name Tehom (there is no article) and related to the Babylonian goddess Tiamat.

4. The first two verses describe the circumstance of the next six paragraphs. The circumstantial character of these verses can be substantiated grammatically (a noun in the construct before a finite verb equals a when-clause, see *UT*, 56 n. 1) and from parallels in the Hebrew Bible (Gen 2:4b) and outside the Hebrew tradition, e.g., *Enuma elish* (for this Mesopotamian epic of creation, see Jacobsen, *The Treasures of Darkness*, 165–91). The point that is sometimes overlooked is that the Hebrew royal scribes were not interested in ultimate origins.

Genesis, a Royal Epic

Day one.⁵

6   Elohim said:
    "Let there be a vault in the midst of the waters.
    Let there be a division between waters and waters."
7   Elohim made the vault.
    He divided between the waters that were under the vault,
    and between the waters that were above the vault.
    So it was.⁶
8   Elohim called the vault heaven.
    There was evening.
    There was morning:
    A second day.⁷

9   Elohim said:
    "Let the waters under the heavens be pooled into one place.
    Let the dry land appear."
    So it was.
10 Elohim called the dry land earth.
    The pools⁸ of waters he called seas.
    Elohim saw that it was good.
11 Elohim said:
    "Let the earth produce vegetation
    (plants that scatter seed, [and] fruit trees that bear fruit
    of their kind in which is their seed)⁹ upon the earth."

5. This is a very strange way of referring to the first day, but as external parallels show (see Fisher, "An Ugaritic Ritual and Genesis I, 1–5") this same expression was used in descriptive ritual texts as a time clause in the final position of each ritual day. Therefore the earlier form of this material could have been grouped around seven ritual days.

6. The LXX puts this phrase at the end of v. 6 (like vv. 9 and 11). The best translation of this phrase is probably, *voilà*.

7. It is important to note that in this time clause we have used an indefinite article. This is the same for each of the following days except "The Sixth Day" which may be by a later editor.

8. The translation "pools," following as it does "be pooled" in v. 9, has the advantage of showing that the Hebrew verb and noun are from the same root.

9. These parenthetical statements (here and in v. 12) in the MT are difficult to translate.

So it was.
12 The earth brought forth vegetation
(plants that scatter seed of their kind, and trees
that bear fruit in which is their seed of their kind).
Elohim saw that it was good.
13 There was evening.
There was morning:
A third day.

14 Elohim said:
"Let there be lights in the vault of the heavens
to divide between the day and between the night;
they will be for signs and seasons and for days and years;
15 they will be for lights in the vault of the heavens to give
light upon the earth."
So it was.
16 Elohim made the two great lights,
the greater light to rule the day
and the lesser light to rule the night,
and the stars.
17 Elohim placed them in the vault of the heavens,
to give light upon the earth,
18 to rule in the day and in the night,
and to divide between the light and between the darkness.
Elohim saw that it was good.
19 There was evening.
There was morning:
A fourth day.

20 Elohim said:
"Let the waters swarm with swarms of living beings.
Let birds fly about—above the earth
and under the vault of the heavens."
21 Elohim formed the great sea monsters,
and all the living beings—
the moving ones who swarmed in the waters—with their kind,
and all the birds of wing with their kind.

Genesis, a Royal Epic

    Elohim saw that it was good.
22 Elohim blessed them saying:
    "Be fruitful, multiply, and fill the waters in the seas,
    and let the birds multiply on the earth."
23 There was evening.
    There was morning:
    A fifth day.

24 Elohim said:
    "Let the earth bring forth living beings with their kind:
      domestic animals, moving ones, and wild animals with their kind."
    So it was.
25 Elohim made the wild animals with their kind,
    the domestic animals with their kind,
    and all the moving ones of the ground with their kind.
    Elohim saw that it was good.
26 Elohim said:
    "Let us make human beings[10] in our[11] image—after our likeness;
    they will supervise the fish of the sea,
    the birds of the heavens, the domestic animals,
    all of the earth, and all the ones who move upon the earth."
27 Elohim formed the human beings in his image;
    in the image of Elohim he formed them;[12]
    male and female he formed them.
28 Elohim blessed them;
    Elohim said to them:
    "Be fruitful and multiply; fill the earth;
    make it a servant; and supervise the fish of the sea,
    the birds of the heavens, and all the living ones
    who move upon the earth."

---

10. The Hebrew word *'adam* is taken here in a collective sense as it must be in v. 27 and in 5:1 and 2.

11. Such plurals refer to members of divine councils in most AML (also see 3:22).

12. Here the singular suffix is taken in the collective sense and thus translated in the plural.

Genesis 1:1—11:26

29   Elohim said:
        "See, I give you every plant that scatters
        seed that is upon all the earth and every tree that scatters
        seed (that is in the fruit of the tree); it will be yours for food.
30   To all the wild animals, to all the birds of the heavens,
        and to all the ones who move upon the earth
        (that are living beings), [I give] all the green plants for food."
    So it was.
31   Elohim saw all that he had made, and behold, it was very
        good.
    There was evening.
    There was morning:
    The sixth day.[13]
2:1   The heavens and the earth were finished and all their entourage.
2   Elohim finished[14] on the seventh day[15] his work that he had been
        doing.
    He rested on the seventh day from all his work that he had done.
3   Elohim blessed the seventh day; he hallowed it,
    because on it he rested from all his work that as Elohim,
    the maker, he had formed.

2:4   ***These are the stories of the heavens and the earth since their formation.***[16]

---

13. This time clause should be "A Sixth Day," and it would work much better just after v. 25. At this point "A Seventh Day" is needed in light of Gen 2:2.

14. The word "finished" (here and in v. 1) is a good translation, because it can have the two meanings of the Hebrew: 1) "to complete," and 2) "to destroy." There was at least one rabbi who understood it in the second sense; in Gen R, Rabbi Efes preached that this meant "destruction." This would make another account of the formation of the world an important next step. See the note on Gen 2:4b.

15. Here the LXX and Sam have "sixth." They had to change it to make sense, but the real problem is with the present form of 1:31.

16. This is a title by the final editor who divided this book with ten titles: 2:4a; 5:1a; 6:9a; 10:1; 11:10a; 11:27a; 25:12; 25:19a; 36:1 (also in 36:9 there is a second title); and 37:2a (see the outline of Genesis in the Introduction). The word "stories" in these titles comes close to the intended meaning, but it is not fully adequate. Here the title mentions "the heavens and the earth," and they have been introduced in 1:1—2:3. In the other titles it works the same way; the person in the title has already been introduced, and the following material deals with subsequent developments and persons.

	On another day[17] when Yahweh-Elohim was about to make earth and heavens,
5	there was as yet no wild shrub on the earth,
	as yet no wild grass had sprouted,
	because Yahweh-Elohim had not sent rain upon the earth,
	and there was no human (*'adam*) to till the ground (*'adamah*),
6	but a flood began flowing from the netherworld,
	and watered the entire surface of the ground,[18]
7	Yahweh-Elohim formed the human [from] the clay[19] of the ground;
	he blew into his nostrils the breath of life;
	the human became a living being.[20]

17. Here we have a second account of the ordering of the cosmos from another source (most give this account to J and the first account to P). If this story was by itself, the best translation of the first words (literally, "In the day") would be "When," but since it follows the story in the first chapter, "On another day when" makes more sense especially if the first work was destroyed. This follows a suggestion by Gordon in "Asymmetric Janus Parallelism," in "'This Time' (Genesis 2:23)," and in "Poetic Legends and Myths from Ugarit," 64. Also see the note on Gen 2:2. It is interesting that when all things are destroyed by the flood, there will have to be another story concerning beginnings. However the above proposal is not the only one on this subject. The second account is usually understood as a much more detailed account of the formation of the humans which makes it useful even though it brings with it, as a second account, many problems. In this case, it is not viewed as a new beginning, but as just another account with material that is useful. (It is like a blow-up or insert on a map showing in great detail a small area.) In the past, such a discussion was not needed when the final editor was seen as a scribe who just used his "cut and paste commands" with very little thought concerning the final meaning; but now the final editor is usually seen as one who has given the entire structure some real thought. It is interesting that with the use of "finished" in Gen 2:1–2, the reader can go either way.

18. This new section begins just like the previous one. Here 4b–6 deals with the circumstance.

19. The Hebrew word (*'apar*) is usually translated "dust" and recently "clod" (in Speiser, AB). This word can mean "dust," "soil," "dirt," "clod," "mud," "particles," "ore," "mortar," "the netherworld," and many other things, so it is very difficult to translate. It refers often to the condition of the soil rather than its content. A translation "mud" would be contextually correct since the entire surface of the ground has just been flooded. It can not be "dust." But, words like "mud" and "clod" can carry derogatory meanings that are sometimes misleading for translating. Here we translate "clay", because in poetry the material of the human body is seen as clay and related to the work of the potter. Note Job 4:19 and 10:9 where "clay" and the traditional "dust" are used in parallel lines. Also, see the note at 3:19.

20. Note that the human is classified as a "living being," and in v. 19 the animals and the birds are also called "living beings."

Genesis 1:1—11:26

8   Yahweh-Elohim planted a garden in Eden, in the east;
    he placed there the human whom he had formed.

9   Yahweh-Elohim caused to sprout from the ground
    every tree desirable in appearance and good for food,
    and the tree of life was in the middle of the garden
    and also the tree of the knowledge of good and evil.
10 (A river flows out of Eden to water the garden,
    and from there it separates; it becomes four branches.
11 The name of the first is Pishon;
    it is the one that flows around the entire land of Havilah,
    in which there is the gold.
12 The gold of that land is excellent.
    The bdellium is there and the *shoham*[21] gems.
13 The name of the second river is Gihon;
    it is the one that flows around the entire land of Cush.
14 The name of the third river is Tigris;
    it runs east of Asshur,
    and the name of the fourth river is Euphrates.)

15 Yahweh-Elohim took the human;
    he settled him in the garden of Eden to till it and guard it.
16 Yahweh-Elohim commanded the human, saying:
        "From every tree of the garden you may certainly eat,
17   except from the tree of the knowledge of good and evil,[22]
        you shall not eat of it,
        because when you eat of it,
        you shall certainly die."

18 Yahweh-Elohim said:
        "It is not good for the human to be alone;
        I will make for him a helper just like him."

---

21. The meaning of this Hebrew word is uncertain.
22. The "knowledge of good and evil" means the "knowledge of everything"; see Gen 3:5, 22; and 31:24. The passage that makes it all clear is 2 Sam 14:17 and 20 (in v. 17 David can understand "good and evil" and hence in v. 20 he knows everything).

19	Yahweh-Elohim formed from the ground all the wild animals and all the birds of the heavens. He brought [them] to the human to see what he called them, and whatever the human called each of the living beings, that was its name.
20	The human gave names to all the domestic animals, to the birds of the heavens, and to all the wild animals, but as for the human, he did not find a helper just like him.
21	Yahweh-Elohim cast a deep sleep upon the human; he slept. He took one of his ribs; He closed the flesh there.
22	Yahweh-Elohim built up the rib, which he had taken from the human, into a woman; he brought her to the human.

23	The human said:
	    "This one, at last, is bone of my bones
	    And flesh of my flesh.
	    This one shall be called woman (*'ishshah*),
	    For from man (*'ish*) this one was taken."

24	Therefore a man leaves his father and his mother; He is joined with his wife; They become one flesh.[23]
25	The two of them were naked (*'arummim*)— the human and his wife, and they were not ashamed.

3:1	Now the serpent was the wisest (*'arum*) of all the wild animals that Yahweh-Elohim had made; he said to the woman:
	    "Indeed, did Elohim really say,
	    'From every tree of the garden
	    you shall not eat?'"

---

23. They can become one flesh, because they are from the same substance. They are soul-mates.

2	The woman said to the serpent:
	"From the fruit of the trees of the garden we may eat,
3	but from the fruit of the tree that is in the midst of the garden,
	Elohim said, 'You shall not eat from it,
	and you shall not touch it,
	or you shall die.'"
4	The serpent said to the woman:
	"Surely, you shall not die;
5	Elohim knows that when you eat from it
	your eyes will be opened;
	you will be like gods—ones who know good and evil."[24]
6	The woman saw that the tree was good for food,
	that it was a delight to the eyes,
	and that the tree was desired to make one wise.
	She took from its fruit; she ate.
	Also when she gave [some] to her husband,
	who was with her, he ate.
7	The eyes of both of them were opened;
	they knew that they were naked (*'erummim*).
	They sewed together fig leaves;
	they made for themselves loincloths.
8	They heard the voice of Yahweh-Elohim,
	who was walking about in the garden at the windy time of day;
	the human and his wife hid from Yahweh-Elohim,
	among the trees of the garden.
9	Yahweh-Elohim called to the human.
	He said to him:
	"Where are you?"
10	He said:
	"I heard your voice in the garden;
	I was afraid,
	because I was naked (*'erom*).
	I hid."

24. See the note on "good and evil" at Gen 2:17. This is a story of how the humans gained all knowledge (see v. 22 and the notes for additional thoughts). It is not a story of "the fall" as understood in later times.

Genesis, a Royal Epic

11 He said:
    "Who told you that you were naked (*'erom*)?
    Did you eat from the tree that I had commanded you not to eat?"

12 The human said:
    "The woman, whom you gave to be with me,
    she gave to me from the tree! I ate."

13 Yahweh-Elohim said to the woman:
    "What is this that you have done?"
The woman said:
    "The serpent deceived me! I ate."

14 Yahweh-Elohim said to the serpent:
    "Because you have done this,
    Cursed (*'arur*) are you—
    More than all domestic animals,
    More than all wild animals.
    On your belly you shall go,[25]
    And dirt[26] you shall eat—
    All the days of your life.

15   Hostility I will put between you
    And between the woman—
    Between your descendants,
    And between her descendants.
    They shall attack you frontally;
    You shall attack them from behind."

16 To the woman he said:
    "I will multiply your pains from your pregnancies;
    In labor[27] you will bear children.
    Your desire is for your husband,
    But he will rule you."[28]

---

25. This is an explanation of why it is that the serpent does not have legs.

26. See 2:7 and the note. This could be "dust," but "dirt" covers all conditions of the soil, and in English it retains the sense of a curse.

27. This word could be translated as in the preceding line, i.e., "pain," but "labor" works well in English and helps to relate this to the next verse.

28. On this last line compare 4:7.

Genesis 1:1—11:26

17   To the[29] human he said:
"Because you listened to the voice of your wife,[30]
You ate from the tree
About which I had commanded you saying,
'You shall not eat from it.'
Cursed (*'arurah*) be the ground on account of you;
In labor[31] you shall eat it[32]—
All the days of your life.

18   Thorns and thistles it shall sprout for you.
You shall eat the wild grass.

19   By the sweat of your brow you shall eat food,
Until you return to the ground,
For from it you were taken.
For you are clay,
And to clay you shall return."[33]

20   The human called forth the name of his wife, "Eve" (*hawwah*),[34] because she was the mother of all living (*hay*).

---

29. Here the vowel has been changed to include the article.

30. Literally "heard the voice of your wife." "Heard the voice" is a phrase that occurs elsewhere in Genesis, and each time most translations usually change it according to the context. But in this translation, we will keep it as "listen to the voice." See Gen 4:23; 16:2; 21:12, 17; 22:18; 26:5; and 27:8. For a fuller explanation see the note at Gen 26:5.

31. See the note for v. 16.

32. Most translations read "of it," and that makes sense. However, the present translation is very literal and in this form it is parallel to the lines in v. 14. If you work the ground you will not only eat from it, but you will eat it.

33. Here again is the Hebrew *'apar* (see the note on 2:7). The traditional translation "For dust you are, and to dust you shall return" (Tanakh) is passable in this case. Job 10:9 is more poetic with the synonyms "mud/clay" and "dust." But in light of 2:7 and the fact that all of the humans will be destroyed by the great flood (except Noah and family), the present translation is contextual. Both the translator and the reader must see the flood as the great divide. Also see the note on 6:3.

34. This naming formula is used many times in Genesis. Most translations shorten it to something like "The man named his wife Eve" (NRSV). However the naming formula was usually a part of some ritual where the name was actually pronounced (this was the case even in very late times as we can see in Luke 1:59 and 2:21). Also the Hebrew scribes knew how to write a shorter form of this. Note Gen 35:18, "Just as her being left her (for she died), she called forth his name, "Ben-oni." His father named him Benjamin."

21	Yahweh-Elohim made for the human and his wife garments of skins;
	he clothed them.
22	Yahweh-Elohim said:
	"Yes, the human has become like one of us,[35]
	knowing good and evil, so now,
	he must not reach out his hand,
	taking also from the tree of life,
	he would eat and live forever!"[36]
23	Yahweh-Elohim sent him from the garden of Eden,
	to till the ground from which he was taken;
24	he drove out the human;
	he stationed, east of the garden of Eden,
	the cherubim and the flaming sword,
	which turned every way to guard the way to the tree of life.
4:1	Now the human knew Eve, his wife.
	She conceived; she bore Cain (*qayin*).
	She said:
	"I have procreated (*qaniti*) a man with Yahweh."
2	Next she gave birth to his brother Abel.
	Abel became a keeper of flocks,
	and Cain became a tiller of the ground.
3	In the course of time,
	Cain brought from the fruit of the ground an offering to Yahweh,
4	and Abel, he also brought from the firstborn of his flock
	and from their choice portions.
	Yahweh paid attention to Abel and to his offering,
5	but to Cain and to his offering he paid no attention.
	Cain became very angry; he became downcast.

---

35. See the note on 1:26.

36. To have all knowledge (i.e., the knowledge of good and evil, see Gen 2:17 and the note) and to be immortal is not allowed for the human; this would mean that the human was a god. The story is etiological and accounts for the fact that humans are mortal, but they do have great knowledge. This is very much like the *Adapa* story (*ANET*, 101–3; *COS* 1.129 [p. 449]) and is understood in Ezekiel 28.

Genesis 1:1—11:26

6   Yahweh said to Cain:
        "Why are you angry?
        Why are you so down?
7   Is it not true [that],
        Either you do well
        [And you] are upbeat,
        Or you don't do well,
        [And so in this case],
        Sin is the demon,[37]
        [Who is] at the door?
        His desire is for you,
        But you will rule him."[38]
8   Cain spoke[39] against Abel, his brother;
    when they were in the field,
    Cain rose up against Abel, his brother;
    he killed him.
9   Yahweh said to Cain:
        "Where is Abel your brother?"
    He said to him:
        "I do not know. Am I my brother's keeper?"
10   He said:
        "What have you done?
        The voice of the blood of your brother is crying to me from
            the ground,
11   and now you are cursed from the ground
        that has opened its mouth
        to receive your brother's blood from your hand.

37. In other words this is a bad demon who will bring one down. The word is an Akkadian loan, *rabiṣum*. It is well known that many ancient people believed that demons often lived at the threshold of dwellings. Also this is the first time that the word "sin" is used in Genesis.

38. For a parallel see 3:16. In both places in this translation the simple future has been used; those who add "will be able to rule" or "can rule" are going beyond what we can know.

39. Most translators think that the Hebrew *'amar* cannot be used in this sense, and they translate something like "Then Cain said . . ." and sometimes add what he said. But here we have a parallel: "Cain spoke against Abel" and "Cain rose up against Abel." "To speak against" can also mean "to plot against." Also see Cassuto's unlikely translation: "Cain appointed a place where to meet Abel" (Cassuto, I, 205, 213–15).

Genesis, a Royal Epic

12	When you till the ground,
	it will never again give its strength to you;
	a vagrant and a wanderer (*nad*) you shall be on the earth."
13	Cain said to Yahweh:
	"My iniquity is too great to be lifted up.
14	It is clear;
	this day you drove me from the face of the ground,
	and from your face I shall hide.
	I shall be a vagrant and a wanderer (*nad*) on earth,
	for anyone who finds me will kill me."
15	Yahweh said to him:
	"Therefore, anyone who kills Cain
	shall receive sevenfold vengeance."
	Yahweh put a mark on Cain,
	so that no one who found him would strike him.
16	Cain went out from the presence of Yahweh;
	he settled in the land of Nod,[40] east of Eden.
17	Cain knew his wife.
	She conceived; she bore Enoch.
	He[41] was the builder of a city.
	He called the name of the city after the name of his son, Enoch.
18	To Enoch was born Irad.
	Irad fathered Mehujael.
	Mehujael fathered Methushael.
	Methushael fathered Lamech.
19	Lamech took for himself two wives.
	The name of the one was Adah,
	and the name of the other was Zillah.
20	Adah bore Jabal.
	He was the "father"[42] of those who dwell with tents and herds.
21	The name of his brother was Jubal.
	He was the "father" of all who are skilled with lyre and pipe.

40. This is a pun on *nad* in vv. 12 and 14.
41. This is Cain.
42. "Father" in this context means the "teacher" or "founder" of a group or a guild, or to put it another way, see v. 22 "the master craftsman."

22   Also, Zillah bore Tubal-Cain,
     the master craftsman of all who are workers with copper and iron
     (and the sister of Tubal-Cain was Naamah).

23   Lamech said to his wives:
         "Adah and Zillah, listen to me;[43]
         Wives of Lamech, give ear to my speech.
         Yes,[44] I have slain a man for my wounds—
         And even a young child for my blows.
24   Yes, Cain will be avenged sevenfold,
         But, Lamech seventy and seven."

25   Adam[45] knew his wife again.
     She bore a son.
     She called forth his name, "Seth," because, [she continued,][46]
         "Elohim set[47] for me another offspring in the place of Abel,
         for his killer was Cain."
26   Also to Seth, a son was born.
     He called forth his name, "Enosh."[48]

     Then it was begun: calling on Yahweh by name.[49]

5:1a   *This is the document of the stories of Adam.*

1b   When Elohim was forming human beings (*'adam*),
       in the likeness of Elohim he made them;

---

43. "To me" is literally "to my voice."

44. Here, the translation "yes" (and also in v. 24) follows the *Ja* of Buber and Rosenzweig.

45. This is the first time that "Adam" is used as a proper name; here it does not have the article.

46. Compare this insertion to Gen 5:29.

47. There may be better translations, but "set" is used, because it sounds like "Seth" just as in the Hebrew. This is a rare example.

48. Verses 25 and 26a are from an unknown source.

49. For a discussion of this phrase see the note on Gen 26:25.

Genesis, a Royal Epic

2   male and female he formed them.
He blessed them; he called forth their name, "Adam,"[50]
when they were formed.[51]

3   **Adam**[52] lived a hundred and thirty years;
he fathered [a son], in his likeness after his image;
he called forth his name, "Seth."

4   The days of Adam were, after he fathered Seth,
eight hundred years. He fathered sons and daughters.

5   When all the days of Adam, that he lived,
equaled nine hundred and thirty years, he died.

6   **Seth** lived a hundred and five years; he fathered Enosh.

7   Seth lived, after he fathered Enosh,
eight hundred and seven years.
He fathered sons and daughters.

8   When all the days of Seth
equaled nine hundred and twelve years, he died.

9   **Enosh** lived ninety years; he fathered Kenan.

10   Enosh lived, after he fathered Kenan,
eight hundred and fifteen years.
He fathered sons and daughters.

11   When all the days of Enosh
equaled nine hundred and five years, he died.

12   **Kenan** lived seventy years; he fathered Mahalalel.

13   Kenan lived, after he fathered Mahalalel,
eight hundred and forty years.
He fathered sons and daughters.

14   When all the days of Kenan
equaled nine hundred and ten years, he died.

---

50. Here one is tempted to translate their name (it means "human beings" as in v. 1b), but it is not a good idea to translate names as noted in Gen 32:31. Here we have a different source. This time we can refer to it as a document.

51. Genesis 5:1b–2 is a statement that follows the tradition of Gen 1:26–27. Therefore, many give this material to P and the material in chapter 4 to J.

52. In v. 1b the word "Adam" is a collective; it is plural. In v. 2 "Adam" is the name given to all the humans as a group. In vv. 1a and 3 it is a proper name for an individual. Here the first human is named, Adam, as in Gen 4:25.

Genesis 1:1—11:26

15	**Mahalalel** lived sixty-five years; he fathered Jared.
16	Mahalalel lived, after he fathered Jared,
	eight hundred and thirty years.
	He fathered sons and daughters.
17	When all the days of Mahalalel
	equaled eight hundred and ninety-five years, he died.
18	**Jared** lived a hundred and sixty-two years; he fathered Enoch.
19	Jared lived, after he fathered Enoch,
	eight hundred years.
	He fathered sons and daughters.
20	When all the days of Jared
	equaled nine hundred and sixty-two years, he died.
21	**Enoch** lived sixty-five years; he fathered Methuselah.
22	Enoch walked with the gods,[53] after he fathered Methuselah,
	three hundred years.
	He fathered sons and daughters.
23	Now all the days of Enoch
	equaled three hundred and sixty-five.
24	Enoch walked with the gods;
	then he was no more, because Elohim took him.
25	**Methuselah** lived a hundred and eighty-seven years;
	he fathered Lamech.
26	Methuselah lived, after he fathered Lamech,
	seven hundred and eighty-two years.
	He fathered sons and daughters.
27	When all the days of Methuselah
	equaled nine hundred and sixty-nine, he died.
28	**Lamech** lived a hundred and eighty-two years; he fathered a son.
29	He called forth his name, "Noah," saying,
	"This one will comfort us from our work,
	And from the toil of our hands,
	From the ground that Yahweh cursed."[54]

53. Here and in v. 24 *haʾelohim* is translated "the gods." This is a real possibility, because we are dealing with pre-flood heroes. Such matters are difficult, but we cannot follow older grammars that tend to opt for the singular unless the speaker is a "heathen" (see Gesenius, §145i, p. 463).

54. This takes us back to Gen 3:17.

30	Lamech lived, after he fathered Noah, five hundred and ninety-five years. He fathered sons and daughters.
31	When all the days of Lamech equaled seven hundred and seventy-seven, he died.
32	When **Noah** was five hundred years old, Noah fathered Shem, Ham, and Japheth.
6:1	When the human beings began to multiply, upon the face of the ground, and daughters were born to them,
2	the sons of the gods saw that the daughters of the human beings were beautiful, they took for themselves wives from any of those they chose.
3	Yahweh said: "My spirit cannot be bottled up[55] in human beings forever, Inasmuch as, they are flesh. Their days will be a hundred and twenty years."
4	The Nephilim[56] were on earth in those days, and afterwards, for the sons of the gods did mate with the daughters of the human beings; they bore [children] to them— they were the heroes of old, the men of renown.

55. The Hebrew *yadon* has always been a problem. This translation "be bottled up" is based upon Arabic and Ugaritic usage of the root *dnn* (see *UT* #680, p. 386). Cassuto was on to this meaning, but he never followed through (Cassuto I, 296). Other translators have come close to the general meaning, but they have lost the color. The root refers to a kind of jar, and so once again we have the human body described as being made out of clay (see Job 4:19).

56. The Nephilim were (as the verse says) "the heroes of old, the men of renown" (for an interesting discussion of this see Kilmer, "The Mesopotamian Counterparts of the Biblical Nepilim." In the ancient world very special people were seen as part divine. But this does not mean that they are immortal; they are made of clay; they are flesh. The great Gilgamesh was part divine, but he finally learned that he was mortal. Tradition has always seen the Nephilim in a very negative way, but this text sees them as great heroes. In such royal literature it is important to deal with the early pre-flood sages, because their knowledge will be passed on to the post-flood population by the hero of the flood. This account is not connected to v. 5ff. where the reason is given for the flood.

Genesis 1:1—11:26

5	Yahweh saw how great was the evil of the human beings on the earth,
	and how every form of the thoughts of their minds was only evil, all of the day.
6	Yahweh regretted that he had made the human beings on the earth.
	He was in labor with his thoughts.[57]
7	Yahweh said:
	"I will blot out the human beings whom I formed,
	from upon the face of the ground—
	from human beings to domestic animals,
	to moving ones, and to the birds of the heavens,
	because I regret that I made them."
8	But Noah found favor in the eyes of Yahweh.
9a	***These are the stories of Noah.***
9b	Noah was a righteous man;
	He was perfect in his generation.
	With the gods,[58] Noah walked.
10	Noah fathered three sons:
	Shem, Ham, and Japheth.
11	The earth was found corrupt before the gods;[59]
	The earth was full of violence.
12	Elohim saw the earth;
	Yes, it was corrupt,
	For all flesh[60] had corrupted their ways upon earth.

---

57. The translation of this phrase is far from literal. A more literal translation would be: "he was suffering to his heart." What we need to remember is that "heart" in Hebrew is usually translated by the word "mind" as in the previous verse. On the word "labor," see 3:16 and 17. Also see 8:21 for an interesting parallel.

58. See the note on 5:22 and note v. 11 below.

59. This is a court scene in the assembly of the gods.

60. "All flesh" (here and elsewhere) refers to all creatures from birds to humans (see 7:21).

Genesis, a Royal Epic

13   Elohim said to Noah:
          "The end of all flesh was declared before me,[61]
          for the earth is filled with violence because of [all flesh],[62]
          and yes, I am the one who shall destroy [all flesh] with the earth.

14   Make for yourself an ark of gopher planks.
          Of reeds[63] you shall make the ark.
          You shall pitch it—inside and outside—with pitch.

15   This is how you shall make it:
          the ark shall be three hundred cubits long,
          its width fifty cubits,
          and its height thirty cubits.

16   A sky-light you shall make for the ark.
          You shall finish it a cubit higher.
          Now you shall put the door of the ark in its side.
          With a lower, a second, and a third [deck] you shall make it.

17   Certainly, I am the one who shall bring the flood—
          waters upon the earth—
          to destroy all flesh that has in it spirit of life under the heavens.
          All which is on the earth will perish.

18   But I will establish my covenant with you;
          you shall come into the ark,
          you and your sons, and your wife,
          and the wives of your sons with you.

19   And from all the living, from all flesh, two from all,
          you shall bring to the ark to live with you;
          male and female, they shall be.

20   And from the birds with their kind,
          and from the domestic animals with their kind,
          and from all the moving ones of the ground with their kind,
          two from all [kinds] will come to you to be kept alive.

---

61. In other words this was a decision of the court.

62. Here and in the next line the Hebrew text has "them." For clarity we have not used the pronoun.

63. This word is usually translated as "rooms" or "compartments." But, this word is in poetic parallel with "gopher planks," and should be read *qanim* from *qaneh*.

21	And you, take for yourself from all food that is eaten;
	you shall gather [it] unto you;
	It will be for you and for them to eat."
22	Noah did according to all that Elohim commanded him, so he did.
7:1	Yahweh said to Noah:
	"Enter, you and all your house, into the ark,
	for I have found that you are righteous before me in this age.
2	From all the clean domestic animals,
	you shall take seven [and] seven, a male and his mate,
	and from the domestic animals that are not clean,
	it is two, a male and his mate,
3	also, from the birds of the heavens,
	seven [and] seven, male and female,
	to keep alive seed upon the face of all the earth.
4	For in seven days, I am the one who shall bring rain upon the earth
	—forty days and forty nights;
	I will blot out all who stand,
	that I made upon the face of the ground."
5	Noah did according to all that Yahweh commanded him.
6	Noah was six hundred years old, and then the flood came—
	waters upon the earth.
7	Noah, with his sons, his wife, and the wives of his sons,
	entered the ark because of the waters of the flood.
8	From the clean domestic animals,
	from the domestic animals that are not clean,
	from the birds, and all the ones that move upon the ground,
9	as pairs, they entered to Noah,
	into the ark, male and female,
	as Elohim had commanded Noah.
10	After seven days, the waters of the flood came upon the earth.
11	In the six hundredth year of Noah's life,
	in the second month,
	on the seventeenth day of the month,

Genesis, a Royal Epic

	on that day, they burst forth all fountains of [the] great deep,[64] and the windows of the heavens were opened.
12	Then came the rain upon the earth, forty days and forty nights.
13	On that very day, Noah entered, with Shem, Ham, and Japheth, the sons of Noah, with his wife, and the three wives of his sons into the ark—
14	they and all the living with their kind: all the domestic animals with their kind, all the moving ones, the ones who move upon the earth, with their kind, and all the birds with their kind—all birds of every wing.
15	They came to Noah, into the ark as pairs, From all the flesh that had within it spirit of life.
16	The ones who entered were male and female from all flesh; They entered as Elohim had commanded them;[65] Yahweh shut them in.
17	The flood was upon the earth forty days. The waters increased. They lifted the ark; it rose above the earth.
18	The waters were mighty; they increased greatly upon the earth. The ark moved upon the face of the waters.
19	The waters became much more mighty upon the earth; covered were all the high mountains, that were under all the heavens.
20	Fifteen cubits higher, the waters were mighty; they covered the mountains.

---

64. See 1:2. This is a return to the chaos that existed before God began to order it.

65. "Them" in this line and the next line is "him" in the Hebrew text and in most translations. If the pronoun refers to Noah, then it should be "him" (as in Gen 7:9). But the singular has to be understood as plural in this context and in many other places.

21 All flesh perished, the ones who move upon the earth:
    the birds, the domestic animals, the [wild] animals,
    the swarmers, the ones who swarm upon earth,
    and all the humans.
22 All that had [the] breath of (spirit of)[66] life in their nostrils,
    all that had been on dry land died.
23 He blotted out all who stand,
    that were upon the face of the ground,
    from humans to domestic animals,
    to moving ones, and to the birds of the heavens;
    they were blotted out from the earth.
    Only Noah was left and those with him in the ark.

24 The waters were mighty upon the earth [for] a hundred and fifty days.

8:1 Elohim remembered Noah
    and all the living and all the domestic animals
    that were with him on the ark.
    Elohim made a wind move upon the earth; the waters decreased.
2   They were closed—
    the fountains of [the] deep,[67]
    and the windows of the heavens.
    It was withheld—
    the rain from the heavens.
3   The waters returned from [being] upon the earth—
    going and returning.
    The waters decreased at the end of a hundred and fifty days.

4   The ark came to rest (*wattanaḥ*),[68]
    in the seventh month, on the seventeenth day of the month,
    upon the mountains of Ararat,

---

66. This is strange; someone has inserted "spirit/wind" to explain "breath."
67. Now there is a return to order—a new cosmos. This is a new beginning.
68. These forms (also vv. 9 and 21) that are transliterated are all built upon the root that means "rest" and from which we have the name Noah.

5	and the waters were going and decreasing until the tenth month.
	In the tenth [month], on the first of the month,
	the tops of the mountains appeared.
6	At the end of forty days,
	Noah opened the window of the ark that he had made.
7	He put out the raven; [the raven] went out—going and returning—
	until the drying up of the waters from upon the earth.
8	He put out the dove, who was with him,
	to see if the waters had decreased from upon the face of the ground.
9	But, the dove could not find a resting place (*Manoaḥ*),
	for the sole of her foot; she[69] returned to him, to the ark,
	for there was water upon the face of all of the earth.
	He put out his hand; he took her;
	he brought her to him, into the ark.
10	He waited for another seven days.
	Again he put out the dove from the ark.
11	The dove returned to him at evening time,
	and there were olive leaves, just picked, in her mouth.
	Noah knew that the waters had decreased from upon the earth.
12	He waited for another seven days.
	He put out the dove, but she did not ever return to him again.
13	It was in the six hundred and first year,
	in the first [month], on the first [day] of the month,
	the waters were dried from upon the earth.
	Noah removed the covering of the ark.
	He saw that the surface of the ground was dry,
14	and in the second month, on the twenty-seventh day of the month,
	the earth was completely dry.
15	Elohim spoke to Noah, as follows:
16	"Come out from the ark,
	you and your wife,
	your sons and the wives of your sons with you.

---

69. There is no way to prove that this is a female dove. The word for dove in Hebrew is feminine and takes feminine forms. But in a story that deals with "all flesh," should we objectify and neuter "all flesh"? English may demand "it," but she allows us to use a "she" here and there. See Gen 22:13 for another example.

Genesis 1:1—11:26

17 All the living that is with you from all flesh:
    from birds, from domestic animals,
    from all the moving ones—
    the ones who move upon the earth,
    bring out with you.
    They will swarm on the earth;
    they will be fruitful and multiply upon the earth."

18 Noah came out, his sons, his wife, and the wives of his sons with him;
19 all the living, all the moving ones, all the birds,
    and all the ones who move upon the earth, with their families,
    they came out from the ark.

20 Noah built an altar to Yahweh.
    He took from all the clean domestic animals
    and from all the clean birds;
    he offered burnt offerings on the altar.

21 Yahweh smelled the soothing (*niḥoaḥ*) odor;
    Yahweh considered:
        "Never again will I despise the ground
        Because of the humans,
        Since the formations,
        In the minds of humans,
        Are evil from their youth.
        Never again will I destroy all life as I did.

22   Throughout all the days of the earth,
        Sowing and reaping,
        Cold and heat,
        Summer and winter,
        Day and night,
        They shall not cease."[70]

---

70. Order in this post-flood world is detailed in this poem. From this point on the stories speak concerning the realities of the world of the Hebrews and their neighbors.

61

9:1		Elohim blessed Noah and his sons; he said to them:
		"Be fruitful and multiply and fill the earth.
2		Your fear and your dread shall be upon all the wild animals,
		and upon all the birds of the heaven,
		[and] in all that moves [upon] the ground,
		and in all the fish of the sea.
		Into your hand they are given.
3		Every moving one that is alive shall be food for you—
		as with [the] green plants, I gave you everything.
4		But, flesh with its being ([that is] its blood) you shall not eat.
5		And surely, [for] the blood of your being I will avenge:
		from the hand of all living I will avenge it,
		from the hand of the human,
		from the hand of a man [for] his brother,
		I will avenge the being of the human.
6		Whoever sheds the blood of the human,
		By the human shall his blood be shed;
		For in the image of Elohim,
		He made the human.
7		And you, be fruitful and multiply;
		swarm on the earth and multiply on it."
8		Elohim said to Noah and to his sons with him as follows:
9		"It is me; I am the one who shall establish my covenant
		with you and with your descendants after you,
10		and with every living being who is with you:
		the birds, the domestic animals, and all the wild animals with you
		(from all the ones who came out of the ark are all the wild animals).
11		I will establish my covenant with you,
		and never again shall all flesh be cut off by the waters of the flood,
		and never again shall there be a flood to destroy the earth."

12	Elohim said:
	"This is the sign of the covenant that I will set between me
	and between you and between every living being who is with you,
	for all future generations.
13	My bow, I have set in the clouds;
	it shall be a sign of the covenant between me
	and between the earth.
14	It will be that when I build up clouds over the earth,
	the bow will appear in the clouds;
15	I will remember my covenant that is between me
	and between you and between every living being among all flesh,
	and never again shall the waters become a flood
	to destroy all flesh.
16	When the bow is in the clouds, I will see it,
	remembering the eternal covenant between Elohim
	and between every living being among all flesh
	that is upon the earth."
17	Elohim said to Noah:
	"This is the sign of the covenant that I have established
	between me and between all flesh that is upon the earth."
18	The sons of Noah who came out of the ark were
	Shem, Ham, and Japheth—
	and Ham, he was the father of Canaan.
19	These three were the sons of Noah,
	and from these all the earth was populated.
20	Noah became a farmer.[71]
	He planted a vineyard.[72]

---

71. The verb in this clause means "began to be." The translation "farmer" comes from "man + the ground," and in this expression "man" is a determinative; the word "man" tells the reader that the next word is an occupation (as in Akkadian). There are many examples in Hebrew such as: "man + war" equals "warrior," "woman + prophetess" equals "prophetess," and "stone + sapphire" equals "sapphire" (in this last example the reader knows that the next word will be some kind of stone).

72. Most translators want to indicate in their translations that Noah "was the first

Genesis, a Royal Epic

21	He drank of the wine.
	He became drunk.
	He uncovered himself within his tent.[73]
22	Ham, the father of Canaan, saw the nakedness of his father.
	He told his two brothers outside.
23	Shem and Japheth took the garment;
	they put it on both their shoulders.
	They walked backwards.
	They covered the nakedness of their father.
	Because their faces were turned the other way,
	the nakedness of their father they did not see.
24	Noah awoke from his wine; he knew what his lesser[74] son had done to him.
25	He said:
	"Cursed be Canaan;
	A slave of slaves
	Shall he be to his brothers."
26	He said:
	"Blessed be Yahweh,
	the God of Shem.
	Let Canaan be a slave to them.
27	May Elohim enlarge (*yapht*) Japheth;
	let him dwell in the tents of Shem;
	let Canaan be a slave to them."

---

to plant a vineyard," but in so doing they use the verb from the first clause in combination with the verb in the second clause. This is not correct, and it is unnecessary because any reader has to assume that Noah is not only the first farmer after the flood, but he also plants the first vineyard after the flood.

73. This should be compared to the story of Lot in Gen 19:30–38.

74. This is very difficult. Most translators have "his youngest son." The sons of Noah are listed in 6:10; 9:18; and 10:1, and the order is "Shem, Ham, and Japheth." Does this indicate the order of birth? Or reverse order as in some genealogies? In 10:2, 6, and 21 they are dealt with in the order of Japheth, Ham, and Shem, and in v. 21 Japheth is said to be the elder. So, many things are possible including an impossible scramble of sources, but as it now stands the best answer to the problem is to understand Ham as the middle son who is "lesser" and unworthy. Shem is probably the youngest of the three, and in epic literature it is the younger who rules the elder. See 25:23; 37:10; 38:29; and 48:19.

28	Noah lived, after the flood, three hundred and fifty years.
29	When all the days of Noah equaled nine hundred and fifty years, he died.
10:1	***These are the stories of the sons of Noah, Shem, Ham, and Japheth***
	(sons were born to them after the flood).
2	The sons of Japheth: Gomer, Magog, Madai, Javan, Tubal, Meshech, and Tiras.
3	The sons of Gomer: Ashkenaz, Riphath, and Togarmah.
4	The sons of Javan: Elishah and Tarshish, Kittim and Dodanim.
5	From these were populated the maritime states with their lands— each with its own language according to their clans within their states.
6	The sons of Ham: Cush, Mizraim, Put, and Canaan.
7	The sons of Cush: Seba, Havilah, Sabtah, Raamah, and Sabteca (The sons of Raamah: Sheba and Dedan).
8	And Cush fathered Nimrod; he was the first to be a hero on the
9	earth; he was the hero of the hunt in the sight of Yahweh,[75] hence, it is said: "Like Nimrod the hero of the hunt in the sight of Yahweh."
10	The heads of his kingdom were Babel, Erech, Accad, and Calneh in the land of Shinar.
11	From that land Asshur went out; he built Nineveh, Rehoboth-Ir,
12	Calah, and Resen between Nineveh and between Calah, she is the great city.
13	Mizraim fathered Ludim, Anamim, Lehabim, Naphtuhim,
14	Pathrusim, Casluhim, the place from where the Philistines came, and Caphtorim.[76]
15	Canaan fathered Sidon, his first born, Heth,
16	the Jebusites, the Amorites, the Girgashites,
17	the Hivites, the Arkites, the Sinites,

75. After the flood Nimrod is the first hero. His title is given by Yahweh.
76. Caphtorim (Crete), not Casluhim, is "the place from where the Philistines came" (see Amos 9:7).

18	the Arvadites, the Zamarites, and the Hamathites.
	Later the Canaanite clans were dispersed.
19	The borders of the Canaanites were from Sidon until you reach Gerar,
	as far as Gaza, and until you reach Sodom, Gomorrah,
	Admah, and Zeboiim, as far as Lasha.
20	These are the sons of Ham according to their clans [and] languages,
	within their lands and their states.
21	Also to Shem [sons] were born;[77]
	he was the ancestor of all the sons of Eber,
	the brother of Japheth, the elder.
22	The sons of Shem: Elam, Asshur, Arpachshad, Lud, and Aram.
23	The sons of Aram: Uz, Hul, Gether, and Mash.
24	Arpachshad fathered Shelah, and Shelah fathered Eber.
25	To Eber, two sons were born; the name of the one was Peleg,
	for in his days the earth was divided (*niphlegah*),
	and the name of his brother was Joktan.
26	Joktan fathered Almodad, Sheleph, Hazarmaveth, Jerah,
27	Hadoram, Uzal, Diklah,
28	Obal, Abimael, Sheba,
29	Ophir, Havilah, and Jobab;
	all these were the sons of Joktan.
30	Their settlements were from Mesha until you come to Sepher,
	the mountain of the east.
31	These are the sons of Shem according to their clans [and] languages,
	within their lands [that belong] to their states.
32	These are the clans of the sons of Noah,
	according to their stories from their states,
	and from these, the states were populated on the earth after the flood.
11:1	Once everyone on the earth had one language
	and the very same vocabulary.

---

77. On this form see Gen 4:26.

2	During their journey from the east, they found a valley in the land of Shinar; they settled there.

3	They said to one another:
	    "Come, let us make bricks,
	    and we will fire [them] with extreme heat."
	For them the brick (*lebenah*) was stone (*le'aben*);
	the bitumen (*ḥemar*) was for them mortar (*ḥomer*).

4	They said:
	    "Come, let us build for ourselves a city
	    and a tower with its top in the heavens;
	    let us make for ourselves a name,
	    or we shall be scattered upon the face of all the earth."

5	Yahweh came down to see the city and the tower that the sons of the humans had built.

6	Yahweh said:
	    "There is one people and one speech for all of them!
	    This is their first endeavor,
	    and now, nothing will be withheld from them
	    that they purpose to do.

7	Come, we will go down; we will confuse their speech, so that, they shall not understand one another's speech."
8	Yahweh scattered them from there upon the face of all the earth; they ceased building the city.
9	Therefore, [Yahweh][78] called forth the name [of the city],[79] "Babel,"[80] because there Yahweh confused (*balal*) the speech of all the earth, and from there Yahweh scattered them upon the face of all the earth.
10	***These are the stories of Shem.*** **Shem** was a hundred years old; he fathered Arpachshad, two years after the flood.

---

78. The Hebrew text has "he called" which is usually taken as "one called."
79. In Hebrew we have literally "her name."
80. Babel refers to Babylon; it means "the gate of god."

Genesis, a Royal Epic

11	Shem lived, after he fathered Arpachshad,
	five hundred years; he fathered sons and daughters.
12	**Arpachshad** lived thirty-five years; he fathered Shelah.
13	Arpachshad lived, after he fathered Shelah,
	four hundred and three years; he fathered sons and daughters.
14	**Shelah** lived thirty years; he fathered Eber.
15	Shelah lived, after he fathered Eber,
	four hundred and three years; he fathered sons and daughters.
16	**Eber** lived thirty-four years; he fathered Peleg.
17	Eber lived, after he fathered Peleg,
	four hundred and thirty years; he fathered sons and daughters.
18	**Peleg** lived thirty years; he fathered Reu.
19	Peleg lived, after he fathered Reu,
	two hundred and nine years; he fathered sons and daughters.
20	**Reu** lived thirty-two years; he fathered Serug.
21	Reu lived, after he fathered Serug,
	two hundred and seven years; he fathered sons and daughters.
22	**Serug** lived thirty years; he fathered Nahor.
23	Serug lived, after he fathered Nahor,
	two hundred years; he fathered sons and daughters.
24	**Nahor** lived twenty-nine years; he fathered Terah.
25	Nahor lived, after he fathered Terah,
	a hundred and nineteen years; he fathered sons and daughters.
26	**Terah** lived seventy years; he fathered Abram, Nahor, and Haran.

PART II
Genesis 11:27—25:18

27 *These are the stories of Terah.*[1]

      Terah fathered Abram, Nahor, and Haran, and Haran fathered Lot.
28   Haran died before Terah, his father,
      in the land of his birth (in Ur of the Chaldeans).
29   Abram and Nahor took for themselves wives;
      the name of the wife of Abram was Sarai,
      and the name of the wife of Nahor was Milcah, the daughter of
          Haran,
      the father of Milcah and the father of Iscah.
30   Now Sarai was barren;
      she had no child.
31   Terah took Abram, his son, Lot, the son of Haran, his grandson,
      and Sarai, his daughter-in-law (the wife of Abram, his son);
      he[2] set out with them from Ur of the Chaldeans
      to go to the land of Canaan.
      They came as far as Haran; they settled there.
32   The days of Terah were two hundred and five years;
      Terah died in Haran.

12:1   Yahweh said to Abram:

---

1. This is the first major block of material in the stories of the fathers. It ends at 25:11.

2. The MT has "they set out." If we accept that reading then "with them" must refer to all of the others that went with them.

Genesis, a Royal Epic

	"Go, yes you,
	from your land,
	your kindred,
	and your father's house,
	to the land that I will show you.³
2	I will make of you a great people;
	I will bless you.
	I will make your name great;
	it will be a blessing.
3	I will bless those who bless you;
	those who curse you I will curse.
	They shall bless themselves through you,
	all the families of the ground."⁴
4	Abram went as Yahweh had commanded him; Lot went with him.
	Abram was seventy-five years old
	at the time of his departure from Haran.
5	Abram took Sarai, his wife, and Lot, the son of his brother,
	and all of their possessions that they had obtained,
	and the persons that they acquired in Haran.
	They set out to go to the land of Canaan;
	they reached the land of Canaan.
6	Abram passed through the land as far as the sanctuary⁵ of Shechem,
	as far as the oak of Moreh⁶
	(The Canaanites were then in the land).
7	Yahweh appeared to Abram; he said:
	"To your descendants I will give this land."

3. This language in form and thought compares to Gen 22:2. For "yes you" compare not only Gen 22:2 but also Gen 27:43.

4. This translation sounds strange, but the use of *'adamah*, "ground" in Genesis seems important. So much so that the untraditional translation is used to call attention to the matter. See 2:7; 7:23; 8:21; and 24:14, 15.

5. The literal meaning of this word is "place," but it can be translated "sanctuary" or "cultic place."

6. "Moreh" means "teacher." This is interesting in light of the discussion of "moriah" in a note to Gen 22:2.

He built there an altar for Yahweh,
the one who had appeared to him.

8   He moved from there to the mountain east of Bethel.
He pitched his tent; Bethel was on the west,
and Ai was on the east.
He built there an altar for Yahweh;
he called on Yahweh by name.[7]
9   Abram departed, going and moving on, toward the Negeb.

10   Now there was a famine in the land.
Abram went down to Egypt to sojourn there,
for the famine was severe in the land.
11   As he was about to enter Egypt, he said to Sarai, his wife:
    "Look now, you[8] know that you are a good looking woman.[9]
12   When the Egyptians see you, they will say,
    'This is his wife!'
    They will kill me,
    and they will let you live.
13   Please say that you are my sister,
    so that it will go well for me because of you;
    I[10] will live on account of you."

14   When Abram entered Egypt, the Egyptians noticed the woman,
because she was very beautiful.
15   The courtiers of Pharaoh saw her; they praised her to Pharaoh.
The woman was taken to the house of Pharaoh.
16   He treated Abram well because of her;
soon he had flocks, cattle, male asses, male slaves, female slaves,
female asses, and camels.

---

7. See the note for Gen 26:25 for a discussion of this phrase.

8. This is taken as an old second person form (see Judg 5:7), but it can also be read as first person.

9. Here the translation "good" in "good looking" is literally "beautiful" as in the description of Rachel in Gen 29:17 and Joseph in Gen 39:6. For Hebrew "good" in "good looking" note the description of Rebekah in Gen 24:16 and 26:7.

10. "I" is literally "my being."

Genesis, a Royal Epic

17	Yahweh plagued[11] Pharaoh and his house [with] great plagues, on account of Sarai, the wife of Abram.
18	Pharaoh summoned Abram; he said:
	"What is this you have done to me?
	Why did you not tell me that she was your wife?
19	Why did you say, 'she is my sister,' so that I took her for my wife?
	And now, here is your wife. Take [her] and go!"
20	Pharaoh put [his] men in charge of [Abram];[12]
	they deported him, his wife, and all that he owned.
13:1	Abram went up from Egypt
	(he, his wife, all that he owned, and Lot was with him)
	toward the Negeb.
2	Now Abram was very wealthy in livestock, silver, and gold.
3	He went on his journeys[13] from the Negeb as far as Bethel,
	as far as the sanctuary where his tent had been at the beginning,[14]
	between Bethel and Ai,
4	to the sanctuary of the altar that he had made there at the first.
	There Abram called on Yahweh by name.[15]
5	Lot, who went with Abram, also had flocks, cattle, and tents.
6	The land could not support them dwelling together,[16]
	For their possessions were great.
	They were not able to dwell together.[17]
7	There were disputes between the herdsmen of Abram's livestock
	and the herdsmen of Lot's livestock.
	(The Canaanites and Perizzites were then dwellers in the land.)
8	Abram said to Lot:

11. There are better translations for this verb (e.g., "afflicted"), but once again this translation is able to show that the verb ("plagued") and the noun ("plagues") are from the same root in the Hebrew text.

12. Hebrew "him."

13. This is plural, because each part of the trip was a journey.

14. See 12:8.

15. See the note on Gen 26:25 for a discussion of this phrase.

16. See Gen 36:7.

17. On this it is interesting to quote Ps 133:1, "Behold, how good and how pleasant, when brothers dwell together." Also compare v. 8.

Genesis 11:27—25:18

>   "Please, let there be no dispute between me and you,
>   between my herdsmen and your herdsmen,
>   for we are kinsmen.[18]

9   Is not all the land before you? Please separate from me.
>   If the left, then I will go right.
>   If the right, then I will go left."[19]

10   Lot lifted up his eyes; he saw[20] all the plain of the Jordan,
>   that all of it was watered (before Yahweh destroyed Sodom
>   and Gomorrah) like the garden of Yahweh,
>   like the land of Egypt as far as Zoar.[21]

11   Lot chose for himself all the plain of the Jordan;
>   Lot departed to the east.
>   They separated from each other.

12   Abram settled in the land of Canaan.
>   Lot settled among the cities of the plain;
>   he tented[22] as far as Sodom.

13   Now the men of Sodom were very evil and sinful before Yahweh.

14   Yahweh said to Abram, after Lot separated from him:
>   "Please, lift up your eyes and see,[23]
>   from the place where you are,
>   to the north and to the south,
>   to the east and to the west,

15   for all the land that you see,
>   to you I give and to your descendants forever."[24]

---

18. "Kinsmen" follows recent translations, but the Hebrew behind this translation is "men" and "brothers" ("brotherly men"). The word "brother" is broad enough to work here, but for the sake of clarity (Lot is the nephew of Abram) we use "kinsmen" with reservations.

19. Since "left" can mean "north" and "right" can mean "south," the Tanakh translates it that way. Their translation is good, but the literal form may be helpful with other parallels.

20. The first part of this verse is a formula used in Ugaritic texts (see UT 76:II:14).

21. Most translations move the clause "as far as Zoar" so that it appears just before the parenthesis.

22. This is what the verb means, and there is no object stated. The verb is used again in v. 18; one could use "camped" for the translation.

23. See v. 10 for the same formula.

24. In royal land grants from this period, the grant is always "forever"; but this does

Genesis, a Royal Epic

16	I will make your descendants as the particles of the earth;
	if one were able to count the particles of the earth,
	even your descendants could be counted.
17	Arise, walk around the land,
	unto its length and unto its breadth,
	for I give it to you."
18	Abram tented; he came;
	he settled at the oaks of Mamre that are in Hebron.
	There he built an altar for Yahweh.
14:1	It happened in the days[25] of Amraphel, king of Shinar, Arioch, king of Ellasar,
	Chedorlaomer, king of Elam, and Tidal, king of Goiim;
2	they made war with Bera, king of Sodom, with Birsha,
	king of Gomorrah, Shinab, king of Admah, Shemeber, king of Zeboiim,
	and the king of Bela (that is, Zoar).
3	All these formed an alliance at the valley of the Siddim
	(that is, the sea of the salt).[26]
4	Twelve years they had served Chedorlaomer,
	and [in] the thirteenth year they rebelled.
5	In the fourteenth year, Chedorlaomer and the kings,
	who were with him came;
	they crushed [the] Rephaim at Ashteroth-karnaim,
	the Zuzim at Ham, the Emim at Shaveh-kiriathaim,
6	and the Horites in the hills of Seir as far as the oak of Paran,
	which is by the wilderness.
7	They returned; they came to En-mishpat (that is, Kadesh);
	they raided all the fields of the Amalekites and also the Amorites,
	the ones who settled in Hazazon-tamar.
8	The king of Sodom, the king of Gomorrah, the king of Admah,
	the king of Zeboiim, and the king of Bela (that is, Zoar) marched forth;

---

not mean that the grant is unconditional.

25. For this formula see Ruth 1:1.
26. Referring to the Dead Sea.

Genesis 11:27—25:18

	they made²⁷ war against them in the valley of the Siddim,
9	against Cherdorlaomer, king of Elam, Tidal, king of Goiim,
	Amraphel, king of Shinar, and Arioch, king of Ellasar—
	four kings against the five.
10	Now the valley of the Siddim had pits [upon] pits of asphalt;
	the king of Sodom and [the king] of Gomorrah fled;
	they fell into them,
	and the survivors fled to the hills.
11	They seized all the possessions of Sodom and Gomorrah,
	and all their provisions.
	They departed.
12	They took Lot and his possessions (the son of the brother of Abram).
	They departed (he was the one who settled in Sodom).²⁸
13	One who had escaped came; he informed Abram, the Hebrew,
	(he was the one who dwelt at the oaks of Mamre, the Amorite,
	brother²⁹ of Eshkol and brother of Aner,
	and they were confederates³⁰ of Abram).
14	Abram heard that his kinsman³¹ had been captured,
	he led forth his commandos,³² born of his house,
	three hundred and eighteen;
	he gave pursuit as far as Dan.
15	He and his servants deployed against them, at night;
	he raided them;
	he pursued them as far as Hobah that is north of Damascus.

27. "Made" is the translation of a Hebrew root meaning "to prepare for war," "to order," or "to arrange."

28. This story has been inserted here. In this present location the reader does not need these parenthetical helps.

29. "Brother" is the literal meaning of the word, but it is also misleading. Here "brother" really means "an equal covenantal partner."

30. Here the literal meaning is "owners/participants of the covenant of Abram."

31. Here again "brother" means "covenantal partner," or in the case of Lot it could mean "kinsman."

32. The meaning of the Hebrew and the text is uncertain. See *ANET*, 328; *COS* 1.32 (pp. 50–52).

16	He recovered all the possessions,
	and even Lot, his kinsman, and his possessions, he recovered
	(and also the women and the troops).[33]
17	The king of Sodom came out to meet him,
	after his return from the battle with Chedorlaomer and the kings, who were with him,
	at the Valley of Shaveh (that is, the Valley of the King),
18	and Melchizedek, king of Salem, brought out food and wine;
	he was a priest of El-Elyon.
19	He blessed him; he said:
	"Blessed be Abram of El-Elyon,
	Procreator of heaven and earth.
20	Blessed be El-Elyon,
	Who gave your foes into your hand."
	He[34] gave him a tenth of everything.
21	The king of Sodom said to Abram:
	"Give me the persons,[35]
	and take the possessions for yourself."
22	Abram said to the king of Sodom:
	"I have lifted up my hand[36] to Yahweh,[37] El-Elyon,
	procreator of heaven and earth, [swearing]:
23	'Not from a thread even unto a sandal-thong!
	I will not take anything that belongs to you.'
	You shall not say, 'I, I made Abram rich.'
24	Nothing for me, except what the soldiers have used up,
	and the share of the men who went with me,
	Aner, Eshcol, and Mamre; they shall take their share."

---

33. The literal meaning is "people." For the meaning "troops" see 1 Sam 13:5 or Judg 5:9.

34. Some translations supply "Abram."

35. In this translation Hebrew *nephesh* is usually translated as "being," but here "person" is better.

36. That is "I have sworn." See *BWL*, 116.

37. "Yahweh" is probably a later addition.

Genesis 11:27—25:18

15:1 After these events, the word of Yahweh came to Abram in a vision saying:
"Do not be afraid, Abram;
I am your benefactor;[38]
Your reward shall be very great."
2 Abram said:
"Lord Yahweh, what will you give me?
Am I going about destitute?
Now the steward (*mesheq*)[39] of my house,
he is Dammesek Eliezer."
3 Abram said:
"Since you have not given me a descendant,
surely, my steward will be my heir."
4 Then the word of Yahweh [came] to him saying:
This one shall not be your heir;
Rather one who issues from your organs,
He shall be your heir."
5 He took him outside; he said:
"Please, look toward the heavens.
Count the stars if you are able to count them."
He said to him:
"So shall be your descendants."
6 He trusted Yahweh; [Yahweh][40] counted it to him [as] a rightful act.
7 He said to him:
"I am Yahweh who brought you out from Ur of the Chaldeans
to give you this land, to possess it."
8 He said:
"Lord Yahweh, how shall I know that I will possess it?"
9 He said to him:
"Bring me a heifer three years old, a female goat three years old,
a ram three years old, a turtledove, and a young bird."
10 He brought him all these;

---

38. This word can also be translated as "shield."
39. This is very uncertain, but this person/official is to be equated with the one in v. 3.
40. Hebrew has "he."

Genesis, a Royal Epic

         he cut them in two.
         He placed each half opposite the other,
         but he did not cut the birds.
11   When the raptors[41] swooped down upon the carcasses,[42]
         Abram frightened[43] them away.

12   Then as the sun was going down, a deep sleep fell upon Abram,
         and a terror, a great darkness fell upon him.
13   He said to Abram:
         "Know well that your descendants shall be immigrants,
         in a land not belonging to them.
         They shall be slaves;
         they shall be oppressed for four hundred years.
14   But even so, of the state that they serve, I am the judge,
         and after that they shall exit with great possessions.
15   And you,
         You shall join your fathers in peace;
         You shall be buried in a good old age.[44]
16   In the fourth generation they shall return here (*hennah*),
         for the punishment of the Amorites is not complete now (*hennah*)."
17   When the sun had set, and it was very dark,
         there was a smoking oven and a flaming torch
         that passed between those pieces.
18   On that day[45] Yahweh cut with Abram a covenant as follows:
         "To your descendants I have granted this land,
         from the river of Egypt to the great river (the river Euphrates):
19   the Kenites, the Kenizzites, the Kadmonites,

---

41. The Hebrew word for this bird means "to scream," so the tradition makes it appear as a "raptor." But raptors do not like dead bodies; "vultures" would work better with dead bodies.

42. This word is used for the name of a month at Ugarit. See *UT*, #2006, 466. Gordon, following Virolleaud, suggests, "that the month is named for funerary sacrifices."

43. The Hebrew word means "to blow."

44. Proper burial is always important.

45. Such a covenant/contract would begin: "From this/that day ..." This appears in contracts from this period and later. Also see the note to Gen 25:31.

20	the Hittites, the Perizzites, the Rephaim,
21	the Amorites, the Canaanites, the Girgashites,
	and the Jebusites."⁴⁶

16:1	Now Sarai, the wife of Abram, had not given birth for him,
	and she had an Egyptian maid, and her name was Hagar.
2	Sarai said to Abram:
	"Note that Yahweh has kept me from bearing.
	Please go into my maid;
	perhaps I will reproduce⁴⁷ through her."
	Abram listened⁴⁸ to the voice of Sarai.
3	Sarai, the wife of Abram, brought Hagar, the Egyptian, her maid
	(after Abram had been settled for ten years in the land of Canaan);
	she gave her to Abram, her husband, for a surrogate.⁴⁹
4	He went in to Hagar; she conceived.
	She saw that she had conceived;
	her mistress was diminished in her eyes.
5	Sarai said to Abram:
	"May my plight⁵⁰ be upon you!
	I, I gave my maid into you bosom;
	she saw that she had conceived;
	I was diminished in her eyes.
	May Yahweh judge between me and between you!"
6	Abram said to Sarai:
	"Hey! Your maid is in your hands;⁵¹

46. As it now stands it appears that the land is granted (in v. 18) along with the people of the land (in vv. 19–21).

47. "Reproduce" is literally "to build up" (Hebrew *banah*); this is a pun on Hebrew *ben*, "son." See Gen 30:3 for a close parallel.

48. See 3:17 for the same phrase. "To listen to the voice" is a literal translation, but there are some good reasons for leaving it in this form (these are discussed in the note for Gen 26:5).

49. Here "woman" means " a concubine who acts as a surrogate" (also see Gen 25:1 and the note). The parallel to this verse is Gen 30:4.

50. This could be translated "my injustice" referring to the wrong that was done to her.

51. This means "in your power" or "under your authority," and it appears again in v. 9.

Genesis, a Royal Epic

         do to her [what seems] good in your eyes."
So Sarai abused her; she ran away from her.

7   The messenger of Yahweh found her,
by the spring of the water in the wilderness,
by the spring on the way to Shur.

8   He said:
"Hagar, maid of Sarai, where have you come from,
and where will you go?"
She said:
"I am a runaway from Sarai, my mistress."

9   The messenger of Yahweh said to her:
"Return to your mistress;
accept abuse from her hands."

10   The messenger of Yahweh said to her:
"I will greatly multiply your descendants;
they shall not be counted because of the multitude."

11   The messenger of Yahweh said to her:
"Certainly, you have conceived;
you are about to bear a son;
You shall call forth his name, 'Ishmael,'[52]
for Yahweh has heard of your abuse.

12   He shall be a wild ass of the steppe;[53]
his hand against everyone,
and the hand of everyone against him.
Over against all his brothers he shall encamp."[54]

---

52. "Ishmael" means "God hears." Here the naming formula is given as a command, and it just does not work as well as when the naming is reported in the third person.

53. The Hebrew behind "steppe" is *'adam* (which may stand for *'adamah*, "ground"). It cannot be translated "man." Perhaps it could be left as "Adam." The above translation rests on Marvin Pope's (AB, *Job*, 86) comments on Job 11:12. Also see Job 24:5 and Gen 49:22 where Joseph becomes the "wild ass" (this is a compliment). It is also important to consider material from the *Gilgamesh Epic* (see *ANET*, 72–99; *COS* 1.132 [pp. 458–60]). In VIII,ii,8–9, in referring to Enkidu it reads, "O my friend, swift-racing mule, wild donkey of the steppe, panther of the open country" (for this translation see *CAD*, A, I, 274). Actually it might be redundant to translate "wild ass of the steppe." The word "steppe" can indicate that the animal is wild.

54. See Gen 25:18.

13	She called the name of Yahweh, the one who spoke to her:
	"You are El-roi,"[55] for she said,
	'Even here, have I not seen after he saw me (*roi*)?'"
14	Therefore the well was called Beer-lahai-roi;[56]
	it is between Kadesh and Bered.
15	Hagar bore a son to Abram.
	Abram called forth the name of his son,
	whom Hagar bore, "Ishmael."
16	Abram was eighty-six years old when Hagar bore Ishmael to Abram.
17:1	When Abram was ninety-nine years old, Yahweh appeared to Abram;
	he said to him:
	"I am El Shaddai.
	Walk before me,
	And be perfect.
2	I will make my covenant,
	Between me and between you.
	I will make you very very great."
3	Abram prostrated himself.[57]
	Elohim spoke with him saying:
4	"I am here; my covenant is with you.
	You shall be Ab-hamon[58] of states.
5	Your name shall not again be called Abram;[59]
	Your name shall be Abraham,[60]
	For I have appointed you Ab-hamon of states.

---

55. This means "God of seeing."
56. The name means "the well of the living one who sees me."
57. The Hebrew literally reads: "Abram fell on his face." It is tempting just to leave it in its literal form, because later in v. 17 we have the same expression but with a different meaning. See *RSP* II, X, 9, 421–22, for a discussion of "prostration formulae."
58. "Ab-hamon" means "father of a multitude."
59. Abram means "exalted father."
60. Abraham probably means "leader of a multitude," but here the author sees it as "the father of a multitude." In other words Abraham sounds something like Ab-hamon.

Genesis, a Royal Epic

6	I will make you very very fruitful.
	I will make of you states.[61]
	Kings shall come forth from you.[62]
7	I will establish my covenant
	Between me and between you,
	And between your descendants after you,
	Throughout their generations for an everlasting covenant,
	To be your God[63] and [the God] of your descendants after you.
8	I will grant to you and to your descendants after you
	The land of your sojourning,
	The entire land of Canaan, for an everlasting holding;[64]
	I will be their God."
9	Elohim said to Abraham:
	"And you, you shall keep my covenant,
	you and your descendants throughout their generations.
10	This is my covenant that you shall keep between me
	and between you and between your descendants after you:
	everyone of your males shall be circumcised.
11	You shall circumcise the flesh of your foreskin;
	that shall be a sign of the covenant between me and between you.
12	At the age of eight days,
	everyone of your males shall be circumcised,
	throughout your generations ([even] the one born at home
	and the one purchased from any foreigner,
	who is not from your descendants).
13	Circumcise the one born in your house
	and the one purchased with your silver;
	my covenant shall be in your flesh as an eternal covenant.
14	An uncircumcised male

---

61. See Gen 12:2.

62. This verse should be compared to Gen 35:11. In both places the fathers are fathers of kings. Also, note v. 16 where Sarah produces kings. This is very important for this royal literature.

63. Here and in the next verse I have translated "Elohim." The context seems to rule out the use of "Elohim" as a title. Elohim is saying, "I will be your God."

64. Royal grants are always forever, but they are not unconditional.

(who has not been circumcised in the flesh of his foreskin):
this person shall be cut off from his people;
he has broken my covenant."

15 Elohim said to Abraham:
"Sarai is your wife;
You shall not call her name Sarai,
For her name is Sarah.
16 I will bless her;[65]
Thus, I will give you a son by her.
I will bless her;
She shall become states;
Kings of peoples shall issue from her."[66]
17 Abraham collapsed[67] with laughter;[68]
he asked himself:
"Can one who is a hundred be a father?
Or, can Sarah who is ninety be a mother?"
18 Abraham said to that God:[69]
"O that Ishmael might live before you!"
19 Elohim said to Abraham:
"Truly, Sarah your wife shall bear for you a son;
you shall call forth his name, 'Isaac.'[70]
Then I will establish my covenant with him
as an eternal covenant for his descendants after him.
20 As for Ishmael, I have heard[71] you; as of now,
I have blessed him: so I will make him fruitful;

---

65. God's blessing is essential for producing an heir. Also note v. 20.

66. See v. 6 above for the same point.

67. The literal translation is: "Abraham fell on his face." The wording is the same as in v. 3, but this cannot be the typical prostration formula. Perhaps in this context we should translate, "Then Abraham collapsed with laughter." But I have left it as is this time around.

68. The literal translation is "He laughed." "Laughed" is a word play on Isaac in v. 19.

69. Here we have a problem. The Hebrew has the article (*ha-ʾelohim*), so I should translate "the/that God/gods." With the article it is not a title. See also the note on Gen 20:6.

70. Meaning "to laugh."

71. This is a play on Ishmael which means "El/god hears."

Genesis, a Royal Epic

	I will increase him more and more.
	He shall father twelve princes;
	I will grant him a great state.[72]
21	But my covenant, I will establish with Isaac,
	whom Sarah shall bear to you at this time next year."
22	He finished speaking with him;
	Elohim went up from Abraham.

23	Abraham took Ishmael, his son, all the ones born in his house,
	and all those purchased with his silver—
	every male from the people[73] of the house of Abraham;
	he circumcised the flesh of their foreskins on that very day,
	as Elohim had spoken to him.
24	Abraham was ninety-nine years old,
	when he was circumcised in the flesh of his foreskin,
25	and Ishmael, his son, was thirteen years old,
	when he was circumcised in the flesh of his foreskin.
26	On that very day, Abraham and Ishmael, his son, were circumcised,
27	and all of the men of his house,
	[even] the one born at home and the one purchased from a foreigner,
	were circumcised with him.

18:1	Yahweh appeared to him[74] by the oaks of Mamre;
	he was sitting at the entrance of the tent in the heat of the day.
2	He lifted up his eyes; he saw:[75]
	there were three men standing near him.
	He saw; he ran from the entrance of the tent to meet them;
	he bowed to the earth.
3	He said:
	"My lord,[76] if I have found favor in your eyes,

---

72. Note that it is the "blessing" which comes before the "birth" of heirs.

73. The word for "people" usually means "men," but sometimes it must be translated "people." See Gen 19:4.

74. This is Abraham.

75. See Gen 13:10 for the same formula.

76. The Hebrew can be read "my lord," "my lords," or "my lord" (referring to

	please do not pass by your servant.
4	Let a little water be brought;
	wash your feet; shade up under the tree.
5	I will bring a little food; nourish yourselves.
	Afterward you will go on.
	For this cause is your journey to your servant."
	They said:
	"You may do as you have said."
6	Abraham hurried into the tent to Sarah; he said:
	"Hurry, three seahs of the best flour!
	Knead and make cakes."
7	Abraham ran to the herd; he took a calf, tender and good;
	he gave [it] to the servant; he was quick to prepare it.
8	He took yogurt, milk, and the calf that had been prepared;
	he set [these] before them. He waited upon them under the tree.
	They ate.
9	They asked him:
	"Where is Sarah, your wife?"
	He answered:
	"There, in the tent."
10	He said:[77]
	"I will certainly return to you at the time of life;[78]
	There will be a son for Sarah, your wife."
	Now Sarah was eavesdropping at the entrance of the tent,
	which was behind him.
11	Abraham and Sarah were old, advanced in days;
	the way of women had ceased to be for Sarah,[79]

Yahweh). The translations are very different on this. At this point in the story, Abraham only sees three men; he knows nothing more. Therefore he is speaking to one of the three in v. 3 and to all of them in the rest of this speech.

77. This translation is literal. The translations vary on this: "Then one said" (AB, NRSV), "The stranger said" (NEB), and "The Lord said" (RSV), but the reader should be allowed to decide on this.

78. This is a literal translation. It has many interpretations. See v. 14 and 2 Kgs 4:16.

79. In other words, menstruation had ceased.

12 Sarah laughed, saying [sarcastically] to herself:[80]
>"After I was withered,
>And my husband was old,
>Passion was mine."

13 Yahweh said to Abraham:
>"Why did Sarah laugh, saying,
>'Really now, shall I be a mother? I am old.'

14 Is anything too difficult for Yahweh?
>To this place, I will return to you at the time of life;
>Sarah shall have a son."

15 Sarah lied saying:
>"I did not laugh" (for she was afraid).

He said:
>"Not? But you did laugh."

16 The men got up from there; they looked down upon Sodom, and Abraham went with them to send them off.

17 Yahweh said:
>"Am I one who conceals from Abraham
>that which I am about to do?

18 Surely Abraham shall become a great and powerful state,
>and all the states of the earth shall bless themselves through him.

19 For I have known him,[81]
>so that he may charge his sons and his house after him;
>they will keep the way of Yahweh—
>doing righteousness and justice,
>In order that Yahweh may accomplish, concerning Abraham,
>that which he has spoken about him."

20 Yahweh said:
>"The crime[82] of Sodom and Gomorrah is so great;

---

80. Compare this phrase to Gen 17:17.

81. "I have known him" means that Yahweh is "related" to him by means of the covenant. See Amos 3:2, "Only you have I known . . ."

82. "Crime" is not a literal translation. The word really means "outcry," i.e. the "outcry" of the victim. Most of the translations are misleading and convey the idea that Sodom and Gomorrah are crying rather than causing the outcry and the suffering. The "crime" causes the outcry and is called "sin" in the next line. In v. 21 a dialectical

	Their sin is so very oppressive.
21	I will go down;
	I will see if they have caused at all
	the outcry that has reached me,[83]
	and if not, I will know."
22	The men turned from there; they went to Sodom,
	but Abraham remained standing before Yahweh.[84]
23	Abraham approached Yahweh; he said:
	"Will you really annihilate righteous with wicked?[85]
24	Perhaps there are fifty righteous ones in the city;
	will you really annihilate and not spare the place
	for the fifty righteous who are in it?
25	[It is] impossible for you to do such a thing as this!
	To kill righteous with wicked,
	so that righteous are as wicked.
	Impossible for you!
	Shall the one who judges all the earth not accomplish justice?"
26	Yahweh said:
	"If I find in Sodom fifty righteous, within the city,
	I will spare the entire place on account of them."
27	Abraham answered; he said:
	"I must venture to speak to my lord, and I am clay and ashes.
28	Perhaps the fifty righteous lack five;

---

variant occurs for this word. Also note Isa 5:7 for the classic passage where Yahweh hopes for justice and finds injustice, "for righteousness (ṣedaqah), but behold, an outcry (ṣe'aqah)."

83. For this phrase in a different context see Exod 3:9.

84. The Masoretic tradition (notes to the Hebrew text) lists eighteen emendations of the scribes. These are known as the *tiqqune ha-sopherim*. According to this tradition, v. 22b originally read: "but Yahweh remained standing before Abraham." This tradition has not been used in the present translation. The MT does read: "but Abraham remained standing before Yahweh" (see Gen 19:27). The verb "standing " is the same word that is translated "waited" in v. 8, and the scribes did not want Yahweh portrayed as serving Abraham. This translation is made with some hesitation, but we are translating the MT (right or wrong), and there may be other places that have been changed and not noted. The desire to get to the original text is usually a foolish desire, because a group of royal scribes could have produced variant texts of this material from the start.

85. This question seems out of order. Yahweh has not talked concerning destruction yet!

Genesis, a Royal Epic

will you destroy, because of the five, the entire city?
He said:
"I will not destroy if I find there forty-five."

29 He continued again to speak to him; he said:
"Perhaps forty will be found there."
He said:
"I will not do it because of the forty."

30 He said:
"Please do not be angry, my lord, and I will speak.
Perhaps thirty will be found there."
He said:
"I will not do it if I find there thirty."

31 He said:
"I must venture to speak to my lord.
Perhaps twenty will be found there."
He said:
"I will not destroy because of the twenty."

32 He said:
"Please do not be angry, my lord, and I will speak this last time.
Perhaps ten will be found there."
He said:
"I will not destroy because of the ten."

33 Yahweh departed, because he had finished speaking to Abraham;
Abraham returned to his place.

19:1 The two messengers entered Sodom in the evening,
and Lot was sitting in the gate of Sodom.
He saw [them]; he rose to greet them;
he bowed low [with his] face to the earth.

2 He said:
"Please, my lords, turn aside to the house of your servant;
spend the night and wash your feet.
You can get up[86] and go on your way."
They said:

---

86. This verb does not actually mean "to get up early" (as in most translations). It means "to get up," "to go up," or "to pack up/get ready." See Gen 19:27; 21:14; and 22:3.

	"No, we will spend the night in the square."
3	He urged them so much that they turned aside to him;
	they entered his house. He prepared drinks for them;
	he baked unleavened cakes; they ate.
4	Before they lay down, the people[87] of the city
	(the people of Sodom) closed in upon the house—
	from young to old, the entire population.
5	They called to Lot; they said to him:
	"Where are the men who came to you tonight?
	Bring them out to us, that we may know them."[88]
6	Lot went out to them, to the entrance; he shut the door behind him.
7	He said:
	"Please, my friends,[89] do no evil.
8	Remember, I have two daughters who have not known a man.[90]
	Allow me to bring them out to you;
	you do to them what is good in your eyes.[91]
	But to these men,[92] do nothing,
	because they have come under the shelter of my roof."
9	They said:
	"Come forward!"[93]
	They said:
	"The one who came here to sojourn, he has acted as a ruler!
	Now, we will do more 'evil' to you than to them."

---

87. "People" is a translation of a Hebrew word that usually means "men." The context, however, forces the translation "people" (as in 1 Chr 16:3 and Gen 17:23). In a parallel story in Judges 19, there is no context that forces this translation. So in Judg 19:22 the translation would be "the men of the city."

88. Here the euphemism is ridiculous; they are going to rape them.

89. Hebrew reads "my brothers."

90. In Hebrew the qualifying phrase, "who have not known a man" is used when referring to virgins.

91. "What is good in your eyes" is a very literal translation. Most of recent translations reduce this to "as you please," and such a translation may be better. However the literal translation is very helpful in comparing this text to Judges 19.

92. "These men" is the usual understanding, but it is actually written "the divine/godly men."

93. Here they command Lot to step forward.

	They pushed hard against the man (against Lot);
	they came forward to break down the door.
10	The men[94] put out their hands;
	they pulled Lot into the house with them;
	they shut the door.
11	Then they struck the people who were at the entrance to the house,
	from the least to the greatest, with the blinding light.[95]
	They were not able to find the entrance.
12	The men said to Lot:
	"Who else belongs to you here?
	Bring out from this[96] place sons-in-law, your sons,
	your daughters, and all who belong to you in the city.
13	For we are about to destroy this place,
	because their crime is great before Yahweh;
	Yahweh sent us to destroy it."
14	Lot went out; he spoke to his sons-in-law,
	who had married his daughters; he said:
	"Get up! Get out of this place,
	because Yahweh is about to destroy the city."
	But he was as a jester in the eyes of his sons-in-law.
15	As dawn broke, the messengers hurried Lot saying:
	"Get up! Take your wife and your two daughters, who are here,
	or you shall be annihilated in the punishment of the city."
16	He hesitated. The men grabbed his hand, the hand of his wife,
	and the hands of his two daughters—
	the compassion of Yahweh was upon him.
	They brought him out; they let him rest outside the city.
17	When they had brought them outside, he[97] said:
	"Flee for your life!
	Do not look behind you.
	Do not stop anywhere in the plain.

---

94. These are Lot's two guests.

95. Here we follow Speiser; see his note on v. 11 (AB, 137) where he says that this is an Akkadian loanword.

96. Literally "the."

97. As in Gen 18:10, this is the literal meaning. It must be one of the men.

Genesis 11:27—25:18

	Flee to the hills,
	Or you shall be annihilated."
18	Lot said to them:
	"Oh no, my lords![98]
19	Obviously, your servant has found favor in your eyes;
	you have multiplied your kindness
	that you did to me in saving my life,
	but I am not able to flee to the hills
	or the evil[99] would possess me; I would die.
20	Here is this town; it is near enough to escape there;
	it is little! Let me flee there. Isn't it little?
	My life will be saved."
21	He said to him:
	"Let it be known, I have given in to you[100] even in this matter;
	there will be no devastation of the city of which you have spoken.
22	Hurry, flee there,
	for I am not able to do anything until your arrival there."
	Hence the name of the city was called Zoar.[101]
23	The sun rose upon the earth as Lot entered Zoar.
24	Yahweh rained upon Sodom and Gomorrah burning rock
	and fire from Yahweh out of the heavens.
25	He devastated those cities and the entire plain
	with all the inhabitants of the cities and the produce of the ground.
26	[Lot's] wife[102] looked back; she became a pillar of salt.
27	In the morning, Abraham went up to the place
	where he had stood before Yahweh.

98. The Hebrew could be read "my lord" (referring to Yahweh), but the same pronunciation gives "my lords" and agrees with "to them." Others delete "to them" and translate "my lord" to agree with the singular "your" in v. 19.

99. This is the literal translation. Most translate "disaster," but this is a translation based upon a hunch. "Evil" does not have to refer to the destruction of Sodom.

100. "I have given in to you" is literally "I have lifted your face." For this expression see Gen 32:21 and Prov 6:35.

101. "Zoar" means "little," and this word was used twice in v. 20.

102. The text reads "his wife." Literally, "she looked behind him" (he was going in the correct direction), and she broke the command of v. 17.

| 28 | He looked down upon[103] Sodom and Gomorrah
| | and the entire landscape of the plain;
| | he saw that the smoke of the land rose like the smoke of a kiln.
| 29 | When Elohim destroyed the cities of the plain,
| | Elohim remembered Abraham.
| | Therefore he removed Lot from the midst of the devastation,
| | when he was about to devastate[104] the cities in which Lot dwelt.

| 30 | Lot went up from Zoar; he settled in the hills with his two daughters,
| | because he was afraid to live in Zoar.[105]
| | He and his two daughters lived in a certain cave.
| 31 | The firstborn said to the younger:[106]
| | "Our father is old. There is not a man on earth
| | to come in to us as is the way of all the earth.
| 32 | Come, let us make our father drink wine,
| | and we will lie with him.
| | We will keep alive descendants from our father."[107]
| 33 | That night they made their father drink wine.
| | The firstborn went in; she lay with her father.
| | He did not know of her lying down or of her getting up.
| 34 | The next day the firstborn said to the younger:
| | "Yes! Last night I slept with my father.
| | Let us make him drink wine again tonight.
| | Go in! Lie with him!
| | We will keep alive descendants from our father."
| 35 | That night also they made their father drink wine.
| | The younger was ready; she lay with him.
| | He did not know of her lying down or of her getting up.
| 36 | The two daughters of Lot were pregnant by their father.[108]

103. For the same expression from the same site see Gen 18:16.

104. "When he was about to devastate" is similar in construction to Gen 2:4b.

105. In v. 19 he was afraid to go to the hills.

106. The Hebrew root for "younger" means "little," and it is the same root that we have in Zoar.

107. This speech in vv. 31 and 32 has a lot in common with the Noah story.

108. The Hebrew word for "hill" and the word for "pregnant" sound alike depending on the form. At any rate, it would be easy at the popular level to relate going to the

37	The firstborn gave birth to a son. She called forth his name, "Moab."[109] He is the father of the Moabites of today.
38	The younger also gave birth to a son. She called forth his name, "Ben-Ammi."[110] He is the father of the Bene-Ammon[111] of today.
20:1	Abraham journeyed from there[112] to the land of the Negeb; he settled between Kadesh and Shur; he sojourned in Gerar.[113]
2	Abraham said of Sarah, his wife, "She is my sister."[114] Abimelech, king of Gerar, sent[115] and took[116] Sarah.

3	Elohim came to Abimelech in a dream that night;
	he said to him:
	  "You are dead, because of the woman whom you have taken.
	  She is a married woman!"[117]

4	Abimelech had not come near to her; he said:

---

hills and becoming like a hill. It is clear that these stories deal with popular etymologies.

109. Here the popular etymology means "from my father."

110. Here the popular etymology means "son of my kinsman."

111. On proper names our policy is to follow the spellings of the modern versions and reference works. But this becomes impossible at times. The name that is common here is "Ammonites," but in ancient texts they are usually listed as Bene-Ammon ("sons/children of Ammon"). The Hebrew behind the translation "Moabites" is simply "Moab."

112. "From there" brings up the question, from where? We do not know; there are many options (see Gen 13:18 and 18:1?). Perhaps it is more important to note that this is like a new beginning in the story of Abraham. This story should be compared to Gen 12:10–20.

113. Gerar is near Gaza, and so Abraham has moved twice in v. 1. When one sojourns that one is an alien. The Hebrew root for "sojourn" can also mean "strife." This is interesting for English speaking people, because of the words "alien" and "alienation."

114. See Gen 12:10 and 26:6.

115. He sent messengers.

116. Most translations have "took" in this context, but it seems that they are too quick to translate this verb as "married" in other contexts (see Gen 38:2).

117. Literally: "She is owned/ruled by a lord/husband"; see Deut 22:22.

	"Adonai,[118] do you really kill righteous people?
5	Did he not say to me, 'She is my sister,'
	while she herself said, 'He is my brother'?
	In the integrity of my heart and with the purity of my hands,
	I have done this."
6	That[119] same God said to him in the dream:
	"Indeed I knew that in the integrity of your heart you did this;
	indeed I kept you from sinning against me.
	Therefore I did not allow you to touch her.
7	Now restore the wife of this man, for he is a prophet.
	He will pray for you, so live!
	But if you are not one who restores,
	know that you shall surely die,
	you and all who belong to you."
8	In the morning, when Abimelech got up, he called to his officials;[120]
	he recounted all these words in their hearing.
	The men were terrified.
9	Abimelech summoned Abraham; he said to him:
	"What have you done to us?
	What sin have I perpetrated against you
	that you should bring a great sin[121] upon me
	and upon my kingdom?
	Things that should not be done, you have done to me."
10	Abimelech said to Abraham:
	"What did you foresee[122] that you did this thing?"

---

118. This means "lord."

119. *Elohim* in this verse has the Hebrew definite article. In this translation this difference is maintained in some way: either "the God," "a certain God," "that God." or in some cases "the gods." *Elohim* is usually kept as a title without the article; one could translate "god" in these cases.

120. The Hebrew literally says "his slaves/servants," but we know that even high officials addressed themselves in this manner when speaking of their relationship to the king. Here we are not reading about the slaves but rather about the men who are "terrified"—the "officials/ministers."

121. The "great sin" is adultery. This is a technical term used in AML. See Moran, "The Scandal of the 'Great Sin' at Ugarit," 180–81; and Fisher, "An International Judgment," 11–21.

122. This is a literal translation; most translations use some form of "think." The literal meaning may be related to the fact that Abraham is called a prophet (v. 7).

11	Abraham said:
	"I said that only because
	there is no fear of Elohim in this place;
	they will kill me because of my wife.[123]
12	Besides, she really is my sister—
	the daughter of my father but not the daughter of my mother;
	she became my wife.
13	So when [the] gods[124] caused me to wander
	from the house of my father,
	I said to her, 'This is your kindness that you shall do to me:
	at every place to which we come, say of me,
	"He is my brother."'"
14	Abimelech took flocks and cattle, male slaves and maidservants;
	he gave them to Abraham; he restored Sarah, his wife, to him.
15	Abimelech said:
	"Here, my land is before you;
	settle where it is good in your eyes."
16	To Sarah he said:
	"Note that I have given your brother a thousand pieces of silver;
	this is your compensation[125] for everything that you experienced.
	From everything you are vindicated."
17	Abraham prayed to the gods.[126]
	Elohim cured Abimelech, his wife, and servant girls; they gave birth.
18	For Yahweh had completely closed every womb of the house of Abimelech

---

123. For this reason David arranged the death of Uriah the Hittite (2 Sam 12:9).

124. The verb is in the plural hence the plural subject.

125. "Compensation" is literally a "covering of the eyes." It is difficult to know just what this means. The gift is somehow a "covering of eyes." Some help is available from Gen 32:21 where it is hoped that a gift will "cover the face." In Prov 6:35, there is an interesting line: "He will not accept any compensation (or "covering")." This example has to do with adultery.

126. Here the word "Elohim" has the definite article, and I have translated "the gods." This is not the only way to handle this situation, but the text demands that we note the difference between this "Elohim" and the next one. Speiser changes Yahweh to Elohim in v. 18.

Genesis, a Royal Epic

because of Sarah, the wife of Abraham.

21:1 Yahweh visited Sarah as he had said;
Yahweh did to Sarah as he had spoken.

2 Sarah became pregnant;[127] she bore a son to Abraham for his old age
(at the appointed time of which Elohim had promised him).

3 Abraham called forth the name of his son
(the one born to him, that is whom Sarah had borne to him),
"Isaac."[128]

4 Abraham circumcised Isaac, his son, [when] he was eight days old,
as Elohim had commanded him.

5 Abraham was a hundred years old when Isaac, his son,
was born to him.

6 Sarah said:
"Elohim has made laughter for me;
Everyone who hears will laugh with me."

7 She said:
"Who has said to Abraham,
'Sarah has nursed children?'[129]
Yet I have borne a son for his old age."

8 The child grew and was weaned;
on the day of the weaning of Isaac,
Abraham prepared a great feast.

9 Sarah saw the son of Hagar the Egyptian
(whom she had borne to Abraham) playing.[130]

---

127. It seems clear that we have another divine birth story. The term "visit" is also used in 1 Sam 2:21 (about the birth of Samuel's brothers and sisters), but the birth of Samuel uses a more restrained language: 1 Sam 1:19b, "and Elkanah knew Hannah, his wife, and Yahweh remembered her."

128. "Isaac" means "laughter." Here is a good example of how most translations cannot remain consistent on the "naming formula." In Gen 19:38 (and elsewhere) "his name" is translated "him" ("she named him Ben-ammi"). But here it is "the name of his son ..." which cannot be shortened to "him." So here the other translations must come up with something like "Abraham gave his son ... the name Isaac."

129. The obvious answer is that no one would say such a thing.

130. The LXX adds, "with her son Isaac." For "playing" with a sexual meaning, see

10   She said to Abraham:
      "Drive out this servant girl and her son,
      because the son of this servant girl
      shall not inherit along with my son, with Isaac."
11   This word was very displeasing in the eyes of Abraham because of
          his son.
12   Elohim said to Abraham:
      "Do not be displeased in your eyes
      because of the boy and your servant girl.
      Whatever Sarah demands of you, listen to her voice,[131]
      because through Isaac descendants will call forth to you.[132]
13   As for the son of the servant girl,
      I will make him into a state,
      for he is your descendant."

14   In the morning when Abraham got up,
      he took food and a skin of water;

Gen 26:8; 39:14, and 17.

131. Literally: "Hear her voice." For a parallel construction see 1 Sam 8:7. See the note for Gen 26:5 for a discussion of "Hear her voice."

132. "Call forth to you" means that the descendants will call forth the name of the father at his grave. It is there that they will receive his blessing. In this passage the verb is translated as an active form. In the MT the form is pointed as a passive ("because through Isaac descendants will be called to you"). This has been paraphrased in the AB as: "for it is through Isaac that your line shall be continued." This certainly presents the important point that it is through Isaac that Abraham will have offspring, but this is not the meaning of v. 12b. The difficulty with the present translation is that it remains unclear to the reader. What does it mean "will call forth to you?" Other passages may help. In Gen 48:16, in the blessing of Joseph's sons, note the phrase "My name and the names of my fathers, Abraham and Isaac, shall be called forth by them. They will become a multitude in the land." Also note Ruth 4:14, with reference to Boaz, "May his name be called forth in Israel." The names of the fathers are called, or the fathers are summoned/invoked as a part of funeral rituals. We now have a funeral ritual from Ugarit where this entire process is described (this text is translated in the "Introduction"). Also this is referred to in Isa 14:20: "You shall not be joined with them in burial, because you destroyed your land; you murdered your people. Let the descendants of evildoers nevermore be called forth." Such people are not to be remembered in the funeral ritual, but the fathers will be remembered or called up to participate in the ritual. This ritual will insure that the present king receives a blessing and will produce an heir.

Genesis, a Royal Epic

	he gave to Hagar the child[133]
	(he placed [the provisions] upon her shoulder).
	He sent her away.
	She departed; she wandered about in the desert of Beersheba.
15	The water from the skin was gone;
	she abandoned the child under one of the bushes.
16	She left; she sat down at a distance opposite him,
	about the distance of a bowshot, for as she said:
	"I can't watch the child die."
	She sat at a distance; she lifted up her voice;[134] she wept.
17	Elohim listened[135] to the voice of the boy.
	The messenger of Elohim called to Hagar from the heavens.
	He said to her:
	"What is with you, Hagar?
	You should not fear,
	because Elohim has listened to the voice of the boy
	from where he is.
18	Come, lift up the boy; hold fast your hand in his,
	for I will make him into a great state."
19	Elohim opened her eyes; she saw a well of water;
	she went; she filled the water skin; she gave the boy a drink.
20	Elohim was with the boy; he grew up; he settled in the desert;
	he became a bowman.
21	He settled in the desert of Paran.
	His mother took a wife for him from the land of Egypt.
22	It was in that time that Abimelech and Phicol,
	the commander of his army, said to Abraham the following:

---

133. In an earlier form of this story the child was probably put upon her shoulder, but in the present narrative sequence the child is too old and the text has been changed. This translation represents what the MT wants the reader to understand. But note that in a Ugaritic myth, the sun goddess places the body of Baal on the shoulders of Anat (UT 62:15).

134. Here is another formula that we know from the Ugaritic texts.

135. "Elohim listened/heard" at the beginning and at the end of this verse has to do with the meaning of the boy's name, but the name Ishmael ("God hears") is never used in this telling of the story (compare Genesis 16). Also see the note for Gen 26:5 for a discussion of "listen to the voice."

Genesis 11:27—25:18

	"Elohim is with you in everything that you do;
23	swear to me by Elohim, here and now,
	that you will not deal falsely with me,
	or with my posterity and progeny,[136]
	but that you will treat me and the land,
	in which you have sojourned,
	as kindly as I have treated you."
24	Abraham said:
	"I will swear."[137]
25	Abraham reproached[138] Abimelech because of the well of water
	that the servants of Abimelech had seized.
26	Abimelech said:
	"I do not know who committed this act,
	and moreover you did not tell me,
	and moreover I have not heard [of it] until today."
27	Abraham took sheep and cattle and gave [them] to Abimelech;
	the two of them made a treaty.
28	Abraham set seven ewe lambs apart by themselves.
29	Abimelech said to Abraham:
	"What are they for—
	these seven ewe lambs that you have set apart?"
30	He said:
	"For this: you will accept seven ewe lambs from my hand,
	because it will be a witness for me that I dug this well."
31	Hence he[139] called that place Beersheba,[140]
	for there the two of them swore an oath.
32	They concluded a treaty at Beersheba.
	Abimelech and Phicol, the commander of his army, left;
	they returned to the land of the Philistines.

---

136. AB translates "kith and kin" which is nice. Either pair reflects the alliteration of the Hebrew pair.

137. This should be future, because in the next verse Abraham still has a problem.

138. Here we could point this as the infinitive absolute which is used in Ugaritic and Phoenician for the past tense.

139. "He" could refer to Abraham.

140. "Beersheba" means "well of seven" / "well of oath."

Genesis, a Royal Epic

33   He[141] planted a tamarisk[142] at Beersheba.
There he called Yahweh, El-Olam,[143] by name.

34   Abraham sojourned in the land of the Philistines many days.

22:1   It was after these events that this God[144] tested Abraham.
He said to him:
"Abraham!"
He answered:
"Here am I."

2   He said:
"Take your son, your only one, whom you love, Isaac,
and go, yes you,[145] to the land of the moriah.[146]
There offer him as a burnt offering upon one of the hills
that I shall make known to you."

3   In the morning when Abraham got up,[147] he saddled[148] his ass;
he took two of his attendants and Isaac, his son, with him. He split the wood for the burnt offering;

---

141. Most translations add "Abraham."

142. In 1 Sam 31:13 Saul and his sons are buried under a tamarisk.

143. "El-Olam" means "eternal El/god." On this formula see the note for Gen 26:25.

144. Here we have "Elohim" with the definite article and a singular form of the verb.

145. "Go, yes you," as in Gen 12:1 (and Gen 27:43), could also be translated "get yourself," but more important than the translation is the relationship of these two chapters (also see the next note).

146. Three Hebrew roots might be related to *moriah* (*yara'* = "to fear," used in v. 12; *ra'ah* = "to see," used in vv. 4, 8, 13 and 14; and *yarah* = "to teach," used in Gen 12:6 as "Moreh" = "teacher"). Second Chronicles 3:1 relates *moriah* to the temple hill. *Moriah* is not a proper name here or in 2 Chr 3:1, because it has the definite article. In light of v. 14, we should probably translate *moriah* as "vision" even though the form for "vision" should be *mar'ah/mar'eh*. But Sarna seems to favor taking *moriah* as a feminine form of *moreh* or "teacher." Also he suggests that Genesis 12 and 22 contain "... the first and last revelation of God to Abraham ... at sites with similar sounding names, ..." (in TC Genesis, Excursus 16, "The Land of Moriah," 391). If this word has the meaning of "female teacher" that is fine, but what does that do for us? Dame Wisdom of Proverbs 8 and 9 does not seem to help us here. The problem has not been solved, so the word is left untranslated.

147. For this formula see Gen 19:2, 27; 20:8; and 21:14.

148. One can translate either "saddled" or "harnessed" depending upon the situation. The Hebrew root means "to bind."

	he got ready; he left for the sanctuary
	that this God had made known to him.
4	On the third day,[149] Abraham lifted up his eyes; he saw the
	sanctuary from afar.
5	Abraham said to his attendants:

        "You stay here with the ass, and I and the boy will go yonder.

        We will worship, and we will return to you."

6   Abraham took the wood for the burnt offering.

    He placed [it] upon Isaac, his son.

    He took in his hand the fire and the knife.

    The two of them walked off together.

7   Isaac spoke to Abraham, his father; he said:

        "My father!"

    He said:

        "Yes, my son."

    He said:

        "Here is the fire and the wood,

        but where is the sheep for the burnt offering?"

8   Abraham said:

        "Elohim will see to it (that is, the sheep for the burnt offering)

            my son."

    The two of them walked off together.

9   They arrived at the sanctuary

    that this God had made known to him.

    Abraham built the altar there;

    he arranged the wood;

    he bound Isaac, his son;

    he placed him upon the altar on top of the wood.

10   Abraham reached out his hand.

    He grasped the knife to kill his son.

11   The messenger of Yahweh called to him from the heavens.

    He said:

        "Abraham! Abraham!"

---

149. In epic literature it is common for a journey to a sanctuary to take three days; see Exod 3:18; and UT, Krt:195.

	He said:
	"Yes."
12	He said:
	"Do not move your hand to the boy!
	Do not do anything to him!
	For now I know that you are a god-fearer;[150]
	You did not withhold your son, your only one, from me."
13	Abraham lifted up his eyes; he saw there a substitute ram,[151]
	who was caught in the thicket by his[152] horns.
	Abraham went; he took the ram;
	he offered him up to be a burnt offering in place of his son.
14	Abraham called forth the name of that sanctuary, "Yahweh-yireh"[153]
	which is expressed today as "On the mountain of Yahweh, he appears."[154]
15	The messenger of Yahweh called to Abraham a second time from the heavens.
16	He said:
	"By myself I have sworn ([this is] an oracle of Yahweh)
	that since you have done this,
	and you have not withheld your son, your only one,
17	so I will indeed bless you, and surely I will make
	your descendants as numerous as the stars of the heavens
	and as the sands that are on the seashore.

---

150. Literally "you are one who fears Elohim."

151. The ancient versions and modern scholars are very much alike; they have had problems with this expression. In the MT we have "ram after," and this makes no sense. Many have made a slight change, and they have come up with "ram one" or "a ram." However, with only a slight change in the pointing we have "another ram" or "a substitute ram"—a ram to substitute for Isaac!

152. In English we must go back to the KJ to find "his" (followed by the RSV but not by the NRSV which tends to neuter everything). We are in the habit of objectifying all that we deem sub-human. However, many who deal with animals on a daily basis would use "his" in a situation like this.

153. "Yahweh will see [to it]." Compare v. 8: "Elohim will see to it."

154. Here the meaning has changed to the passive. Perhaps this should be left as "which is expressed today, *behar Yahweh-yera'eh*."

Genesis 11:27—25:18

	Your descendants shall take possession of the gates of their enemies.
18	Through your descendants all the states of the earth shall bless themselves, because you listened to my voice."[155]
19	Abraham returned to his attendants. They got ready; they left together for Beersheba. Abraham settled in Beersheba.
20	It was after these events that it was reported to Abraham as follows: "Milcah, too, has borne sons to Nahor, your brother:
21	Uz, the firstborn, Bus, his brother, Kemuel, the father of Aram,
22	Chesed, Hazo, Pildash, Jidlaph, and Bethuel
23	(Bethuel fathered Rebekah)." These eight Milcah bore to Nahor, the brother of Abraham.
24	His concubine whose name was Reumah also bore: Tebah, Gaham, Tahash, and Maacah.[156]
23:1	A hundred and twenty-seven years were the life of Sarah— the years of the life of Sarah.[157]
2	Sarah died in Kiriath-arba (that is, Hebron) in the land of Canaan. Abraham went in to lament for Sarah and to weep [for] her.
3	Abraham got up from before his dead. He spoke to the sons of Heth as follows:
4	"I am a resident alien[158] among you;

---

155. Here the translation "listened to my voice" is given, because the general meaning "voice" is all that is intended. Many would translate this "obeyed my command," but when the Hebrew text wants to be explicit, it can tell you in no uncertain terms what is contained within the word "voice" (for an example see Gen 26:5).

156. In these main lists there is always twelve (as with Ishmael and Jacob).

157. This verse has textual problems. Most translators add "the years of" and delete the final clause with the LXX. Then it would read: "And, the years of the life of Sarah were a hundred and twenty-seven years."

158. Literally "a sojourner and a settler" or in other words one who could not buy real estate.

Genesis, a Royal Epic

	grant[159] to me [my] own[160] sepulcher among you,
	and I will bury my dead [wife who] is with me."
5	The sons of Heth[161] answered Abraham as follows:
6	"Pray,[162] hear us, my lord!
	You are the prince of Elohim[163] in our midst.
	In the choicest of our sepulchers, bury your dead.
	None of us will deny you his sepulcher for burying your dead."
7	Abraham bowed low to the people of the land, to the sons of Heth;
8	he spoke with them as follows:
	"If you really want me to bury my dead [wife who] is with me,
	hear me, and intercede for me with Ephron, the son of Zohar.
9	Let him sell[164] me the cave of the Machpelah[165] that he owns,
	which is at the end of his field.
	For the full price,[166]
	let him sell it to me in your midst for [my] own sepulchre."
10	Ephron was sitting with the sons of Heth, so Ephron, the Hittite,

---

159. "Grant" seems to work well here. The basic meaning of the Hebrew word is "give" and in stories such as this one it is clear that it can also mean "to sell." If it is used as a euphemism for "sell" then perhaps the euphemism should be allowed to stand (as in v. 11), but in v. 9 we must translate "sell."

160. "[My] own" is the translation of one Hebrew word that means "inheritable property." This is the most important term in this transaction, because a sepulchre that could be the property of descendants was essential. The children had to hold certain funeral rituals for their fathers in order to receive a blessing; this blessing made certain that they would have heirs to continue the royal line.

161. Most translations have "Hittites" for this except for Speiser in AB who has "children of Heth" (for Heth see Gen 10:15). In this chapter there are several terms and phrases that refer to the citizens of Hebron. At this point in our studies it seems best to let them stand in a literal fashion. The word for "Hittite" does appear in v. 10.

162. This translation follows that of Speiser in AB. The word "pray" in the MT is attached to v. 5 (just as in vv. 14 and 15). In doing this the MT reads it as "to him," but we read it with the following verse as a precative particle ("but please"). This makes grammatical sense and it appears this way in v. 13. Speiser could have made a stronger case for his translation if he had translated v. 13 in the same way.

163. Or "an exalted prince."

164. See v. 4 n. 159.

165. *Machpelah* means "double." It is not a proper name.

166. The term "full price" is literally "with full silver." It is a common term in contracts and appears in 1 Chr 21:22, 24 where David is buying a threshing floor. Also see 2 Sam 24:18–25.

	answered Abraham in the hearing of the sons of Heth
	from all who entered the gate of his city,[167] as follows:
11	"No! My lord, hear me.
	The field I give to you;
	the cave that is in it,
	I give to you;
	in the presence of the sons of my people,
	I give it to you.
	Bury your dead!"
12	Abraham bowed low before the people of the land;
13	he spoke to Ephron in the hearing of the people of the land, as
	follows:
	"Only if you, pray, hear me.
	I have offered the price of the field;
	accept it from me, and I will bury my dead there."
14	Ephron answered Abraham as follows:
15	"Pray[168] my lord, hear me!
	The land is four hundred shekels of silver!
	Between me and between you, what is that?
	So bury your dead!"
16	Abraham listened to Ephron; Abraham weighed out for Ephron
	the silver of which he spoke in the hearing of the sons of Heth—
	four hundred shekels of silver at the exchange rate of the
	merchants.
17	The field of Ephron that was in the Machpelah, before Mamre,
	the field and the cave that was in it and all the trees that were in the
	field
	(that were within all its boundary lines) was deeded
18	to Abraham as a purchase in the presence of the sons of Heth,
	from all who entered the gate of his city.
19	After that, Abraham buried Sarah, his wife,
	in the cave of the field of the Machpelah,
	before Mamre (that is, Hebron), in the land of Canaan.
20	The field and the cave that was in it was deeded to Abraham

---

167. For this difficult phrase note v. 18.
168. As in v. 6 so here "pray" belongs to the preceding verse.

for [his] own sepulchre from the sons of the Hittites.

24:1 Abraham was old, advanced in years,
and Yahweh had blessed Abraham in every way.
2 Abraham said to his servant,[169] the oldest of his house,
who was in charge of all that he owned:
"Put your hand under my thigh,[170]
3 and I will make you swear by Yahweh,
the God of the heavens and the God of the earth,[171]
that you will not take a wife for my son
from the daughters of the Canaanites,
among whom I am living,
4 but to my land and to my kindred[172] you will go;
you will take a wife for my son, for Isaac."
5 The servant said to him:
"Suppose that the woman does not want to follow me to this land,
should I take your son back to the land from which you came?"

169. This servant is not named. There is no way to know if this is the same servant as in Gen 15:2.

170. Most scholars think that "thigh" refers to the genital organ. This is correct, and note that in Gen 46:26 "his own issue/offspring" (as translated by most) is literally "those who came out of his thigh" (also see Exod 1:5 and Judg 8:30—the total number in these examples is seventy). In Gen 47:29 we have another last request of a father. Here Jacob says to Joseph, "Place your hand under my thigh," but this time the oath has to do with proper burial. But both stories have the same goal. With Abraham the oath has to do with obtaining the right wife in order to produce an heir; with Jacob the oath has to do with proper burial from which issues blessing and hence the birth of an heir. One thing is clear: such an oath could result in a curse for noncompliance or a blessing for compliance.

171. "Yahweh, the god of the heavens and the god of the earth" only appears here in the Hebrew Bible. The name Yahweh may have been inserted here; without it the translation would be "I will make you swear by the gods of the heavens and the gods of the earth. In oaths and covenants from the ancient Mediterranean, the gods of heaven and earth were invoked as witnesses (see PRU IV, p. 139, for an example from Ugarit). Heaven and earth, without divine determinatives, are used in this way in Deut 4:26; 30:19; 31:28; 32:1; and Isa 1:2.

172. For "my land" and "my kindred" see Gen 12:1, "Go, yes you, from your land, your kindred . . ." The word for "kindred" can mean "birth" (Gen 11:28), but here it cannot mean "birth."

Genesis 11:27—25:18

6	Abraham said to him:
	"Watch yourself so that you do not take my son back there!
7	Yahweh, the God of the heavens,
	who took me from the house of my father
	and from the land of my kindred,
	who spoke to me, and who swore to me saying:
	'To your descendants I will grant this land,'
	he will send his messenger before you;
	you shall take a wife for my son from there.
8	And if the woman does not want to follow you,
	you shall be cleared from this oath to me,
	but you shall not take my son back there."
9	The servant placed his hand under the thigh of Abraham, his lord;
	he swore to him concerning this matter.
10	The servant took ten camels (from the camels of his lord);
	he left with every kind of gift from his lord in his hand;
	he got underway;
	he went to Aram-naharaim,[173] to the city of Nahor.
11	He made the camels kneel outside the city
	by the well of water at evening time,
	at the time when the women who draw water come out.
12	He prayed:
	"O Yahweh, god of my lord Abraham,
	Please make it happen before me today;[174]
	Maintain kindness with my lord Abraham.
13	Here I stand beside the spring of water;
	When girls[175] from the town come to draw water,
14	So let it be: the girl to whom I say,
	'Please now, lower your jar that I may drink,'
	Who says, 'Drink! I'll water your camels too,'

---

173. *Aram-Naharaim* was translated in the LXX as "Mesopotamia" or the land "between the two rivers." But it really means "Aram on the river/Euphrates." In the Amarna texts it is called Naharima. The city of Nahor must be Haran.

174. This line really means "Make this my lucky day."

175. "Girls from the town" is literally "the daughters of the men/citizens of the town." I have taken just a bit of poetic license here in order to keep down the English syllable count.

Genesis, a Royal Epic

> She is the one that you have appointed—
> Appointed[176] for your servant, for Isaac.
> And by this I shall in fact really know,
> That you have maintained kindness with my lord."

15 Before he had finished praying, there was Rebekah,
who was born to Bethuel, son of Milcah, the wife of Nahor,
the brother of Abraham,
coming out with her jar on her shoulder.

16 This girl was very good looking,[177]
a young woman[178] whom no man had known.
She went down to the spring; she filled her jar;
she came up.

17 The servant ran to meet her; he said:
> "Please give me a little swallow of water from your jar."

18 She said:
> "Drink, my lord."

She hurried; she lowered her jar upon her hand;
she gave him a drink.

19 She had finished giving him a drink; she said:
> "I will draw for your camels as well,
> until they have finished drinking."[179]

20 She hurried; she emptied her jar into the trough;
she ran back to the well to draw; she drew for all his camels.

21 The man constantly watched[180] her;
he was silently learning

---

176. "Appointed" has been repeated to lengthen the line. The next line is literally "And by this I shall know." In both cases extra syllables are needed for the poem. I have not done this for every poem, but one has to do something for exalted expression.

177. For "good looking" see Gen 12:11; 26:7; 29:17; and 39:6.

178. This "young woman" is a virgin, but we know that because of the following qualifying phrase. Most translate "a virgin whom no man had known," but this is redundant. In Gen 19:8 we have "two daughters who have not known a man." No one would change "daughters" to "virgins." Also in Isa 7:14 the same Hebrew word is used for "young woman"; but in this case it is usually left as "young woman" because she is pregnant.

179. This was a difficult chore. It seems that she had to go down into the well, and then carry the water up the steps (see vv. 16 and 45). Ten camels would drink a lot of water.

180. "Watched" or "gazed" is a good guess but nothing more.

Genesis 11:27—25:18

	whether Yahweh had made his journey successful or not.
22	When the camels had finished drinking, the man took a gold ring weighing a half-shekel[181] and two gold bracelets for her wrists weighing ten shekels.[182]
23	He said: "Whose daughter are you? Please tell me. Is there [in] the house of your father a place for us to lodge?"
24	She said to him: "I am the daughter of Bethuel, the son of Milcah, whom she bore to Nahor.
25	She said to him: "We have plenty of straw and feed, even a place to lodge."[183]
26	The man bowed and prostrated himself before Yahweh.
27	He prayed: "Blessed be Yahweh, the god of my lord Abraham, who has not withheld his kindness and his truth from my lord. I was on this journey; Yahweh guided me to the house of my lord's kinsmen."
28	The girl ran and recounted to her mother's household about these events.
29	Rebekah had a brother, and his name was Laban. Laban ran to the man at the spring outside [the city][184]—

---

181. Some translators insert at this point "and he put it on/in her nose." This insertion is based on v. 47 and the Sam text. The best argument for this insertion is that "for her wrists" is literally "upon her wrists." Verse 47 does not support this insertion; in fact it argues the other way. In v. 47 the man asks who she is before he puts on the ring and bracelets. So it follows that in v. 22, he has them ready, but he does not put them on her (if this was narrated here it would stand between vv. 25 and 26; compare v. 47b).

182. "Ten shekels" is literally "ten gold shekels"; but it seems to make better sense to allow "gold" to modify "bracelets."

183. It is not narrated, but according to v. 47 the man puts on the ring and bracelets at this point. She is wearing them in v. 30.

184. "Outside" is used in v. 11 and it is related to the city.

30	after seeing the ring and the bracelets upon the wrists of his sister
	and after hearing the words of Rebekah, his sister,
	namely, "Thus spoke the man to me;"
	he approached the man there,
	who was standing by the camels near the spring.
31	He said:
	"Come, O Blessed of Yahweh!
	Why do you stand outside [the city]?[185]
	I have prepared the house
	and a place for the camels."
32	The man went to the house; he unloaded the camels.
	[Laban][186] gave straw and feed to the camels
	and water for washing his feet
	and the feet of the men who were with him.
33	[Food] was set before him to eat.
	He said:
	"I will not eat until I have told my story."
	He said:
	"Speak."
34	He said:
	"I am the servant of Abraham.
35	Yahweh has greatly blessed my lord;
	he has become great.
	He has given him: flocks and cattle, silver and gold,
	servants and maidservants, and camels and asses.
36	Sarah, the wife of my lord,
	has borne a son for my lord in her old age;[187]
	he has deeded him everything that he owns.[188]
37	My lord made me swear to the following:
	'You shall not take a wife for my son

---

185. See the note to v. 29.

186. The MT reads "he gave," but it must be Laban.

187. When one is blessed in this literature, that person has not only been given riches but also has been given an heir.

188. See Gen 25:5. To give property while still living is not common; but there are a few texts that deal with this practice (RS 16.129 in PRU III; or see Fisher, "An Amarna Age Prodigal").

	from the daughters of the Canaanites
	in whose land I am living,
38	but you shall go to the house of my father,
	to my clan, and you shall take a wife for my son.'
39	I said to my lord,
	'Suppose that the women will not follow me?'
40	He said to me, 'Yahweh, with whom I have walked,
	will send his messenger with you;
	he will make your journey successful.
	You shall take a wife for my son
	from my clan and from the house of my father.
41	Then you shall be cleared from my curse,[189]
	because you came to my clan, and if they refuse you,
	you shall [also] be cleared from my curse.'
42	I arrived at the spring today and prayed,
	'O Yahweh, god of my lord Abraham,
	if you are really the one,
	who makes successful my journey
	on which I am the traveler,
43	note that[190] I stand beside the spring of water,
	and so let it be: the young woman who comes out to draw,
	[to whom][191] I shall say, "Please give me
	a little water from your jar,"
44	and who will say to me, "For you, drink!
	And I will also draw for your camels,"
	she is the woman
	whom Yahweh has appointed for the son of my lord.'
45	Before I had finished praying silently,[192]
	there was Rebekah coming out with her jar on her shoulder.

189. An oath carries with it curses for noncompliance and blessings for compliance. Here Hebrew *'alah*, "curse" or "ban" is used, and it must be distinguished form the traditional "oath."

190. "Note that" is from the same Hebrew word (*hinneh*) as "Here" in v. 13; but the context in v. 43 (following the "if" clause of v. 42) demands a different translation.

191. This addition is influenced by v. 14.

192. "Silently" is from a Hebrew phrase meaning "to my heart/mind."

	She went down to the spring and drew.
	I said to her, 'Please give me a drink.'
46	She hurried; she lowered her jar from upon her;
	She said, 'Drink! And I will also water your camels.'
	I drank, and she also watered the camels.
47	I questioned her; I said, 'Whose daughter are you?'
	She said, 'The daughter of Bethuel, son of Nahor,
	whom Milcah bore to him.'
	Then I put the ring on her nose
	and the bracelets on her wrists.
48	I bowed and prostrated myself before Yahweh;
	I blessed Yahweh, the God of my lord Abraham,
	who led me on a journey of truth
	to take the daughter of my lord's kinsman[193] for his son.
49	Now, if you are the ones
	who will do kindness and truth with my lord,
	tell me, and if not, tell me,
	that I may turn right or left."
50	Laban and Bethuel[194] answered; they said:
	"This event has issued from Yahweh;
	we are not in a position to speak of evil or good[195] to you.
51	Here is Rebekah before you; take [her], and go.
	She shall become a wife to the son of your lord,
	as Yahweh has directed."
52	When the servant of Abraham heard their words,
	he bowed to the earth before Yahweh.
53	The servant brought out articles of silver, articles of gold,
	and clothing which he gave to Rebekah;
	also he gave presents to her brother and to her mother.[196]

---

193. "Kinsman" is the translation of the common Hebrew word meaning "brother." This is used is the same way in v. 27, but there it is in the plural. "Brother" can be used in this sense.

194. Most agree that the inclusion here of Bethuel is very strange.

195. This really means, "we are not in a position to say anything to you."

196. These gifts to Rebekah and to her family may be like the "gifts" in Gen 34:12, but they are probably not related to the "brideprice" of Gen 34:12 or Exod 22:15 and

54	He and the men who were with him ate; they drank;
	they spent the night.
	In the morning, when they got up, he said:
	"Send me to my lord."
55	Her brother and her mother said:
	"Let the girl stay with us a few days, say ten?
	After that she shall go."
56	He said to them:
	"Do not detain me;
	Yahweh has made my journey a success.
	Send me; I will go to my lord."
57	They said:
	"We will call the girl. Let us ask for her response."[197]
58	They called Rebekah; they said to her:
	"Will you go with this man?"
	She said:
	"I will go."
59	They sent away their sister Rebekah, her nurse,[198]
	the servant of Abraham, and his men.
60	They blessed Rebekah; they said to her:
	"Our sister, surely you are.
	Be thousands and myriads.
	Your descendants shall conquer,
	[Conquer] the gates of their foes."[199]

---

16. This does not means that a bride price was not paid.

197. "For her response" is literally "her mouth." In English we have some expressions like this, but they are usually so negative: "don't give me any lip" or "don't take any mouth." There are more positive uses such as "from the mouths of babes," but we do not "ask her mouth." All of this just points up some difficulties of translation. More important is the fact that since it has all been settled by Yahweh, there is no question that Rebekah will go with the servant; the only question that they can ask her is "When do you want to go, now or in ten days?"

198. In Gen 35:8 Rebekah's nurse (Hebrew *meneket*, also see Exod 2:7) is called Deborah. In TC Genesis, Sarna makes an interesting point: "In Mesopotamia the wet nurse, Akkadian *museniqtum*, 'the one who suckles,' frequently had the additional duties of *tarbitum*, bringing up the child and acting as guardian . . . Interestingly, Targum [Pseudo-]Jonathan renders *meneket* by *padgogthah*, from Greek *paidagogos*, 'tutor,' a meaning that echoes the Akkadian *tarbitum*."

199. See Gen 22:17 for "and your descendants shall take possession of the gates of

Genesis, a Royal Epic

61 Rebekah and her maids got ready; they rode on the camels.
They followed after the man.
The servant took Rebekah; he departed.

62 Isaac had come to the entrance of Beer-lahai-roi;
he was living in the land of the Negeb.

63 Isaac went out to walk in the field toward evening;
he lifted his eyes; he saw: there were camels coming.

64 Rebekah lifted up her eyes; she saw Isaac.
She jumped from the camel.

65 She said to the servant:
> "Who is the man out there,
> who is walking in the field to meet us?"

The servant said:
> "He is my lord."[200]

She took the veil; she covered herself.[201]

66 The servant recounted to Isaac everything that he had done.

67 Isaac brought her to the tent of Sarah, his mother.[202]
He took Rebekah; she became his wife.
He loved her.
Isaac was comforted after his mother's [death].[203]

25:1 Once again Abraham took a woman[204] and her name was Keturah.[205]

---

their enemies." These two phrases are the same in Hebrew except for the last word in each (foes and enemies).

200. Here "lord" refers to Isaac. Abraham is dead at this point (compare v. 62 above with Gen 25:11).

201. In Gen 38:14, we give a more literal translation of this word, "double wrap" (contextually it works better in Gen 38:14 and 19). But here "veil" is better.

202. "Sarah, his mother" is seen as an addition by many. However it could be that this is very important. In other words, Rebekah takes the place of Sarah.

203. The Hebrew text says "after his mother."

204. Here "woman" (as in Gen 16:3) means "concubine," but here Keturah is not a surrogate. In v. 6 both Hagar and Keturah would be included among Abraham's "concubines" (also see 1 Chr 1:32 where Keturah is listed as a concubine).

205. The addition of Keturah is narrated here (after the death of Sarah and before the death of Abraham). According to the epic pattern used in Genesis, this is the place for additional words concerning the descendants. This corresponds to Gen 35:22–26

Genesis 11:27—25:18

2   She bore for him: Zimran, Jokshan, Medan, Midian, Ishbak, and Suah.
3   Jokshan fathered Sheba and Dedan.
    The sons of Dedan were the Asshurim, the Letushim, and the Leummim.
4   The sons of Midian were Ephah, Epher, Enoch, Abida, and Eldaah.
    All of these were the sons of Keturah.
5   Abraham deeded everything that he owned to Isaac.
6   To the sons of Abraham's concubines, Abraham gave gifts.
    While he was still living, he sent them away from his son Isaac, eastward, to the land of Kedem.[206]

7   These are the days of the years of the life of Abraham,[207]
    who lived a hundred and seventy-five years.
8   Abraham expired; he died at a ripe old age, old and satisfied.
    He was gathered to his people.
9   Isaac and Ishmael, his sons, buried him in the cave of the Machpelah,
    in the field of Ephron, the son of Zohar the Hittite, that was before Mamre,
10 the field that Abraham purchased from the sons Heth;
    there Abraham was buried and Sarah his wife.
11 It was after the death of Abraham that Elohim blessed Isaac, his son,[208]
    and Isaac settled near Beer-lahai-roi.

12 **These are the stories of Ishmael**, the son of Abraham,
    whom Hagar, the Egyptian, the maid of Sarah, bore to Abraham.[209]

(after the death of Rachel and before the death of Isaac). This account relates to a much earlier time, probably after he took Hagar but surely before the birth of Isaac.

206. In vv. 5 and 6 we have a legal action by which the other sons are "cleared" from the estate. For a biblical parallel see 2 Chr 21:3, and note the Ugaritic parallel with a detailed discussion in Fisher, "An Amarna Age Prodigal."

207. This has been left in a literal form, because it is rare and used only here, Genesis 47 and 2 Sam 19:35.

208. Proper burial brings with it a blessing.

209. This is the title for this very short section on Ishmael. Between each major cycle there is a minor cycle (compare Gen 36:1—37:1).

13	These are the names of the sons of Ishmael
	(with their names [taken] from their stories):[210]
	Nabaioth, the firstborn of Ishmael, Kedar, Adbeel, Mibsam,
14	Mishma, Dumah, Massa,
15	Hadad, Tema, Jetur, Naphish, and Kedmah.
16	These are the sons of Ishmael,
	and these are their names
	from their villages and from their encampments,
	twelve princes according to their tribes.
17	(These are the years of the life of Ishmael:
	a hundred and thirty-seven years.
	He expired; he died; and he was gathered to his people.)
18	They dwelt from Havilah, by Shur, which is near Egypt, until you reach Asshur,
	and over against all their brothers, they fought.[211]

---

210. For this usage compare Gen 10:32 ("according to their stories"). For these short sections the names are taken, but the narrative material is not included.

211. This last clause is the same as the last clause in Gen 16:12 except for the verb.

PART III
Gen 25:19—37:1

19   *These are the stories of Isaac*, the son of Abraham.[1]

       Abraham fathered Isaac;
20   Isaac was forty years old when he took for his wife Rebekah,
       the daughter of Bethuel the Aramean from Paddan-aram,
       the sister of Laban the Aramean.
21   Isaac made a petition[2] to Yahweh on behalf of his wife,
       for she was barren.
       Yahweh responded to him;
       Rebekah, his wife, conceived.
22   The children were being crushed inside her; she said:
          "If this is the case, why me?"[3]
       She went to seek Yahweh.
23   Yahweh said to her:
          "Two states are [now] within your womb;
          Two peoples shall come from your body.
          One shall be stronger than the other,

---

     1. In Gen 11:27 there is the title *These are the stories of Terah*, and these stories are about Abraham. *These are the stories of Isaac* is another title and here we have the stories of Jacob. An interesting question is where is the title *These are the stories of Abraham*? If there ever was such a section it would have contained stories about Isaac. But we have very little material about Isaac, and most of what we have was put into Genesis 24 and 26. This is the second major block of tradition concerning the fathers. It ends at 35:29.

     2. See Judg 13:8 and 9 for the use of this word in a birth story.

     3. "Why me?" from "why am I this [way]?"

Genesis, a Royal Epic

	And the elder shall serve the younger."[4]
24	Her days were fulfilled to give birth; there were twins in her womb.[5]
25	The first one came out red, all of him like a hairy mantle. They called forth his name, "Esau."[6]
26	Next his brother came out with his hand grasping the heel of Esau. He called forth his name, "Jacob."[7] Isaac was sixty years old when they were born.
27	The boys grew up. Esau became a hunter,[8] a man of the wild.[9] Jacob was a complete man, one who dwelt in tents.[10]
28	Isaac loved Esau, because [Esau's][11] game was in his mouth, and Rebekah loved Jacob.
29	Jacob cooked a stew; Esau came in from the field; he was famished.
30	Esau said to Jacob: "Give me a taste of the red, this red [stew], for I am famished."

---

4. This is one of the main themes in royal epic. It will appear again in Genesis 38 and in the Joseph story.

5. This verse is very much like Gen 38:27, but it is not the same.

6. "Red" (Hebrew *'admoni*) is used in 1 Sam 16:12 and 17:14 to describe David. In Egypt and at Ugarit a ruddy complexion was a sign of a great warrior. Here it is used for a word play on Edom. Also "hairy" (Hebrew *śe'ar*) is a word play on Seir (another name for Edom). For Edom = Esau see v. 30 and Gen 36:1. Perhaps the most interesting point here is that Esau's hairy body invites a comparison with Enkidu in the *Gilgamesh Epic*; Enkidu's body is covered with hair (see in *ANET*, 72–99).

7. The name Jacob comes from the same root as the word for "heel."

8. Literally "a man who knows hunting." Here again the word "man" is not translated. As in Akkadian the word "man" can determine that what follows is an occupation. See the note to Gen 9:20.

9. Literally "a man of the field." But in these texts "an animal of the field" means "a wild animal."

10. This description of Jacob is not easy to understand. Most of the translations are not correct. But it is certain that Jacob is being praised as one who is fit to be the father of kings (Gen 35:11).

11. We have added "Esau's" for clarity.

(Therefore his name was called Edom)[12]
31 Jacob said:
  "Sell me your birthright as of now."[13]
32 Esau said:
  "Here am I; I am about to die.
  So why should I have a birthright?"
33 Jacob said:
  "Swear to me as of now."
  He swore to him; he sold his birthright to Jacob.
34 So Jacob sold[14] bread and lentil stew to Esau.
  He ate; he drank; he got up; he left.
  Esau despised the birthright.

26:1 Now there was a famine in the land,
  in addition to the first famine that was in the days of Abraham.
  Isaac went to Abimelech, king of the Philistines, in Gerar.
2 Yahweh appeared to him; he said:
  "Do not go down to Egypt;
  dwell in the land that I shall make known to you.[15]
3 Sojourn in this land, and I will be with you.
  I will bless you, for to you and to your descendants,
  I will give all these lands.
  I will re-establish[16] the oath that I swore to Abraham, your father:
4 I will make your descendants as numerous as the stars of the heavens;
  I will give all these lands to your descendants;
  through your descendants all the states of the earth shall bless themselves,

---

12. This is Esau.

13. "As of now," here and in v. 33, is important in any sales agreement. Legal texts of this sort start with "From this day . . ."

14. Literally "Jacob gave," but it is obvious that it was not a gift.

15. For this phrase see Gen 22:2 and 9.

16. "Re-establish" is usually taken as "fulfill," but the present translation makes sense in light of Gen 17:21.

Genesis, a Royal Epic

5	because Abraham listened to my voice[17]—
	he kept my charge, my commandments, my statutes, and my teachings."
6	Isaac settled in Gerar.[18]
7	The men of the place asked concerning his wife. He said:
	"She is my sister,"[19]
	for he was afraid to say, "My wife," [for he thought]:[20]
	"The men of the place might kill me on account of Rebekah, for she is good looking."[21]
8	Now after he had been there for many days,[22]
	Abimelech, king of the Philistines, looked down[23] from the window;[24]
	he saw Isaac making love[25] with Rebekah, his wife.
9	Abimelech summoned Isaac; he said:
	"So she really is your wife!
	How could you have said, 'She is my sister?'"
	Isaac said to him:
	"Because I thought that I might die on account of her."
10	Abimelech said:

---

17. Once again "listened to my voice" is left in a very literal state (see Gen 3:17; 16:2; 21:12, 17; 22:18; and 27:8). Yes, the phrase could be translated "obeyed my command" or with others "obeyed me," but why should we interpret when the text goes on to tell us what it means? This is why we have retained "voice" in some places where we could have made it more explicit. In those places the text may intend to keep things very general. Another possibility is that here in 5b we have a later hand who brings an explicit interpretation to this text.

18. See Gen 20:1.

19. This is the third time that the "wife-sister" motif has been used (Gen 12:13 and 20:2).

20. This insertion is presupposed by the following construction (see v. 9).

21. For the same description see Gen 12:11; 24:16; 29:17; and 39:6.

22. Literally "And it was that the days were long to him there, ... "

23. "Looked down" suggests looking down from a high vantage point as in Gen 18:16 and 19:28 where the same verb is used. It was from such a vantage point that David watched Bathsheba (2 Sam 11:2).

24. This is the main window of the palace.

25. The basic meaning of this verb is laughter, and it is used in the name Isaac. In most places it does mean "to laugh," "to jest," or "to play" (as in Gen 21:9), but here and in Gen 39:14 and 17 the context demands more than "playing with" or "laughing."

Genesis 25:19—37:1

> "What is this you have done to us?
> Just a little longer and someone[26] might have laid your wife;
> you would have brought guilt upon us."

11 Abimelech charged all the people as follows:
> "The one who touches this man or his wife shall be put to death."

12 Isaac sowed in that land.
He reaped in the same year a hundred [measures] of barley.[27]
Yahweh blessed him.[28]

13 The man became great; he continued growing until he was very great.

14 He had a flock of sheep, a herd of cows, and a large labor force.[29]
The Philistines hated[30] him.

15 And all the wells that the servants of his father had dug
(in the days of Abraham, his father),
the Philistines ruined them; they filled them with dirt.[31]

16 Abimelech said to Isaac:
> "Go away from us, for you have become too great for us."[32]

17 Isaac departed from there;
he encamped by the wadi[33] of Gerar.
He settled there.

---

26. Literally "one of the people."

27. Here we follow the LXX and read "barley" by using the same consonants. The traditional translation of "a hundredfold" is a guess.

28. See Fisher, "From Ugarit to Gades: Mediterranean Veterinary Medicine," 213, for a discussion of how the great leaders are also great farmers. Or note Gordon, who suggests that the story about Isaac's farming is "a statement worth recording because in the heroic age the aristocratic leaders are landowners, who personally excel in agriculture between military campaigns"; *The Ancient Near East*, 126.

29. See Job 1:3 for this term. The term is singular but it could refer to slaves and work-animals.

30. They "hated" him because they were jealous ("jealous" is the basic meaning of the root). To say that they "envied him" (as some translations) is not strong enough.

31. "Dirt" or perhaps "rubble." See the note for Gen 2:7 where we translated "clay."

32. Some translations use the comparative ("greater than we"), and this is possible. But it does not make much sense if the command is really a command.

33. "Wadi" is Arabic for a "stream-bed" (which is the meaning of the Hebrew root) and is used in geographical names.

18	When Isaac returned, he dug out the wells of water
	that they had dug in the days of Abraham, his father
	(the Philistines ruined them after the death of Abraham);
	he called them [by the same] names as the names
	that his father called them.
19	The servants of Isaac dug by the wadi;
	they found there a well with running water.[34]
20	The shepherds of Gerar contended[35] with Isaac's shepherds saying:
	"The water is ours!"
	He called forth the name of that well, "Esek,"[36]
	because they contended with him.
21	They dug another well; they also contended over that one;
	he called forth its name, "Sitnah."[37]
22	He moved from there; he dug another well.
	They did not contend over it. He called forth its name, "Rehoboth."[38]
	He said:
	"For now Yahweh has made room[39] for us;
	we can increase[40] in the land."
23	From there he went up to Beersheba.
24	Yahweh appeared unto him that night;
	he said:
	"I am the god of Abraham, your father.
	Fear not for I am with you;
	I will bless you;[41]

---

34. "Running water" stands for what is literally "living waters." In any case this well had water running into it; in other words it was a well and not a cistern. Some translate "spring water," but the Hebrew word for "spring" (literally "eye") is not used in this verse.

35. The Hebrew root for "contended" can mean "to contend in court." This is not the same word that is translated "contended" in the second part of this verse.

36. "Esek" appears as a personal name at Ugarit (UT 147:4), and it means "contention." The same Hebrew root is used in the following explanation translated "they contended."

37. "Sitnah" is a feminine form of a root known from its popular use in later times as "satan;" it means, "adversary."

38. This word means "room."

39. Here we translate the same root as we have in "Rehoboth."

40. Or "be fruitful."

41. Again Yahweh's blessing results in an increase of offspring.

>   I will multiply your descendants,
>   For the sake of Abraham, my servant."
>
> 25 There he built an altar;
>   he called on Yahweh by name.[42]
>   There he pitched his tent.
>   There the servants of Isaac began digging[43] a well.
>
> 26 Then Abimelech came to him from Gerar with Ahuzzath, his counselor,[44]
>   and Phicol, the commander of his army.[45]
>
> 27 Isaac said to them:
>   "Why have you come to me?
>   Surely you hate me!
>   You sent me away from you."
>
> 28 They said:
>   "Certainly we have seen that Yahweh has been with you.
>   We have said, 'Let there be sanctions between us
>   (between us and between you);
>   we will make a treaty with you:
>
> 29 you shall not do us harm,[46] since we did not touch you,
>   and since we did with you only good.
>   We sent you away in peace;
>   you are now the blessed of Yahweh.'"
>
> 30 He made for them a banquet.
>   They ate; they drank.

42. This phrase has been used in Genesis several times up to this point (Gen 4:26; 12:8; 13:4; and 21:33). None of the translations make much sense when constructed as follows: ". . . the name of Yahweh/the Lord." In this way of doing it the problems multiply when one uses "the Lord" (it is even more of a problem in Gen 4:6). The emphasis has to be on "Yahweh." Speiser (in the AB) discusses this in connection with Gen 4:6 but fails to follow his rule in Gen 21:33. This has also caused some problems for translators in 1 Kgs 18:24–26 (in v. 26 it must read, ". . . and they called the *ba'al* by name. . . ." I think that we are not given the *ba'al*'s name—though we are told in our grammars that "the *ba'al*" = "Baal.").

43. The verb here is different than in the preceding verses. I follow Speiser's note (in the AB) that suggests that this root means that the digging has been started but not finished. Then again the two verbs could be synonymous (but see Num 21:18).

44. The basic meaning of the Hebrew root is "friend."

45. See Gen 21:22 for the same person.

46. "Harm" or literally "evil."

Genesis, a Royal Epic

31   In the morning they got up.
     They swore an oath to each other.[47]
     Isaac sent them away.
     They left in peace.[48]

32   It was on that day that the servants of Isaac arrived.
     They told him about the well that they had dug.
     They said to him:
         "We found water!"
33   He called it Shibah;[49]
     therefore the name of the city is called Beersheba[50] to this day.

34   When Esau was forty years old, he took as wife Judith,
     the daughter of Beeri, the Hittite,
     and Basemath, the daughter of Elon, the Hittite.[51]
35   They were ill-natured toward Isaac and Rebekah.[52]

27:1 When Isaac was old, his eyes were too dim to see.
     He called Esau, his elder son; he said to him:
         "My son."
     He answered him:
         "Yes."[53]
2   He said:
         "Notice that I have grown old;

---

47. "To each other" is literally "each to his brother." In such treaties the word "brother" is used for "a covenant partner."

48. Here we have the same words as in vv. 27 and 29 but the content is very different. In v. 27 "sent" could be translated as "drove," and in v. 29 "in peace" does not really describe the situation.

49. "Shibah" means "oath."

50. Or "well of oath."

51. This information is quite different than the information in Gen 36:2 and 3, and yet critics go to great lengths to argue that the two passages are both from the source P. See Genesis 36 for additional comments.

52. This line is very difficult. "Ill-natured" is literally "bitter/strong of spirit/wind"; this provides one with all kinds of options. But the difficulty has to do with prepositions. Most translations see the wives as "a source of bitterness to Isaac and to Rebekah." This material is continued in Gen 27:46.

53. In Gen 21:1, 7, and 11, we varied these responses (literally "behold me").

Genesis 25:19—37:1

	I do not know the day of my death.
3	Now then, take your gear, your quiver and your bow,
	and go out in the wild[54] and hunt some game for me.
4	Prepare for me the tasty food that I love,
	and bring it to me. I will eat it,
	so that my very being may bless you before I die."[55]
5	Rebekah was listening when Isaac spoke to Esau, his son.
	Esau went into the wild to hunt game to bring back.
6	Rebekah said to Jacob, her son, as follows:
	"I just heard your father speaking to Esau,
	your brother, saying:
7	'Bring me game, and prepare for me tasty food.
	I will eat it;
	I will bless you in the presence of Yahweh before my death.'
8	Now, my son, listen to my voice,[56]
	to what I command you.
9	Go to the flock, and from there get me two fat young goats;
	with them I will prepare the tasty food
	for your father that he loves.
10	You shall bring [it] to your father; he will eat,
	so that he may bless you before his death."
11	Jacob said to Rebekah, his mother:
	"But Esau, my brother, is a hairy man;[57]
	I am a smooth man.[58]

54. "Wild" is literally "field." For a note on this see Gen 25:27.

55. This is a very special formulation of the blessing, because it will be the final blessing. In vv. 19, 25, and 31 there is the same formulation with "being." Also note that here and in these other verses the meal is necessary for the blessing. This is not only the case for the "death-bed" blessing, but it is also necessary in a funeral ritual. Proper "care and feeding " of the dead brings blessing.

56. As we have noted several times (Gen 3:17; 16:2; 21:12; 22:18; and 26:5 with note), it is best to leave "voice" in its literal form if the explanation follows.

57. We discussed at Gen 25:25 the fact that Esau was hairy. Here we seem to have a play on words or at least a preparation for a play on words. Since the Hebrew word for "hairy" sounds just like the word for a buck goat, it is interesting that Jacob will be wearing the skins of these kids (v. 16).

58. Jacob is a "smooth man." The Hebrew root for "smooth" also can mean that he was a "smooth talker" and "deceptive."

12	What if my father touches me?
	I will be in his eyes as one who mocks.[59]
	I will bring upon myself a curse and not a blessing."
13	His mother said to him:
	"Be upon me your curse, my son!
	Just listen to my voice.[60]
	Go and get [them] for me."

14	He went and got [them]; he brought [them] to his mother.
	His mother prepared the tasty food that his father loved.
15	Rebekah took the finest clothes of Esau, her older son,
	which were with her in the house;
	she outfitted Jacob, her younger son.
16	She put the skins of the young goats on his hands[61]
	and on the nape of his neck.
17	She placed the tasty food and the bread that she had made
	in the hands of Jacob, her son.

| 18 | He went to his father; he said: |
| | "My father." |

---

59. In this story this is a great line, and it is ruined by most translations. Here the blind father just might see with his fingers. To bring this out the literal phrase "in his eyes" has been left as such. Most translations avoid any connection with the verb "to see." They translate "I will seem/appear/look like" or even change the subject and say, "he will think/know." If one wants to move from the literal "in his eyes," then it should be "Then I will be seen by him. . . ." The blind father can see! The second part of the line is also usually botched. This is done in several ways. The NRSV (and others, e.g., Westermann [*Genesis 12–36*] and AAT) makes the mistake of ruining the double entendre by the following: ". . . I shall seem to be mocking him, ..." The word "mocking" is great, but it is the "him" (referring to the father) that ruins the double entendre. He is mocking Esau in the sense of "imitation," but he is also in "contempt" with such a "delusion" with reference to Isaac. The phrase must be kept open. Jacob mocks Esau, Isaac and their customs. Instead of using "mocks" in this double sense some translations want to soften the entire issue with words like: "trickster" (Tanakh), "frivolous" (AB), or "impious" (AAT). But even after these "soft touches" with the whitewash, many commentaries feel the necessity to make excuses for Jacob. Such apologies miss the mark. This is royal epic and the younger must rule the elder.

60. This is literally "listen to my voice" as in v. 8.

61. The word for "hand" can mean "wrists" (Gen 24:47), and it is tempting to translate "wrists" here.

Genesis 25:19—37:1

He said:
"Yes, who are you, my son?"

19   Jacob said to his father:
"I am Esau, your firstborn. I have done as you told me.
Come now, sit up and eat of my game,
so that your very being may bless me."

20   Isaac said to his son:
"What is this? You have succeeded so quickly, my son.
He said:
"Because Yahweh, your god, made it happen before me."

21   Isaac said to Jacob:
"Come closer. I will touch you, my son.
Are you my son, Esau, or not?"

22   Jacob came close to Isaac, his father. He touched him; he said:
"The voice is the voice of Jacob,
but the hands are the hands of Esau."

23   But he did not identify him, for his hands were hairy,
like the hands of Esau, his brother.

[Isaac] blessed him:[62]

24   He said:
"Are you my son Esau?"
He said:
"I am."

25   He said:
"My son, serve me, and I will eat game, so that
my very being may bless you."
(He served him; he ate. He brought wine for him; he drank.)

---

62. Most translations do not try to make much sense at this point. Speiser does try (in the AB) to do something meaningful, and I am attracted to his solution. He translates ". . . Still, as he was about to bless him, (24) he asked again, . . ." With this translation he does not have two blessings like most of the translations, because in v. 27b he can say, ". . . Then, at last, he blessed him, saying . . ." Speiser explains how this is possible, but it seems very difficult with the consecutive *waw*. But he is aware of the problem. A better solution has been proposed by Westermann (*Genesis 12-36*), who sees vv. 24-29 as a ritual of blessing, and this is the way in which we have formatted it. We have in the ritual the following: 1) identification, 2) the meal, 3) the kiss, and 4) the actual pronouncement of blessing.

Genesis, a Royal Epic

26   Isaac, his father, said to him:
     "Come closer, and kiss me, my son."
27   (He came close; he kissed him; he smelled the odor of his clothes.)
     He blessed him; he said:
     "Yes! The odor of my son
     Is like the smell of a field[63]—
     A field that Yahweh has blessed.
28   And may that God grant to you,
     From the dew of the heavens,
     And from the fat[64] of the earth,
     Abundance of grain and wine.[65]

29   Peoples shall serve you;
     States shall bow down to you.
     Be the ruler of your brothers;
     The sons of your mother shall bow down to you.
     Cursed be those who curse you;

---

63. In this section "field" has been translated "wild," but here it is used in a more general sense. It is a bit odd that Esau's best clothes retained this odor (but this poem may not fit in an exact way the context).

64. "Fat" or "oil."

65. Here we are translating the MT, or in other words, one understanding of the text. We correct the text when it appears that there is some accidental mistake or when there is just no understanding in the tradition of the text, but here those situations do not present themselves. This is a situation where a more original form of this poem was changed at some point to avoid any theological embarrassment. The parallels with Ugaritic poetry have been pointed out many times. One of the best places to check this out is in *RSP* (vol I, II 207 and 208; III 117; vol. III, II 4; IV 5). In the *Anat* text from Ugarit (*Anat* II:39–40), the goddess Anat is washing in "... the dew of heaven, the oil of earth, the showers/rain of Cloud-Rider ..." For the *Anat* text see Gordon, *Ugarit and Minoan Crete*, 52. This is a striking parallel and it probably means that at some earlier time v. 28 was quite different. First the word "abundance," Hebrew *rb*, was at the earlier time *rbb* ("rain" in Ugaritic). Then they had three gifts from the gods, dew, oil, and rain. These gifts were from Heaven, Earth, Dagan (sometimes "grain" in Hebrew), and Tirosh ("wine" in Hebrew). When such a blessing was first used in Israel it meant that now it is Yahweh who gives dew, oil, and rain—all of these once belonged to and were given by these other gods but no more. At that stage v. 28 might have read: "So may that God grant to you,/ From the dew of Heaven,/ And from the oil of Earth,/ And from the rain of Dagan and Tirosh." However I think that a shorter form would be more likely: "May Yahweh grant to you,/ The dew of Heaven,/ The oil of Earth,/ And the rain of Cloud-Rider" (see Ps 68:4).

Genesis 25:19—37:1

        Blessed be those who bless you."[66]

30   Now when Isaac had finished blessing Jacob,
      in fact Jacob had just left the presence of Isaac, his father,
      Esau, his brother, came in from his hunt.

31   He too prepared tasty food. He came to his father;
      he said to his father:
          "Let my father get ready and eat of his son's game,
          so that your very being may bless me."

32   Isaac, his father, said to him:
          "Who are you?"
      He said:
          "I am your son, your firstborn, Esau."

33   Isaac broke into uncontrollable and ever increasing trembling;[67]
      he said:
          "Who then is the one that hunted game and came to me?
          I ate of everything before you returned.
          I blessed him, so blessed he will be."

34   When Esau heard the words of his father,
      he broke into uncontrollable and ever increasing bitter crying.
      He said to his father:
          "Bless me, even me, my father."

35   He said:
          "Your brother came in disguise; he took your blessing."

36   He said:
          "Is that why his name is Jacob?[68]
          He has cheated me these two times:
          'My birthright he took,[69]
          And just now, really,

---

66. For an exact parallel to the last two lines see Num 24:9b, and also this can be compared to Gen 12:3.

67. In the Ugaritic texts there is a similar formula that is used to introduce a speech by someone who fears the worse (see Anat III:29-32, in Gordon, *Ugarit and Minoan Crete*, 53).

68. "Jacob" in its verbal forms means "to supplant," "to cheat, or "to overreach." It is used in the next line and translated "cheated." This line is literally, "Is that why he called forth his name, "Jacob."

69. See Gen 25:29-34.

Genesis, a Royal Epic

He took my blessing!'"
He said:
"Haven't you kept a blessing for me?"
37 Isaac answered; he said to Esau:
"Note that I have made him your ruler;
I have given all of his brothers to him for servants.
With grain and wine I have sustained him.
What is there that I can do for you, my son?"
38 Esau said to his father:
"Have you just one blessing, my father?
Bless me too, my father."[70]
Esau lifted up his voice; he wept.
39 Isaac, his father, answered; he said to him:
"Far from the fat of the earth,
Shall be your dwelling—
And from the dew of the heavens above.
40 By your sword you shall live,
And you shall serve your brother.
But someday, when you rebel,
You shall break his yoke from your neck."

41 Esau hated Jacob on account of the blessing that his father had given him.
Esau spoke his mind:[71]
"The days of mourning for my father are drawing near;
I will kill Jacob, my brother."
42 The words of Esau, her older son, were reported to Rebekah.
She sent [a message]; she summoned Jacob, her younger son.
She said to him:
"Beware! Esau, your brother,
is consoling himself at your [expense]—
with [talk of] killing you!
43 Now, my son, listen to my voice:[72]

---

70. Here the LXX inserts, "Isaac said nothing."

71. Most translations have something like "Esau said to himself." This cannot be correct, because in v. 42 Rebekah finds out what Esau has been saying.

72. Once again this phrase has been left in literal form. It can be interpreted as

	Quick! Flee, yes you,[73] to Laban, my brother, in Haran.
44	You shall stay with him a few days,
	until your brother's anger subsides,
45	until your brother's wrath turns from you.
	He will forget what you have done to him.
	I will send [for you]; I will take you from there.
	Why should I lose the two of you [in] one day?"
46	Rebekah said to Isaac:[74]
	"I hate my life because of the daughters of Heth;[75]
	if Jacob should be one who takes a women
	from the daughters of Heth like these,
	from the daughters of this land,
	what purpose is life for me?"
28:1	Isaac summoned Jacob; he blessed him;
	he commanded him; he said to him:
	"You shall not take a wife from the daughters of Canaan.
2	Get up! Go to Paddan-aram, to the house of Bethuel,
	Your mother's father and take from there a wife for yourself,
	from the daughters of Laban, your mother's brother.
3	May El Shaddai bless you:
	May he make you fruitful;
	May he make you many—
	You shall be a community of peoples.

"obey me," "hear me," or today we could even say "read my lips." See the note for Gen 26:5.

73. See Gen 12:1 and 22:2 for this expression.

74. Some would place Gen 26:34 and 35 just before 27:46. Genesis 26:34 and 35 read: "When Esau was forty years old, he took as wife Judith, the daughter of Beeri, the Hittite, and Basemath, the daughter of Elon, the Hittite, and they were ill-natured toward Isaac and Rebekah." These verses plus Gen 27:46 and 28:1–9 are usually given to P (usually seen as a late source), but the search for the right wife is very important to the structure of the narrative. Therefore this material or something just like it was a part of the earliest tradition. Jacob flees for his life (Genesis 27), but he also goes to get a wife.

75. See Gen 23:5 for the "sons of Heth" (Speiser in AB translates "children of Heth" in Gen 23:5, but here he goes with the majority and translates "Hittite women."). Those who translate "children of Heth" in Gen 23:5 have real problems when they get to Gen 27:46. The NRSV avoids all of this by just translating "Hittites."

4	May he grant to you the blessing of Abraham—
	To you and to your descendants who are with you,
	So that you may possess the land of your sojourning,
	That Elohim granted to Abraham."[76]
5	Isaac sent Jacob away; he went to Paddan-aram, to Laban,
	the son of Bethuel the Aramean, the brother of Rebekah,
	the mother of Jacob and Esau.
6	Esau saw that Isaac had blessed Jacob.
	He had sent him to Paddan-aram to take a wife from there for himself.
	In blessing him, he had commanded him saying:
	"You shall not take a wife from the daughters of Canaan."
7	Jacob listened to his father and to his mother;
	he went to Paddan-aram.
8	Esau saw that the daughters of Canaan were evil in the eyes of Isaac, his father.
9	Esau went to Ishmael. He took to be his wife,
	in addition to the wives he had, Mahalath,
	the daughter of Ishmael (the son of Abraham) [and] the sister of Nebaioth.
10	Jacob set out from Beer-sheba and went toward Haran.
11	He came upon a sanctuary and lodged there for the sun had set.
	He took [a stone] from the stones of the sanctuary.
	He placed [it] at his head.
	He lay down in that sanctuary.
12	He dreamed:
	There a stairway[77] was built to the earth;
	its top reached to the heavens.
	There the messengers of Elohim
	were ascending and descending on it.

76. This blessing does two things: it grants heirs and land. These two things are central to the royal epic. See Gen 35:11–12 and 48:3–4.

77. The root meaning of "stairway" is "to lift up." It is used in dealing with ramps and roads. This is a solid stairway, and it brings to mind the great stairways leading up to the tops of Mesopotamian ziggurats.

13	There Yahweh stood upon it.[78]
	He said:
	"I, Yahweh, am the god of Abraham,
	your father, and the god of Isaac.
	The land on which you are lying,
	I will give to you and to your descendants.
14	Your descendants shall be as the particles of the earth.
	You shall spread out to the west and to the east,
	to the north and to the south.
	They shall bless themselves through you and your descendants,
	all the families of the ground.
15	Yes! I am with you; I will guard you wherever you go;
	I will bring you back to this ground,
	for I will not leave you until I have done what I promised to you."
16	Jacob awoke from his sleep; he said:
	"Surely, Yahweh is in this sanctuary,
	and I did not know it."
17	He was afraid; he said:
	"How awesome is this sanctuary.
	This is none other than the house of Elohim.
	This is the gate of the heavens."[79]
18	Jacob got up in the morning.
	He took the stone that was there at his head.
	He set it up [as] a sacred pillar.
	He poured oil on its top.
19	He called forth the name of that sanctuary, "Bethel,"
	but Luz was the name of the city[80] at its beginning.
20	Jacob vowed a vow saying:
	"If Elohim will be with me,
	if he will guard me on this journey that I am making,

---

78. Some translate "beside him" for "upon it."

79. The phrase "the gate of heavens" reminds us that what we have here is another "Tower of Babel" story as in Gen 11:1–9. "Babel" not only refers to Babylon but means "the gate of God."

80. "City" can also mean "temple quarter."

	if he will give me food to eat and clothing to wear,
21	if I return in health to the house of my father,
	and if Yahweh will be for me, O Elohim,[81]
22	then, this stone that I have set up [as] a sacred pillar
	shall be the house of Elohim,
	and of all that you give to me, a tenth I will give to you."
29:1	Jacob directed his feet[82] to the land of the Bene-qedem.[83]
2	He saw there a well in the field.
	There were three flocks of sheep beside it,
	because the flocks were watered from that well.
	The stone over the mouth of the well was large.
3	When all the flocks[84] were gathered there,
	they would roll away the stone from the mouth of the well;
	they would water the sheep;
	they would put the stone back over the mouth of the well in its place.
4	Jacob said to them:
	"My brothers, where are you from?"
	They said:
	"We are from Haran."
5	He said to them:
	"Do you know Laban, the son of Nahor?"
	They said:
	"We know [him]."
6	He said to them:

---

81. Many see this line as a later insertion and as part of the vow rather than as one of the conditions. But as such it is very clumsy. Jacob in this account is dealing with two gods, and this line is one of the conditions; both gods must help (The vow is made to Elohim, so he must make sure that Yahweh does his part). This vow has been compared (see Fisher, "Literary Genres in the Ugaritic Texts," 147–52) to the vow of Keret in a like situation (See UT, Krt:199b–206). This line could be translated as "and if Yahweh will [also] be my God . . . "

82. Literally, "Jacob lifted up his feet and went . . ."

83. "Bene-qedem" has been translated "sons/people of the East," Easterners," or "Kedemites." Also see Gen 19:38 and the note on Bene-ammon.

84. Some of the translations change the word "flocks" to "shepherds," but there is really no reason to do that.

"Is he well?"[85]
They said:
"[He is] well! There is Rachel, his daughter, coming with the
flock."
7 He said:
"There is still a lot of this day left;
it is not time to gather the cattle.[86]
Water the sheep. Go and graze."
8 They said:
"We can't until all the flocks are gathered.
They will roll the stone from the mouth of the well;
we will water the sheep."

9 While he was speaking with them,
Rachel arrived with the sheep that belonged to her father,
for she was a shepherdess.
10 As soon as Jacob saw Rachel, the daughter of Laban
(the brother of his mother), Jacob went up;
he rolled the stone from the mouth of the well.
He watered the sheep of Laban (the brother of his mother).
11 Jacob kissed Rachel; he lifted up his voice; he wept.
12 Jacob told Rachel that he was her father's kinsman,[87]
and that he was Rebekah's son.
She ran; she told her father.
13 As soon as Laban heard the report of Jacob, the son of his sister,
he ran to meet him; he embraced him; he kissed him.
He brought him to his house.
[Jacob][88] recounted to Laban all these things.
14 Laban said to Jacob:

---

85. "Well" is the translation of Hebrew "*shalom*" (perhaps it should be left in its Hebrew form?).

86. "Cattle" could be translated "herds" or "large animals," and this could include sheep. But it seems that the sheep are already coming in for water but not the other animals such as cattle.

87. See Gen 13:8 for "kinsman." Here the Hebrew is literally "brother."

88. The Hebrew has "he."

Genesis, a Royal Epic

                "Surely, you are my bone and my flesh."[89]
                He stayed with him [for] a whole month.

15   Laban said to Jacob:
          "Just because you are my kinsman,
          should you serve me for nothing?
          Tell me, what is your wage?"
16   Laban had two daughters:
      the name of the older one was Leah,
      and the name of the younger one was Rachel.
17   Leah's eyes were soft, and Rachel was well-built and good looking.[90]
18   Jacob loved Rachel.
      He said:
          "I will serve you seven years for Rachel,
          your younger daughter."
19   Laban said:
          "It is better that I give her to you
          than that I should give her to another man;
          stay with me."
20   Jacob served seven years for Rachel.
      In his eyes they were as a few days—
      he was in love with her.
21   Jacob said to Laban:
          "Give me my wife for my time is fulfilled;
          I want to go in to her."
22   Laban gathered all the men[91] of the [home] place.
      He prepared a feast.[92]
23   When evening came, he took Leah, his daughter;

---

89. See Gen 2:23 for "bone" and "flesh" plus Judg 9:2; 2 Sam 5:1; 19:13 and 14. Some translators change this to the English idiom "flesh and blood." But for comparative work it is best to keep this in its Hebrew form.

90. For this usage see Gen 12:11; 24:16; 26:7; and 39:6.

91. "Men" can be translated "people," but at marriage feasts the men and the women usually had separate parties (see Judges 14 and Psalm 45). As in other places it could be translated "men of the place/sanctuary" (see Judg 14:18 for "men of the city").

92. For a seven day feast see Judges 14 and v. 27 below.

Genesis 25:19—37:1

        he brought her to [Jacob].[93]
        He went in to her.

24   (Laban gave Zilpah, his maidservant, to Leah, his daughter,
        for her maidservant.)

25   When morning came, there she was, Leah!
        He said to Laban:
            "What is this you have done to me?
            Was it not for Rachel that I served you?
            Why have you deceived me?"

26   Laban said:
            "It is not done so in our place to give the younger
            before the firstborn.

27   Complete the seven [day feast] of this [one].
            In addition we will give you this [other one]
            for service that you will render me for another seven years."

28   Jacob did so. He completed the seven [day feast] of this [one];
        [Laban][94] gave Rachel, his daughter, to him for a wife.

29   (Laban gave to Rachel, his daughter, Bilhah, his maidservant,
        for her maidservant.)

30   [Jacob][95] also went in to Rachel.
        Moreover, he loved Rachel more than Leah.
        He served [Laban][96] yet another seven years.

31   Yahweh saw that Leah was unloved;[97]
        he opened her womb
        (Rachel was barren).

32   Leah conceived; she bore a son.
        She called forth his name, "Reuben," for she said:

---

93. The Hebrew text has "him."
94. The Hebrew text has "he."
95. The Hebrew text has "he."
96. The Hebrew text has "him."
97. "Unloved" is from a Hebrew word that means, "to hate" (as in 2 Sam 13:15), but most translators think that "hate" is too strong in this situation (in v. 30 he loves Rachel "more than" Leah). For a detailed explanation of this situation and the use of both "love" and "hate" see Deut 21:15-17.

Genesis, a Royal Epic

           "Because Yahweh has seen[98] my distress,
             surely now my husband will love me."
33   She conceived again; she bore a son.
       She said:
           "Because Yahweh has heard[99] that I was unloved,
             he has also given to me this [son]."
       She called forth his name, "Simeon."
34   She conceived again; she bore a son.
       She said:
           "Now, this time, my husband will be joined[100] to me,
             for I have borne him three sons."
       Therefore, he called forth his name, "Levi."
35   She conceived again; she bore a son.
       She said:
           "This time I will praise[101] Yahweh."
       Therefore she called forth his name, "Judah."
       She stopped bearing.

30:1 Rachel saw that she did not give birth for Jacob.
       Rachel was jealous of her sister; she said to Jacob:
           "Give me sons![102] If not, I am dead."
2   Jacob burned with anger against Rachel; he said:
           "Am I in the place of Elohim
       who has withheld from you [the] fruit of [the] womb?"
3   She said:
           "Here is my servant girl, Bilhah; go in to her.
           She will bear upon my knees;[103]

---

98. The Hebrew behind "seen" makes up the first part of the name Reuben; Reuben means, "see, a son."

99. The Hebrew word for "heard" stands behind the name "Simeon."

100. Here the Hebrew sounds like Levi.

101. Here the Hebrew is related to Judah. She will praise Yahweh through Judah. This gives Judah an important place.

102. Many translate "children" here, but Rachel wants sons, and she is pleased that Elohim has listened to her (see v. 6 below).

103. This is a form of adoption, i.e. to bear or place a child upon the knees.

Genesis 25:19—37:1

           I will reproduce,[104] even I, through her."
4   She gave him Bilhah, her maidservant, for a surrogate;[105]
       Jacob went in to her.
5   Bilhah conceived; she bore Jacob a son.
6   Rachel said:
           "Elohim has judged[106] me;
           he has also listened to my voice;[107]
           he has given me a son."
       Therefore she called forth his name, "Dan."
7   She conceived again; Bilhah, the maidservant of Rachel,
       bore Jacob a second son.
8   Rachel said:
           "[In] wrestlings [before the] gods,[108]
           I have wrestled[109] with my sister.
           Moreover I have prevailed."
       She called forth his name, "Naphtali."

9   Leah saw that she had stopped bearing.
       She took Zilpah, her maidservant.
       She gave her to Jacob for a surrogate.[110]
10   Zilpah, the maidservant of Leah, bore Jacob a son.
11   Leah said:
           "[I'm] in luck!"[111]

104. "Reproduce" is literally "to build up" which is a word play on the Hebrew word for "son." See Gen 16:2 for the same idiom.

105. Here the Hebrew word for "woman" means "a concubine who is a surrogate." See Gen 16:3 for the same translation.

106. The Hebrew root in "judged" is also the root for "Dan."

107. See Gen 26:5 for a discussion of this idiom.

108. This clause is literally "wrestlings of Elohim/gods." In the courts and homes of this period, certain judgments were made before the gods. This happened when there was a lack of evidence, and the issue had to be settled by ordeal. One ordeal was to wrestle before the gods. The winner was innocent of all charges. In Gen 31:30 Laban's gods are mentioned.

109. "Wrestled" is from the same Hebrew root as "Naphtali."

110. Hebrew "woman." See v. 4 above and the note.

111. "Luck" in Hebrew is "Gad." At one time this line may have been longer. It was sometimes read as "luck has come," but it also could have been "with the help of Gad" (Gad was a god of luck). Note Gen 4:1, "I procreated a man with Yahweh."

She called forth his name, "Gad."
12 Zilpah, the maidservant of Leah, bore Jacob a second son.
13 Leah said:
"I'm honored[112] that young women count me honorable."
She called forth his name, "Asher."

14 In the days of the wheat harvest,
Reuben went out and found mandrakes[113] in the field;
he brought them to Leah, his mother.
Rachel said to Leah:
"Please give me some of your son's mandrakes."
15 She said to her:
"Was your taking my husband such a little thing
that you can take my son's mandrakes as well?"
Rachel said:
"So, he may lie with you tonight
in return for your son's mandrakes."
16 Jacob came from the field in the evening;
Leah came out to meet him.
She said:
"You shall come in to me,
for I have actually hired[114] you with my son's mandrakes."
He lay with her that night.
17 Elohim listened to Leah.[115]
She conceived; she bore Jacob a fifth son.
18 Leah said:
"Elohim has paid my hire,[116]
for I gave my maidservant to my husband."
She called forth his name, "Issachar."

---

112. One term for "honored" in Hebrew is "Asher." See Hanson, "'How Honorable!' 'How Shameful!': A Cultural Analysis of Matthew's Makarisms and Reproaches."

113. The fruit of the mandrakes was thought to be an aphrodisiac.

114. "Hired" is from the same Hebrew root that is in the name "Issachar."

115. As usual we have translated "listened" even though it means that Elohim listened and acted accordingly (as he did below in v. 22 with Rachel).

116. Here is a second explanation for the name Issachar. Issachar could mean "he (God) pays."

19	Leah conceived again; she bore Jacob a sixth son.
20	Leah said:
	"Elohim has presented[117] me with a precious present;
	this time my husband will exalt[118] me,
	for I have borne him six sons."
	She called forth his name, "Zebulun."
21	Later she bore a daughter; she called forth her name, "Dinah."[119]
22	Elohim remembered Rachel.
	Elohim listened to her.
	He opened her womb.
23	She conceived; she bore a son.
	She said:
	"Elohim has taken away my disgrace."
24	She called forth his name, "Joseph," saying:
	"May Yahweh add[120] another son for me."
25	After Rachel had given birth to Joseph, Jacob said to Laban:
	"Set me free. I will go to my place and my country.
26	Give me my women and my children
	for whom I have served you.
	I will go, for you yourself know my work that I did for you."
27	Laban said to him:
	"When I have found favor in your eyes,
	I have been prosperous.[121]
	Yahweh has blessed me on account of you."
28	He said:
	"Lay[122] your price on me! I will give it."

---

117. The Hebrew root is *zabad*. At least it starts like Zebulun.

118. Here the Hebrew root is *zabal*. This is much better. However Speiser in AB thinks that Zebulun may go back to Akkadian *zubullu*, "a bridegroom's gift."

119. The mention of Dinah prepares the reader for Genesis 34.

120. "Joseph" means "to add."

121. "Prosperous" is the Akkadian meaning of this root, and it works well (as suggested by Sarna in TC Genesis).

122. The meaning of this word is uncertain.

Genesis, a Royal Epic

29   [Jacob]¹²³ said to him:
         "You yourself know how I have served you
         and how your stock has been under me,
30   for the little that you had before my [time] has become much.
         Yahweh has blessed you since my arrival.
         Now when will I, even I, work for my house?"
31   He said:
         "What will I give you?"
      Jacob said:
         "You shall not give me anything!¹²⁴
         I will return; I will shepherd;
         I will guard your flocks, if you will do for me the following:
32   let me go through your entire flock today,
         removing from there all speckled and spotted sheep
         (all colored sheep) with their lambs
         and all [the] spotted and [the] speckled from the goats.
         Such shall be my earnings.
33   My honesty will answer for me.
         In the future when you bring my earnings before you,
         everyone that is not speckled and spotted among the goats
         and colored among the lambs with me shall be judged stolen."
34   Laban said:
         "Granted. Let it be according to your word."
35   On that day [Laban]¹²⁵ removed the striped and spotted billy goats,
         all the speckled and spotted nanny goats
         (everyone that had white¹²⁶ on it),
         and everyone that was colored from the lambs.
         He put [them] under the supervision of his sons.¹²⁷
36   He set a distance of three days' journey between himself and Jacob
         (Jacob was still in charge of the rest of Laban's flock).

---

123. Hebrew reads "he."

124. "Give" as used in v. 28 and now in this verse is better than "pay." Jacob does not want gifts (real or in Laban's mind) but rather his earnings.

125. Hebrew has "he."

126. "White" in Hebrew is *laban*. Also see v. 37 below.

127. Laban agreed to Jacob's proposal and wages, and then he steals the wages.

Genesis 25:19—37:1

37	Jacob took fresh shoots of poplar, almond, and plane;
	he peeled white stripes on them,
	laying bare the white of the shoots.
38	He placed the shoots, that he had peeled,
	in front of the flock in the troughs ([that is] in the watering troughs)
	to which the flock came to drink.
	They came in heat when they came to drink.
39	The flock bred facing the shoots; the flock reproduced striped, speckled, and spotted.
40	Jacob separated the lambs:
	he moved[128] the flock to the speckled
	and the multicolored in the flock of Laban.[129]
	He made for himself a separate flock
	(he did not put them with the flock of Laban).
41	Whenever the best ewes[130] of the flock came in heat,
	Jacob put the shoots before the flock in the troughs
	for breeding near the shoots.
42	For the worse of the flock, he did nothing.
	The worse became Laban's and the best Jacob's.
43	The man[131] became very prosperous.
	He had many flocks, maidservants, manservants, camels, and asses.
31:1	[Jacob][132] heard the following words of the sons of Laban:
	"Jacob has taken everything that belonged to our father;

---

128. Literally "he set the faces of the flock to . . ." means, "he set out/moved."

129. He may have moved the flock in his charge to the flock under the supervision of his sons.

130. "The best ewes" is literally "the strong" (a fem. form). "The worse" in v. 42 is literally "the weak." The best ewes will breed first hence the tradition in some of the early versions that there is a comparison between the early breeders and the late breeders.

131. "The man" seems like a strange way to refer to Jacob, but this is the way to state such conclusions. Isaac is "the man" in Gen 26:13-14: "The man became great; he continued growing until he was very great. He had a flock of sheep, a herd of cows, and a large labor force. The Philistines hated him."

132. The Hebrew text has "he."

Genesis, a Royal Epic

	from that which belonged to our father,
	he has made all of this wealth."
2	Jacob saw that the manner of Laban toward him was not as it had been in the past.
3	Yahweh said to Jacob:
	"Return to the land of your fathers and to your kindred;[133]
	I will be with you."[134]
4	Jacob sent [a messenger];[135]
	he summoned Rachel and Leah to the field where his flock was;
5	he said to them:
	"I have seen that the manner of your father toward me
	is not as it has been in the past,
	but the God of my father has been with me.
6	Certainly you know that I have served your father with all my strength.
7	Your father has cheated me; he has changed my wages ten times,
	but Elohim has not allowed him to harm me.
8	If he should say, '[The] speckled shall be your wage,'
	all the flock would reproduce speckled,
	and if he should say, '[The] striped shall be your wage,'
	all the flock would reproduce striped.
9	Elohim has reclaimed[136] the herd of your father;
	He has granted [it] to me.
10	Once when the flocks were breeding,
	I lifted up my eyes and saw in a dream [the following]:
	the billy goats were mounting the flocks—

133. "Kindred" or "family" can also mean "place of birth." In Gen 11:28 we translated "birth" because of the word "land" (this is also the case for v. 13 below), but this could not be done in Gen 24:4 or in 12:1. Here "kindred" works best, and in 32:10 "family" works well in that prayer.

134. See Gen 28:15.

135. The addition of "a messenger" may be helpful; it is sometimes left out, but not always (see Gen 32:4).

136. "Reclaimed" and "granted" form a word pair; this pair appears in Aramaic legal texts. Its counterpart in Akkadian appears in documents from Ugarit. See *PRU* III, RS 16.239, 79.

Genesis 25:19—37:1

	[they were] striped, speckled, and spotted.
11	In the dream the messenger of the gods said to me:
	'Jacob.'
	I said:
	'Yes.'
12	He said:
	'Lift up your eyes and look!
	All the billy goats who are mounting the flocks are striped, speckled, and spotted,
	for I have seen all that Laban has been doing to you.
13	I am the God of Bethel[137] where you anointed a sacred pillar,
	and where you made a vow to me.
	Now get up and depart from this land;
	Return to the land of your birth.'"
14	Rachel and Leah answered;
	they said to him:[138]
	"Is there still for us a share and an inheritance in the estate of our father?
15	Are we not considered by him as foreigners?
	[Yes!] Because he sold us; he completely devoured our silver.[139]
16	Yes! All the wealth that Elohim has reclaimed from our father belongs to us and to our children.
	Now, do all that Elohim has said to you."
17	Jacob complied; he put his children and his wives on the camels;
18	he drove all his livestock and all his property that he had acquired
	(the livestock [from] his earnings that he had acquired in Paddan-aram)
	to Isaac, his father—to the land of Canaan.

137. The LXX and Targums insert after "God" the phrase "who appeared to you in," and they do not need "of." This is tempting, but we are translating the MT. It is true that there are grammatical problems with the above translation. If compared to Gen 35:7 we might add another Hebrew *ʾel* and translate "I am the God of El-bethel."

138. "Answered" and "said:" this is a regular word pair.

139. "Our silver" is usually interpreted as "our purchase price" or "the money paid for us." But we have left it in a literal form, because this may not be connected to the sale.

Genesis, a Royal Epic

19	Laban had gone to shear his flocks.
	Rachel stole the household gods[140] that belonged to her father.
20	Jacob deceived[141] Laban, the Aramean,
	by not informing him that he was one who runs away.
21	He fled (he and all that he had); he got underway;
	he crossed the river;[142]
	he set his face toward the hill country of the Gilead.
22	On the third day Laban was informed that Jacob had fled.
23	He took his allies with him and pursued after him—
	a journey of seven days.[143]
	He caught up with him in the hill country of the Gilead.
24	Elohim came to Laban, the Aramean, in a dream that night;
	he said to him:
	"Watch yourself! Do not plot anything against Jacob."[144]
25	Laban overtook Jacob. Jacob had set up his tents on the mountain.
	Laban camped with his allies in the hill country of the Gilead.
26	Laban said to Jacob:
	"What have you done? You have deceived me;
	you have marched off with my daughters
	like captives of [the] sword.
27	Why did you make a secret escape? You deceived me;
	you did not inform me. I would have sent you off:
	with joy and with songs, with tambourine and with lyre.
28	You did not allow me to kiss my [grand]sons and [grand]daughters.[145]

140. "Household gods" or "teraphim" are called "gods" in vv. 30 and 32. They may have something to do with acquiring a legal title to the property of an estate.

141. This is the Euphrates.

142. "Deceived" is literally "stole the heart/mind of." This verb "to steal" is used in vv. 19, 20, 26, 27, 30, 32, and 39.

143. In royal epic important journeys would usually be "seven days." At Ugarit in the *Epic of Keret*, he travels seven days when he goes after his wife (see Gordon, *Ugarit and Minoan Crete*, 104).

144. The word "plot" is literally "to speak," but it can be used in this way (also see RS 1957.1 in CRST where the King of Amurru is ordered not "to speak/plot with his sister). The word "anything" is literally "from good to evil." Again this phrase means "everything" as in Gen 2:17; 3:5, 22; and 2 Sam 14:17 and 20.

145. The text has "sons" and "daughters;" it seems appropriate to add "grand" be-

	You have done a foolish thing!
29	I have the power to do you harm,
	but the God of your father spoke to me last night saying:
	'Keep yourself from plotting anything against Jacob.'
30	Now, you just had to go,
	for you were very homesick for the house of your father,
	[but] why did you steal my gods?"
31	Jacob answered; he said to Laban:
	"I was afraid, because I thought
	that you would kidnap your daughters from me.
32	The one with whom you find your gods shall not live!
	In the presence of our allies,
	identify what is yours among my things, and take yours."
	(Jacob did not know that Rachel had stolen them.)
33	Laban went into the tent of Jacob, into the tent of Leah,
	and into the tent of the two servant girls,
	but he found nothing. He left the tent of Leah;
	he entered the tent of Rachel.
34	Rachel had taken the household gods.
	She put them in the camel saddle; she sat on them.
	Laban rummaged through the entire tent, but he found nothing.
35	She said to her father:
	"Let there be no anger in the eyes of my lord,
	because I am unable to rise in your presence
	for the way of women is mine."
	He searched, but he did not find the household gods.
36	Jacob became angry; he initiated legal proceedings against Laban.
	Jacob responded; he said to Laban:
	"What is my crime? What is my felony,
	that has caused you to track me down,
37	that has caused you to rummage through all my things?
	What have you found from all the items of your house?
	Put [it] before my allies and your allies;
	they will decide between the two of us.
38	These twenty years I have been with you;

---

cause we are not informed that any of Laban's sons went with Jacob.

	your ewes and your nanny goats have not aborted;
	I have not eaten the rams of your flock.
39	I did not bring you a torn carcass; I bore the loss myself;
	from my hand you demanded it—
	a loss by day or a loss by night.[146]
40	I was in the day consumed by heat and by frost in the night;
	my sleep fled from my eyes.
41	This I have, twenty years in your house:
	I served you fourteen for your two daughters
	and six years for your flocks.
	Ten times you changed my wages.
42	If the God of my father, the God of Abraham,
	and the Paḥad[147] of Isaac, had not been for me,
	by now you would have sent me away with nothing.
	Elohim saw my affliction and the weakness of my hands.
	He gave judgment last night."
43	Laban answered; he said to Jacob:
	"The girls are my [grand]daughters;
	the boys are my [grand]sons;
	the flocks are my flocks;
	everything that you see is mine!
	What can I do this day for these daughters of mine
	or for the children that they have borne?
44	Come now, we will make a covenant, you and I;
	it will be a treaty between me and between you."
45	Jacob took a stone; he raised it up [as] a sacred pillar;[148]
46	Jacob said to his allies:
	"Gather stones."
	They took stones;
	they made a mound;
	they ate there upon the mound.

---

146. According to ancient Mediterranean law, a shepherd was not liable for a loss due to a predator; see *The Code of Hammurapi* §266 in *ANET*, 177; and *COS* 2.131 (p. 350); as well as Exod 22:11.

147. "Paḥad" is usually translated "Fear." The term is uncertain.

148. This is what he did in Gen 28:18.

Genesis 25:19—37:1

47 Laban called it, *Yegar-śahaduta*;[149] Jacob called it, *Gal-ʿed*.[150]
48 Laban said:
    "[From] today this mound is a witness between me and
        between you."
    Therefore he[151] called forth its name, *Gal-ʿed*.
49 And "the Mizpah"[152] of which he said:
    "May Yahweh watch between me and between you,
    When we are separate, each from the other.[153]
50 If you oppress my daughters,
    or take wives in addition to my daughters—
    though no one is with us,
    consider that Elohim is a witness between me and between
        you."
51 Laban said to Jacob:
    "Here is this mound, and here is the sacred pillar
    that I have set between me and between you.[154]
52 This mound is a witness, and the sacred pillar is a witness
    that I will not go past this mound to you
    and that you shall not go past this mound
    or this sacred pillar to me for harm.[155]
53 May the God of Abraham and the God of Nahor
    (the gods of their fathers) judge between us."
    Jacob swore by the Paḥad of his father Isaac.
54 Jacob offered a sacrifice on the hill;
    he called to his allies to break bread.
    They broke bread; they spent the night on the hill.

149. Aramaic for "mound of witness."

150. Hebrew for "mound of witness."

151. It is not clear who the subject is at this point. Most avoid the problem, while creating a few more, and say, "it was named..."

152. Something may be missing at this point. "Mizpah" is a place name meaning, "watch-tower."

153. This contains a threat, and it is certainly not a blessing. Here the gods are called upon to enforce the treaty.

154. Something seems wrong here. Jacob set up the sacred pillar!

155. In this royal literature we have an important point made concerning the border between Aram and Israel. This was a matter of dispute in the time of the monarchy (see 1 Kgs 22:1–4).

Genesis, a Royal Epic

32:1   In the morning Laban got up;
  he kissed his [grand]sons and his [grand]daughters;
  he blessed them; he left; he returned to his place.

2   Jacob went on his way; the messengers of Elohim met him.
3   When he saw them, Jacob said:
   "This is the camp of Elohim!"
  He called forth the name of that sanctuary, "Mahanaim."[156]

4   Jacob sent messengers ahead of him[157] to Esau, his brother,
  to the land of Seir, the country of Edom;
5   he commanded them as follows:
   "Thus you shall say:
   'To my lord, to Esau,
   thus your servant Jacob has said:
   "I have been staying with Laban;
   I have remained until now.
6   I have acquired cattle, asses, sheep,
   menservants, and maidservants.
   I have sent to inform my lord in order
   to find favor in your eyes."'"[158]

7   The messengers returned to Jacob saying:
   "We came to your brother, to Esau;
   moreover he is on his way to meet you—
   with him are four hundred men."
8   Jacob was terrified; he was backed into a corner.
  He divided the people who were with him
  (also the flocks, the cattle, and the camels) into two camps.
9   He said:

---

156. "Mahanaim" or "Two Camps" is important to this story. The word "camp(s)" also appears in vv. 8, 9, 11, and 22. Also this word sounds like the word for gift in vv. 14, 19, and 21. In v. 22 both words appear: "gift" and "camp."

157. "Ahead of him" is literally "before his face." The word face also appears in this story in vv. 17, 18, 19, 21 (see notes), and 22. All of this is leading up to the story in vv. 23-33 concerning Peniel or "the face of God."

158. This letter is very much like other letters in AML. For examples and discussion note *RSP* II, 206.

	"If Esau comes against the one camp and attacks
	it, then the other camp will be free."
10	Jacob prayed:
	"God of my father Abraham
	And God of my father Isaac,
	Yahweh, the one who said to me,
	'Return to your country
	And to your family;[159]
	I will deal well with you.'
11	I am so insignificant before all the kindness and truth[160]
	that you have shown to your servant;
	for with my staff I crossed this Jordon,
	and now I have become two camps.
12	Deliver me, please, from the hand of my brother,
	from the hand of Esau, for I am afraid of him;
	he may come and strike me, [the] mothers,
	and in addition [the] children.
13	You yourself have said, 'I will certainly deal well with you;
	I will make your descendants like the sands of the sea,
	which cannot be counted because of an infinite number.'"[161]
14	He spent that night there.
	He selected from that which was with him[162] a gift for Esau, his brother:
15	two hundred nanny goats and twenty billy goats,
	two hundred ewes and twenty rams,
16	thirty lactating camels and their young,[163]
	forty cows and ten bulls,
	twenty female asses and ten male asses.
17	He put his servants in charge of each herd by itself.
	He said to his servants:

159. See the note for Gen 31:3.
160. Note that the same idiom ("kindness and truth") is used in Gen 24:49.
161. "An infinite number" may be a bit strong; it is a huge multitude that is impossible to count.
162. Literally: "From that which came in his hand."
163. Literally: "their sons."

Genesis, a Royal Epic

              "Go on ahead of me,[164]
              and keep a space between each herd."
18   He commanded the first as follows:
              "When Esau my brother meets you,
              he will ask you the following:
              'To whom do you belong?
              Where are you going?
              Whose [animals] are these ahead of you?'[165]
19   You shall answer, 'To your servant, to Jacob;
              it is a gift sent to my lord, to Esau;
              and [Jacob] himself is just behind us.'"
20   Also, he commanded the second, the third,
              and all the others who were driving the herds saying:
              "You shall say this same thing to Esau when you find him.
21   Also, you shall say,
              'Now your servant, Jacob, is just behind us.'"
            For he said:
              "I will change the expression of his face,[166]
              With the gift that goes before my face.
              Afterwards when I shall see his face,
              Perhaps he will lift up my face."[167]

---

164. See the note for v. 4 (literally, "before my face").

165. See the note for v. 4 (literally, "before your face").

166. The word "face" is important here, but to keep it does make things difficult for the reader. A translation that is even more literal is useful at this point: "I will cover his face with the gift that goes before my face. Afterwards when I shall see his face, perhaps he will lift up my face." This means that "I will change his angry face to a happy face with the gift that goes before me. Afterwards when I shall go before him [and bow down with my face to the ground (Gen 33:3)], perhaps he will lift up my face." If this happens Jacob will be able to see Esau's face (note Gen 32:31 and 33:10), and it will mean that Esau is pleased and will save Jacob. Most translations are like the following translation of the NRSV: "I may appease him with the present that goes on ahead of me, and afterwards I shall see his face; perhaps he will accept me." Perhaps this should be related to Gen 20:16 where there is a gift that becomes a "covering of the eyes." It is important to also compare this with 2 Sam 21:1–13 (note v. 3); Prov 6:35; and 16:14 (also v. 15). Why is it important to keep the word "face" in these four lines? Because the word for "face" appears five times in vv. 21 and 22 (plus vv. 4, 17, and 18) as we prepare for the story about Peniel/Penuel, "the face of God" in vv. 23–33.

167. "Lift up my face" can mean "to agree with" (as in Gen 19:21), "to grant," or "to accept," but here it means "to be generous."

Genesis 25:19—37:1

22   The gift (*minḥah*) went on before his face;[168]
      he remained that night in the camp (*maḥaneh*).

23   During that night, he got up and took his two wives,
      his two maidservants, and his eleven children;
      he crossed the ford of the Jabbok.

24   He took them; he brought them across the stream;
      and he brought over his possessions.

25   Jacob was left alone;
      a man wrestled with him until the break of the dawn.

26   He[169] saw that he could not prevail over him;[170]
      he struck the socket of his hip—
      Jacob's hip socket was dislocated,
      as he wrestled with him.

27   He said:
        "Let me go, for the dawn has broken."
    He said:
        "I will not let you go, unless you bless me."

28   He said to him:
        "What is your name?"
    He said:
        "Jacob."

29   He said:
        "Your name shall no longer be called Jacob,[171] but Israel,[172]
        because you have wrestled with Elohim and men;
        you have prevailed."[173]

30   Jacob asked and said:

---

168. "Before his face" means "ahead of him," but the literal form is interesting following v. 21.

169. Most assume that "he" = "the man."

170. Most assume that "him" = "Jacob."

171. "Jacob" is a play on the Hebrew word for "heel" (see Gen 25:26).

172. "Israel" means "God wrestles."

173. At Nuzu when a judge could not decide a case, the two parties were brought to court, and they would wrestle. The winner was innocent. It is not clear in this story who wins. It may be a draw; Jacob is crippled, but his opponent is held down. It appears that Jacob does not really win, but in another sense he does; he is blessed. It is really God who wrestles and who prevails.

Genesis, a Royal Epic

"Please make known your name."
He said:
"Why is it that you asked for my name?"
He blessed him there.

31   Jacob called forth the name of the sanctuary,[174] "Peniel,"[175]
because [he said]:
"I have seen Elohim face to face,
and my being has been preserved."

32   The sun rose on him as he passed Penuel;[176]
he was limping on account of his hip.

33   (Therefore the Israelites do not eat the muscle of the thigh that is on the socket of the hip until this day, for he struck the socket of Jacob's hip at the muscle of the thigh.)[177]

33:1   Jacob lifted up his eyes; he saw:[178]
there was Esau coming, and four hundred men were with him.
He divided the children among Leah, Rachel, and the two maidservants.

2   He put the maidservants and their children first,
Leah and her children next, and finally Rachel and Joseph.

3   He himself went on before them.
He bowed to the earth seven times[179] until he was near his brother.

4   Esau ran to meet him;
he embraced him;
he fell on his neck;
he kissed him;
they wept.

5   He lifted up his eyes; he saw the women and the children.
He said:

---

174. "The sanctuary" or "The place."
175. "Peniel" means "the face of God" or "the face of El."
176. Another spelling for Peniel.
177. This statement seems to be a late insertion into Genesis.
178. This introductory phrase is also used at Ugarit at the beginning of narratives sections, and it is left in its literal form. See *RSP* III, 214.
179. This custom of bowing seven times or even twice seven times is well known from the letters of this period. See *RSP* II, 421 and 422.

           "Who are these with you?"
      He said:
           "The children with whom Elohim has favored your servant."
6   The maidservants drew near, they and their children; they bowed.
7   Also Leah and her children drew near; they bowed.
      Finally, Joseph and Rachel drew near; they bowed.
8   He said:
           "What [is in it] for you—all this company that I met?"
      He said:
           "To find favor in the eyes of my lord."
9   Esau said:
           "I have a great deal, my brother; what is yours shall be yours!"
10   Jacob said:
           "Never, please! If I have found favor in your eyes,
           you shall accept my gift from my hand,
           for I saw your face—
           it was like seeing the face of Elohim.[180]
           You were pleased with me.
11   Please accept my present[181] that was sent to you,
           because Elohim has favored me with everything I have."[182]
      He urged him; he accepted.

12   He[183] said:
           "Let us get ready; we will go; I will go beside you."
13   He said to him:
           "My lord knows that the children are young;
           the flocks and herds, which are lactating,
           are [a burden] to me;
           If they are driven hard one day, all the flocks will die.
14   Let my lord go on ahead of his servant;

---

180. Here the reader is asked to remember Gen 32:31.

181. Literally, this is "my blessing." Jacob once took Esau's blessing, and now he is giving one (Gen 27:35).

182. Literally, this is "and because I have everything," but the two phrases should be related. In any case other interpretations such as, "I have enough/plenty" do not work. See Gen 39:4, 5, and 8 for the normal use of this phrase.

183. "He" = Esau.

	I will move slowly after the livestock
	that is before me and after the children
	until I come to my lord in Seir."
15	Esau said:
	"Allow me to station with you some of the troops that are with me."
	He said:
	"Why is this? I will do the right thing in the eyes of my lord."[184]
16	On that day, Esau started back on his way to Seir.
17	Jacob journeyed to Succoth; he built quarters for himself;
	he made shelters for his livestock.
	Therefore he called forth the name of that place, "Succoth."[185]
18	Jacob came in peace[186] to the city of Shechem,
	which is in the land of Canaan, on his journey from Paddan-aram;
	he camped before the city.
19	He bought the parcel of the field where he pitched his tent
	from the sons of Hamor, the father of Shechem,[187]
	for a hundred *qesitahs*.[188]
20	He set up an altar there; he called it, "El-elohe-Israel."[189]
34:1	Dinah, whom Leah had borne to Jacob,

184. Literally, "I will find favor in the eyes of my lord." In other words, "you do not have to watch me." Most of the translations seem to be really wild on this one.

185. "Succoth" means "shelter/booth."

186. He was peaceful, and this was the reason that he was able to buy the land. Josh 24:32 makes this same point. There is another tradition that points to the violent overthrow of Shechem (see Genesis 34 and 48:22). Most translations miss the point by saying, "Jacob arrived safely." Also some have taken the word "peace" as a geographical name: "Jacob came to Salem, the city of Shechem (in this case Shechem would be the person of v. 19 and of the next chapter rather than the city).

187. "Shechem" here probably means the person whom we meet in the next chapter.

188. "Qesitahs" is unknown. It is some unit or measure of unknown value. This term appears only here, Josh 24:32; and Job 42:11.

189. Or "El, the God of Israel." Even as Shechem can be a place or a person, so "Israel" can refer to the state, to Jacob, or to both.

Genesis 25:19—37:1

	went out to visit with the daughters of the land.
2	Shechem, the son of Hamor the Hivite,[190] prince of the land, saw her.
	He seized her;
	he raped her;[191]
	he humiliated her.
3	[But], his being was captured by Dinah,[192] the daughter of Jacob:
	he loved the maiden;
	he spoke to the maiden's heart.
4	Shechem said to Hamor, his father:
	"Take for me this girl for a wife."
5	Jacob heard that [Shechem][193] had defiled Dinah, his daughter;
	his sons were with his cattle in the field;
	Jacob remained silent until their return.
6	Hamor, the father of Shechem, went out to Jacob to speak with him.
7	The sons of Jacob had come from the field when they heard;
	the men were distressed; they were very angry,[194]
	because he[195] had committed this grave offense in Israel,
	to rape the daughter of Jacob. This is not done![196]
8	Hamor spoke with them:[197]

---

190. "Hivite" = one of the terms for the Hurrians.

191. Literally "he laid her." This is also the same in v. 7.

192. In v. 2, Dinah is raped; in v. 3, she is loved. It seems necessary to add "[But]." The literal translation is, "His being clung to Dinah." There are some very strange translations of this line in v. 3. Note in Westermann, "But he remained true to Dinah" (*Genesis 37-50*, 533). Such a translation is influenced by Gen 2:24, but there the situation is very different.

193. Hebrew = "he."

194. This might be translated, "he (i.e. Shechem) angered them very much," but the above translation is better. The proof comes from such passages as Gen 31:36.

195. "He" = Shechem.

196. The reference to Israel is an anachronism. The language is that of 2 Sam 13:12 and the story of the rape of Tamar.

197. In v. 6 he came to speak "with him," but now Jacob's sons are there as well. This is understandable, but later in this verse the "your" in "your daughter" is plural (?).

Genesis, a Royal Epic

	"Shechem, my son, is as one with your daughter.[198]
	Please give her to him for a wife.
9	Intermarry with us; give your daughters to us,
	and take our daughters for yourselves.[199]
10	You may settle with us, and the land shall be before you.
	Dwell and trade[200] therein and acquire property in it."
11	Shechem said to her father and to her brothers:
	"Let me find favor in your eyes,
	and whatever you ask of me, I will give.[201]
12	Greatly increase for me a brideprice and gift;[202]
	I will give whatever you ask of me.
	Give to me the maiden for a wife."
13	The sons of Jacob answered Shechem and Hamor, his father, with deceit;
	they plotted, because he had defiled Dinah, their sister;
14	they said to them:
	"We are not able to do this thing,
	to give our sister to a man who is uncircumcised,
	for that would be a disgrace for us.
15	But only in this [way] will we agree with you:
	if you will become like us,
	every male among you must be circumcised.
16	We will give our daughters to you;
	your daughters we will take for ourselves;
	we will settle with you; we will be one people.

---

198. Literally, this phrase is, "his being is attached to your daughter." This is just a little different than v. 3.

199. See Deut 7:3 for the negative form of this verse.

200. This translation is close to Gordon's in "Abraham and the Merchants of Ura," 29. Speiser (in the AB, 265) has argued that this should not be "trade" but "move freely about." Even if one accepted Speiser's arguments, it would not mean that the patriarchs were just "pastoral folk" as Speiser claims. See Gen 42:34 where Speiser takes the same approach in spite of the context.

201. Or "give" can be translated "pay."

202. See the note for Gen 24:53. This terminology, "brideprice and gift," can be seen in Akkadian marriage contracts. For a cross-cultural analysis of dowry, brideprice, and indirect dowry, see Goody and Tambiah, *Bridewealth and Dowry*; and Hanson, "The Herodians and Mediterranean Kinship, Part III: Economics."

Genesis 25:19—37:1

17	If you do not listen to us about being circumcised,
	we will take our daughters. We will leave."
18	Their words[203] appeared good in the eyes of Hamor
	and in the eyes of Shechem, the son of Hamor.
19	The young man did not delay in doing this word,
	for he desired the daughter of Jacob,
	and he himself was the most important of all
	[in] the house of his father.[204]
20	Hamor and Shechem, his son, went to the gate of the city;[205]
	they spoke to the men of their city as follows:
21	"These men are peaceful; they are with us;
	they will settle in the land; they will trade therein.
	The land here is wide open before them.
	We will take their daughters for ourselves for wives,
	and we will give our daughters to them.
22	But only in this [way] will the men agree with us,
	to settle with us, to be one people:
	[if] every male among us be circumcised
	as they are circumcised.
23	Their livestock, their property, and all their cattle,
	will they not be ours?
	But we must agree with them;
	they will settle with us."[206]
24	They listened to Hamor and to Shechem, his son—
	all who went out the gate of his city;
	every male was circumcised—
	all who went out the gate of his city.[207]
25	On the third day, when they were in pain,
	two of the sons of Jacob, Simeon and Levi, brothers of Dinah,

---

203. "Words" comes from the same Hebrew root that was translated "plotted" in v. 13. This is a clever use of words.

204. Hence others would follow him.

205. The "gate" was where the "town meetings" took place.

206. There seems to be some "plotting" with both parties.

207. This phrase should be compared to Gen 23:10 and 18 where it is those who "come in" rather than those who "go out."

Genesis, a Royal Epic

	each took his sword;
	they attacked the unsuspecting city; they killed every male.
26	Hamor and Shechem, his son, they put to the sword;
	they took Dinah from the house of Shechem; they went out.
27	The sons of Jacob came upon the slain;
	they sacked the city that[208] had defiled their sister.
28	They took their flocks, their cattle, and their asses
	that were in the city and that were in the fields.
29	They captured all their army,[209] all their children, and all their women;
	they plundered everything that was in the palace.

30   Jacob said to Simeon and to Levi:
        "You have distressed me by making me odious
        among those who dwell in this land,
        the Canaanites and the Perizzites. I have [only] a few men;[210]
        [if] they join forces against me and attack me,
        I will be destroyed, I and my house."

31   They said:
        "Should he treat our sister like a prostitute?"

35:1   Elohim said to Jacob:
        "Arise, go up to Bethel; settle there,
        and make there an altar for the God[211]
        who appeared to you when you were fleeing
        from the face of Esau, your brother."

2   Jacob said to his household and to all who were with him:
        "Get rid of the foreign gods that are in your midst;

---

208. Regardless of how this is translated (i.e. with a relative or "because they had defiled . . .") there is an interesting shift here from Shechem, the person, to Shechem, the city.

209. This could be translated "wealth" (as it should be in Num 31:9), but in this verse there is first a list of captives. The real problem with the above translation is that v. 25 says that all males were killed. These captured army units must have been outside the city and "off guard."

210. Literally: "I have men of number." In other words, "I have a few men; you can count them; they are not beyond number or countless."

211. "God" = "El." This is the same in v. 3.

	purify yourselves, and change your garments.
3	We will prepare; we will go up to Bethel;
	I will make there an altar for the God
	who answered me in the day of my distress
	and who has been with me during the journey that I have taken."
4	They gave to Jacob all the foreign gods in their possession
	and the rings that were in their ears;
	Jacob buried them under the terebinth that was near Shechem.
5	They departed.
	Since the terror of Elohim was upon the cities round about them,
	they did not pursue the sons of Jacob.
6	Jacob came to Luz (that is, Bethel) in the land of Canaan,
	he and all the people who were with him.
7	He built there an altar; he called the sanctuary El-Bethel,[212]
	for there the gods[213] were revealed to him
	when he was fleeing away from his brother.
8	Deborah, the nurse of Rebekah, died;
	she was buried below Bethel, under the oak;
	he called forth its name, "Allon-bacuth."[214]
9	Again, Elohim appeared to Jacob
	upon his arrival from Paddan-Aram; he blessed him.
10	Elohim said to him:
	"Your name is Jacob;
	Not again will your name be called forth, 'Jacob';
	But Israel shall be your name."[215]
	He called forth his name, "Israel."

212. "El-Bethel" = "The God of Bethel."

213. Here "Elohim/gods" takes the plural form of the verb. This does not refer to the messengers of Elohim in Gen 28:12 but rather to Elohim and Yahweh. It is not surprising that the ancient and modern versions have never translated the plural form in this text.

214. "Allon-bacuth" = "the oak of weeping."

215. Compare the naming in Gen 32:29.

Genesis, a Royal Epic

11 Elohim said to him:
   "I am El Shaddai.[216]
   Be fruitful and multiply;
   A people, [yeah], a community of peoples,
   Shall come from you;
   Kings shall come forth from your loins.[217]
12 The land that I gave to Abraham and to Isaac,
   To you, I give it;
   To your descendants, [the ones who] follow you,[218]
   I will give the land."

13 Elohim went up from him,
   from the sanctuary in which he had spoken with him.
14 Jacob set up a sacred pillar in the sanctuary
   in which he had spoken with him (a sacred pillar of stone).
   He offered a libation on it; he poured oil on it.
15 Jacob called forth the name of the sanctuary,
   where Elohim had spoken with him, "Bethel."

16 They departed from Bethel.
   When there was still some distance to go to Ephrath,
   Rachel gave birth; she had great pain during her labor.
17 When her labor was at its hardest, the midwife said to her:
   "Fear not for it is another son for you."
18 Just as her being left her (for she died),
   she called forth his name, "Ben-oni."[219]
   His father called him Benjamin.[220]
19 Rachel died.
   She was buried on the road to Ephrath (that is Bethlehem).
20 Jacob set up a sacred pillar on her grave.

216. This is like Gen 17:1.

217. This is also said about Abraham and Sarah in Gen 17:6c and 16. The fathers are the fathers of the kings of Israel.

218. See Gen 28:1–4 and 48:3–4.

219. "Son of my suffering."

220. "Son of the right/south." This verse is interesting in that both forms are used for naming: to call forth his name and to call/name him.

Genesis 25:19—37:1

It is the sacred pillar of Rachel's grave to this day.

21 Israel departed.
    He pitched his tent beyond Migdal-eder.
22 While Israel was staying in that land, Reuben came,
    and he laid[221] Bilhah, his father's concubine.
    Israel found out.

    The sons of Jacob were twelve.
23 The sons of Leah: Reuben (the firstborn of Jacob), Simeon, Levi,
    Judah, Issachar, and Zebulun.
24 The sons of Rachel: Joseph and Benjamin.
25 The sons of Bilhah, Rachel's maid: Dan and Naphtali.
26 The sons of Zilpah, Leah's maid: Gad and Asher.
    These are the sons of Jacob who were born to him in Paddan-aram.

27 Jacob came to Isaac, his father, [at] Mamre/Kiriath-arba
    (that is, Hebron),[222] where Abraham and Isaac had sojourned.
28 The days of Isaac were one hundred eighty years.
29 Isaac expired.
    He died; he was gathered to his people, old and full of days.
    Esau and Jacob, his sons, buried him.

36:1 *These are the stories of Esau* (that is, Edom).

2   Esau took his wives from the daughters of the Canaanites:
    Adah, the daughter of Elon, the Hittite;
    Oholibamah-bat-Anah,[223] the [grand]daughter of Zibeon, the
        Hivite;
3   Basemath, the daughter of Ishmael, the sister of Nebaioth.

---

221. These passages are difficult, i.e., this one and Gen 34:2. Here it could be "lay with," but in Gen 34:2 we do have the sign of the direct object. It cannot be translated, "he lay with her" in 34:2; it is either "he raped her" or "he laid her."

222. See Genesis 23 for these place names.

223. This name could be given as "Oholibamah, the daughter of Anah, the [grand]daughter of Zibeon," but in v. 25 the above rendering works better. There is no need to change "daughter" to "son" as is the custom with many translations (here and in v. 14 plus v. 39).

Genesis, a Royal Epic

4	Adah bore to Esau Eliphaz;
	Basemath bore Reuel;
5	Oholibamah bore Jeush, Jalam, and Korah.
	These are the sons of Esau who were born to him
	in the land of Canaan.
6	Esau took his wives, his sons, his daughters,
	all the members of his household, his cattle, all his animals,
	and all his belongings that he acquired in the land of Canaan;
	he went to a land away from his brother.[224]
7	For their possessions were too great for them to live together;
	the land of their sojourning was not able to support them
	along with their livestock.
8	Esau settled in the hills of Seir (Esau is Edom).
9	**These are the stories of Esau**, the father of Edom, in the hills of Seir.[225]
10	These are the names[226] of the sons of Esau:
	Eliphaz, the son of Adah, the wife of Esau,
	Reuel, the son of Basemath, the wife of Esau.
11	The sons of Eliphaz were Teman, Omar, Zepho, Gatam, and Kenaz.
12	Timna was a concubine of Eliphaz, the son of Esau;
	she bore to Eliphaz, Amalek.
	These are the sons of Adah, the wife of Esau.
13	These are the sons of Reuel: Nahath, Zerah, Shammah, and Mizzah.
	These were the sons of Basemath, the wife of Esau.

---

224. Here in the story of Esau, we have a very different explanation from what we had in the story of Isaac.

225. It is usual in Genesis to have a brief "story" between the major "stories" (see Gen 25:12–18), and that is how Gen 36:1—37:1 functions. But it is not usual to have a second title for a new location after the first title (see 36:1). In any case this second document has much more detail. This second title in this section is mentioned in the list of titles in the note for Gen 2:4. Here they used two documents for the same section.

226. Following the title in v. 9, "These are the names" equals the structure of Gen 25:12 and 13. For these brief sections/stories the names are listed without the narrative material.

Genesis 25:19—37:1

14   These were the sons of Oholibamah-bat-Anah, the [grand]daughter of Zibeon:
she bore to Esau, Jeush, Jalam, and Korah.

15   These are the chiefs[227] of the sons of Esau.
The sons of Eliphaz, the firstborn:
chief Teman, chief Omar,
chief Zepho, chief Kenaz,
16   chief Korah, chief Gatam, and chief Amalek;
these are the chiefs of Eliphaz in the land of Edom.
These are the sons of Adah.
17   These are the sons of Reuel, the son of Esau:
chief Nahath, chief Zerah, chief Shammah, and chief Mizzah;
these are the chiefs of Reuel in the land of Edom.
These are the sons of Basemath, the wife of Esau.
18   These are the sons of Oholibamah, the wife of Esau:
chief Jeush, chief Jalam, and chief Korah;
these are the chiefs of Oholibamah-bat-Anah, the wife of Esau.
19   These are the sons of Esau; these are their chiefs (he is Edom).
20   These are the sons of Seir, the Horite, who settled in the land:
Lotan, Shobal, Zibeon, Anah,
21   Dishon, Ezer, and Dishan;
these are the chiefs of the Horites,
the sons of Seir in the land of Edom.
22   The sons of Lotan were Hori and Hemam;
the sister of Lotan was Timna.
23   These are the sons of Shobal:
Alvan, Manahath, Ebal, Shepho, and Onam.
24   These are the sons of Zibeon:
Aiah and Anah
(he is the Anah who discovered the sea[228] in the desert

---

227. "Chiefs" or some type of ruler is better than the translation, "clans" in recent works. These chiefs are called "sons;" it is difficult to refer to a "son" as a "clan." It is also the case that the same word is used this way in Ugaritic lists.

228. The word "sea" in Hebrew is *Yam* (from the root *ymm*). Here we have *ymm* that many want to read *mym* or "water." "Water/spring" is much better than the usual "hot springs," and Gen 26:19 and 32b uses this terminology in the case of springs. However, the word "sea" is what we have, and it could work.

Genesis, a Royal Epic

	while pasturing the asses of Zibeon, his father).
25	These are the children of Anah:
	Dishon and Oholibamah-bat-Anah.
26	These are the sons of Dishon:
	Hemdan, Eshban, Ithran, and Cheran.
27	These are the sons of Ezer:
	Bilhan, Zaavan, and Akan.
28	These are the sons of Dishan:
	Uz and Aran.
29	These are the chiefs of the Horites:
	chief Lotan, chief Shobal, chief Zibeon, chief Anah,
30	chief Dishon, chief Ezer, and chief Dishan.
	These are the chiefs of the Horites,
	attached to their divisions[229] in the land of Seir.
31	These are the kings[230] who ruled in the land of Edom
	before any king ruled the Israelites.
32	Bela, the son of Beor, ruled in Edom,
	and the name of his city was Dinhabah.
33	Bela died;
	Jobab, the son of Zerah of Bozrah, ruled in his place.
34	Jobab died;
	Husham of the land of the Temanites ruled in his place.
35	Husham died;
	Hadad, the son of Bedad
	(who defeated Midianites in the fields of Moab), ruled in his place;
	the name of his city was Avith.
36	Hadad died;
	Samlah of Masrekah ruled in his place.
37	Samlah died;
	Saul[231] of Rehoboth-hannahar[232] ruled in his place.

229. This is some type of military unit.

230. Here we have a king list; this is very important. All of these countries kept a list of the kings.

231. Or "Shaul," but why make it different than the name we know?

232. "Rehoboth-hannahar" = "Rehoboth [on] the river" but not the Euphrates. See *RSP* II, 329.

38	Saul died;
	Baal-hanan, the son of Achbor, ruled in his place.
39	Baal-hanan, the son of Achbor, died;
	Hadad[233] ruled in his place;
	the name of his city was Pau;
	the name of his wife was Mehetabel-bat-Matred,
	the [grand]daughter of Me-zahab.
40	These are the names of the chiefs of Esau according to their families,
	according to their localities, [and] with their names:
	chief Timna, chief Alvah, chief Jetheth,
41	chief Oholibamah, chief Elah, chief Pinon,
42	chief Kenaz, chief Teman, chief Mibzar,
43	chief Magdiel, and chief Iram.
	These are the chiefs of Edom
	according to their settlements in the land that they hold
	(Esau, he is the father of the Edomites).
37:1	Jacob settled in the land where his father sojourned—
	in the land of Canaan.[234]

---

233. "Hadad" in the Hebrew text is Hadar; this is a common mistake (confusion of *r* and *d* in Hebrew), and we know from other lists that "Hadad" is the correct name (1 Chr 1:43–51). Probably during the reign of this Hadad (II), David defeated Edom (see 2 Sam 8:13 and 14). Another note concerning a later Hadad is in 1 Kgs 11:14–22.

234. This verse stands alone as does a similar note in Gen 47:27.

PART IV

Genesis 37:2—50:26

37:2 *These are the stories of Jacob*.[1]
Joseph was seventeen years old. He was shepherding with his brothers among the flocks. He was an assistant to the sons of Bilhah and to the sons of Zilpah, the wives of his father. Joseph brought their bad record to their father.[2] 3 Israel loved Joseph more than any of his sons, for he was the child of his old age. He made him a royal robe.[3] 4 His brothers saw that their father loved him more than any of his brothers. They hated him, and they could not overcome his perfect speech.[4] 5 Joseph had a dream. He told [it] to his brothers. They hated him even more.

1. In the first two major cycles concerning the fathers (Gen 11:27—25:11 and 25:19—35:29), the narrative materials were very brief; they set the stage for conversation/speeches that followed. But in Gen 37:2—50:26 ("The Stories of Jacob"—containing the story of Joseph), we have something different. See note 55 in the Introduction for details. We have a well-written story. The segments of the story function like those in the previous cycles, but there is more narrative with some conversation and a few speeches. All of this is very clear when this material is compared to Genesis 38. This chapter was inserted into the Joseph material, and since it is very much like the earlier cycles, the differences between the two styles seem to stand out.

2. His father instructs him to do this again in v. 14.

3. "Royal robe" is a possible translation. In 2 Sam 13:18 the same term is used, and this time it is described as something that the king's daughters wore. At Ugarit there is a garment in a list, and it is modified by the same root (*psm*). For a full discussion see *RSP* II, 120–23. In this case Joseph, the younger, has the royal robe and shall rule the elder brothers.

4. "Perfect speech" will be important for Joseph in Egypt. The Egyptian king, Meri-ka-Re, was taught: "Be a craftsman in speech" (see *ANET*, 415; *COS* 1.35 [p. 62]). The above translation is not difficult, but most translations assume that the "speech" is that of the brothers (hence something like, "they could not speak a word of peace to him.").

6 He said to them: "Please listen to this dream that I dreamed: 7 There, we were binding sheaves in the field; There, my sheaf stood up and presided; There, your sheaves surrounded and bowed down to my sheaf."

8 His brothers said to him, "Indeed! Are you going to be king over us, or shall you really have dominion over us?" They hated him even more for his dreams and for his words.[5]

9 He had another dream. He recounted it to his brothers; he said, "Yes, I had another dream. In it the sun, the moon, and eleven stars bowed down to me." 10 He had narrated [it] to his father and to his brothers.

His father scolded him; he said to him, "What is this dream that you had? Indeed, shall we really come, I, your mother,[6] and your brothers, to bow down to the earth before you?"

11 His brothers were jealous of him. His father observed the situation. 12 His brothers had gone to pasture their father's flocks in Shechem.

13 Israel said to Joseph, "Are not your brothers shepherding in Shechem? Come, I will send you to them."

He said, "I'm willing."

14 He said to him, "Please go! Note the health of your brothers and the well-being of the flocks and bring back word to me."

He sent him from the valley of Hebron. He arrived in Shechem. 15 A man found him wandering about there in the fields.

The man asked him, "What are you looking for?"

16 "I'm looking for my brothers," he said. "Please tell me where they are shepherding."

17 The man said, "They have moved from here. They were the ones that I heard saying, 'Let's go to Dothan.'"

This is not the case, and it is made clear in v. 8. Another possibility is "they were unable to answer his speech/words." See Gen 45:3 for another situation like this.

5. Joseph's robe, his speech, and his dreams show that Joseph will rule. His brother's hate will also contribute; it will send him to Egypt.

6. Rachel died in Gen 35:19, but this is a different story. In this story, these first events either take place while Rachel is still alive or since there are eleven stars (brothers) perhaps the reference is to Rachel in her tomb! It is sometimes amusing to see the explanations of how it is that Rachel could be in this story or how this is really Bilhah—all for the sake of harmony and our sequential minds.

Joseph went after his brothers. He found them in Dothan. 18 They saw him from a distance, and before he reached them, they plotted [against] him to kill him.

19 They said to one another, "There comes that master-dreamer. 20 Now come on! We will kill him and throw him into one of the pits. We will say, 'An evil beast devoured him.' We shall see how his dreams turn out."

21 Reuben overheard; he [wanted] to rescue him from their hands. He said, "We must not destroy [this] person!" 22 Reuben said to them, "You shall not shed blood! Throw him into this pit which is in the desert, but do not lay a hand on him." ([This he said] in order to deliver him from their hands and to restore him to his father).

23 So when Joseph reached his brothers, they stripped Joseph of his robe, the royal robe that was his. 24 They took him; they threw him into the pit. The pit was empty; there was no water in it. 25 They sat down to eat a meal; they lifted up their eyes; they saw:[7] there was a caravan of Ishmaelites coming from Gilead. Their camels were carrying gum, balm, and resin;[8] they were making a run down to Egypt.

26 Judah said to his brothers, "Where is [the] profit,[9] if we kill our brother and if we cover his blood? 27 Come, we will sell him to the Ishmaelites; our hands will not touch him, for he is our brother; he is our flesh."

His brothers agreed.[10]

28 [Meanwhile], some Midianite traders passed by. They pulled; they brought up Joseph from the pit. They sold Joseph to the Ishmaelites for twenty [shekels] of silver;[11] they brought Joseph to Egypt. 29 Reuben returned to the pit, and there was no Joseph in the pit! He tore his clothes.[12]

---

7. For this formula see Gen 33:1.

8. There is a great deal of uncertainty concerning these items. They appear again in Gen 43:11. The gum might be "gum-tragacanth," and the resin is usually related to Greek, Latin, and Assyrian *ladanum*.

9. Actually "unjust gain."

10. Literally, "His brothers heard." The above translation follows most of the others and is an interpretation.

11. The Midianites sold Joseph before his brothers got around to it.

12. This is a sign of Reuben's mourning.

Genesis 37:2—50:26

30 He went back to his brothers; he said, "The boy, he is not there! And I, where will I go?"

31 They took the robe of Joseph; they slaughtered a billy goat; they dipped the robe in the blood. 32 They sent the royal robe [ahead]. They came to their father.

They said, "We found this. Please observe. Is it the robe of your son or not?"

33 He recognized it. He said, "My son's robe! An evil beast has devoured him; yes, Joseph has been torn up!"[13]

34 Jacob tore his clothes; he put sackcloth on his loins; he mourned his son many days. 35 All his sons and all his daughters tried to comfort him; he refused to be comforted.

He said, "In mourning, I will go down to my son in Sheol."[14] His father wept for him.

36 The Medanites[15] sold [Joseph][16] in Egypt to Potiphar, an officer of Pharaoh (the head of his stewards.)[17]

---

13. This is very bad, because Jacob has nothing to bury.

14. "Sheol" is the dark and silent place of the dead.

15. Most translations read "Midianites." This does not make much sense if we compare v. 28 above and Gen 39:1 with v. 36. The usual explanation is that we are dealing with two different sources. That may be, but when two sources are put together the scribes try to make sense out of the final form. The scribes probably meant to write "Medanites" here and identified this group with the Ishmaelites.

16. Hebrew has "him."

17. Since this story now shifts to a story about Judah the reader must wait until Gen 39:1 to get back to the Joseph story.

Genesis, a Royal Epic

38:1 It was in that time[18] that Judah parted[19] from his brothers;
he camped[20] near an Adullamite,[21] and his name was Hirah.

2 There Judah saw the daughter of a Canaanite, and his name was Shua.
He took her; he went in to her.[22]

3 She conceived; she bore a son.
He called forth his name, "Er."

4 She conceived again; she bore a son.
She called forth his name, "Onan."

5 She repeated again; she bore a son.
She called forth his name, "Shelah."

18. Genesis 38 was inserted at this point in the Joseph story by royal scribes in the time of the monarchy. This has caused a major break in this story, but it accomplished the purpose of the scribes. They wanted to provide genealogical material leading to David (this material plus the book of Ruth gives a complete picture). Genesis 38 is an independent tradition that we could entitle *These are the stories of Judah* following the custom of the final editors of Genesis. We do not have all of this Judah cycle, but we do have the beginning. It begins like Gen 25:19—35:29 (*These are the stories of Isaac*). It would be great to have the rest of this cycle. Given this understanding, it is very difficult to give a good translation of this first phrase. "That time" refers to the time of the patriarchs as viewed from the time of the monarchy (or to be more exact, the "time" when the brothers were still together). But, in its present position, the reader assumes that the word "time" refers to a particular moment in the Joseph story. Also note that in the Joseph story, Judah continues to play a major role. Recent attempts to handle this by making the time indefinite (Tanakh, "About that time") really do not work for any situation. It is a definite time that can only be misunderstood in its present context; but this was the plan of the scribes—they have related it to the Joseph story.

19. The translation "parted" really means "went down." Perhaps it should be left in its literal form. This would picture Judah going down from the hills, or it can also be translated as "going south" (this translation is used in the NEB). The Hebrew root meaning "to go down" is also used in the word Jordon, and the Jordon River runs south.

20. "Camped" is a translation of a Hebrew root that means "to pitch," and it is usually followed by the word "tent." Here the verb stands alone without an object. In Gen 13:12 and 18 we find the opposite situation. The root meaning "tent" is used verbally with no object.

21. In the Hebrew text the word "man" appears before the word "Adullamite," but this is another case where the word "man" is probably a determinative (see the note to Gen 9:20). In the next verse, the word "Canaanite" is determined by "man."

22. This translation is literal, and it is more like the KJ. Most recent translations euphemize the first phrase (translating "he married her"), and they remove the Hebrew euphemism for the second phrase (translating "he had intercourse with her").

	He[23] was in Chezib when she bore him.
6	Judah took a woman for Er, his firstborn;
	her name was Tamar.

7	Er, the firstborn of Judah, was evil in the eyes of Yahweh;
	Yahweh killed him.[24]
8	Judah said to Onan:
	"Go in to the wife of your brother;
	be a brother-in-law to her;
	raise up a descendant for your brother."
9	Onan knew that the descendant would not be his,
	and whenever he went in to the wife of his brother,
	he wasted [his semen][25] on the ground so as not to give a descendant to his brother.
10	What he did was evil in the eyes of Yahweh;
	he killed him as well.
11	Judah said to Tamar, his daughter-in-law:
	"Dwell as a widow in the house of your father
	until Shelah, my son, grows up."
	(He said that, for he too might die like his brothers.)
	Tamar left, and she lived in the house of her father.

12	After many days, the daughter of Shua, the wife of Judah, died.
	Judah was comforted;[26] he went up to the shearers of his flocks at Timnah
	—he and Hirah, his friend,[27] the Adullamite.
13	It was made known to Tamar:

23. "He" = Judah (as in v. 3). The LXX reads "she."

24. Here in the beginning of the line of David, Yahweh punishes as he does in David's own time (see 2 Sam 12:15).

25. The Hebrew text does not provide the object, but it is clear that we should add "his semen," hence *coitus interruptus*.

26. Recent translations mention at this point that the period of mourning was complete, or in AAT Meek translates, "After completing the mourning ceremonies,..." This is interesting, and it is true that in these stories proper burial provides a blessing that insures offspring, but all of this is an attempt to understand what stands behind the word "comforted" rather than a translation of the text.

27. The word "friend" can refer to an official adviser.

	"Now, your father-in-law is going up to Timnah
	to shear his flocks."
14	She removed her widow's garments;
	she covered herself with a double wrap.²⁸
	She was disguised.
	She sat down in the gate of Enaim, which is on the road to Timnah,
	for she realized that Shelah had grown up, yet she had
	not been given to him for a wife.
15	Judah saw her;
	he took her for a harlot,
	for she had covered her face.
16	He turned to her by the road.
	He said:
	"Give, please, I will go in to you"
	(for he did not know that she was his daughter-in-law).
	She said:
	"What will you pay me for coming in to me?"
17	He said:
	"Surely I will send a kid from the flock."
	She said:
	"Only if you give a pledge²⁹ until you send it."
18	He said:
	"What is the pledge that I shall give you?"
	She said:
	"Your seal, your belt, and your staff that is in your hand."³⁰
	He gave [them] to her;
	he went in to her;
	she conceived by him.
19	She got up;
	she left.

28. "Wrap" for the common translation "veil."

29. See *UT*, 461, #1915 for a discussion of this word. Note Ugaritic ʿrbn, Hebrew ʿerabon, Akkadian ú-ru-ba-nu, Greek *arrabon*, Latin *arrabo*, and French *les arrhes*.

30. The "pledge" consists of three items not two. Instead of "your belt" many see this as the cord on which the seal is carried, but the belt was a very important item for an important person. In the courts at Nuzu, "belt-wrestling" was used to determine the guilty party. If your belt was taken from you, you were guilty, and you had to pay the damages to get it back. Here Tamar gets Judah's belt; he is guilty, and he must pay.

She removed her wrap;
she put on her widow's garments.

20 Judah sent the kid in the possession of his friend, the Adullamite,
to redeem the pledge from the possession of the woman.
But, he did not find her.

21 He asked the men of her sanctuary:[31]
"Where is the cult-prostitute?
She was in Enaim by the road."
They said:
"No cult-prostitute has been here."

22 He returned to Judah.
He said:
"I did not find her. Moreover, the men of the sanctuary said,
'No cult-prostitute has been here.'"

23 Judah said:
"Let her keep [the pledge] for herself,
for we might become involved in a scandal. Note that I did send this kid,
but you did not find her."

24 It was about three months later when it was made known to Judah:
"Tamar, your daughter-in-law, has become a harlot!
Moreover, now she is pregnant from harlotry."
Judah said:
"Bring her out! She will be burnt."

25 As she was being brought out, she sent to her father-in-law the following:
"By the man to whom these belong I am pregnant!"
She said:
"Please observe! To whom do these belong,
the seal, the belt, and the staff?"

26 Judah knew.
He said:
"She is more in the right than I,
inasmuch as I did not give her to Shelah, my son."

---

31. "Sanctuary" is a possible translation of the Hebrew for which the basic meaning is "place." If we are going to translate "cult-prostitute" in the next line, then this translation makes sense.

Genesis, a Royal Epic

    (He never again knew her.)
27 When the time of her delivery came,
    there were twins in her womb.[32]
28 During her delivery, one presented a hand;
    the midwife took [it];
    she bound scarlet[33] upon his hand saying:
      "This one came out first."
29 But just as he was drawing back his hand,
    his brother came out.
    She said:
      "What a break you have made for yourself!"
    [Judah][34] called forth his name, "Perez."[35]
30 Afterward his brother came out,
    on whose hand was the scarlet.
    [Judah][36] called forth his name, "Zerah."[37]

39:1 Joseph was brought down to Egypt; an Egyptian, Potiphar, an officer of Pharaoh (the head of the stewards), purchased him from the hand of the Ishmaelites who had brought him down there.[38]

---

32. Compare Gen 25:24 dealing with the birth of Jacob and Esau.

33. Most translators translate "scarlet thread" or something like that, but the text just says "scarlet." This is interesting in that the same word can also mean "second." The first received the "scarlet" but became the "second." Note that in the patriarchal birth stories it is always the elder who serves the younger. Also it is interesting that Esau came out "red."

34. Hebrew = "he."

35. "Perez" means "a break" as a "break" in a wall or in a relationship. We have used "break" because it can mean many things all at the same time. He broke out; he broke a relationship; and he had a lucky break. He would rule his brother.

36. Hebrew = "he."

37. The Hebrew root means "brightness."

38. This verse functions in the final form as a "review" of Gen 37:36, and brings the reader back to the Joseph story. The scribe that gave us this review sees the Ishmaelites and the Medanites as the same group.

2 Yahweh was with Joseph; he was a successful man; he was over[39] the household of his master, the Egyptian.[40] 3 His master saw that Yahweh was with him, and Yahweh made successful in his hands everything that he was doing. 4 Joseph found favor in his eyes; he attended him. [The Egyptian][41] appointed him over his household; he put all of his possessions under his supervision. 5 From the time that he appointed him over his household and over all of his possessions, Yahweh blessed the household of the Egyptian on account of Joseph; so that the blessing of Yahweh was upon all his possessions in the house and in the field.[42] 6 He left all his possessions under the supervision of Joseph, and he did not have common knowledge with him [about] anything except the food that he was eating.[43] Joseph was well built and good looking.[44]

7 It was after these events that the wife of his master lifted up her eyes to Joseph;[45] she said, "Lie with me."

8 He refused! He said to the wife of his master: "Here is my master; he does not have common knowledge with me [about] what is in the house; all his possessions he has put under my supervision. 9 He is not greater in this house than I; he has not withheld anything from me except you, because

---

39. "Over" is not the most common meaning of this Hebrew preposition, but in v. 5 it is used in this way.

40. These three statements provide us with a "table of contents" for the following paragraph.

41. Hebrew = "he."

42. "House" and "field" = "the totality of all his possessions."

43. This is very difficult. Literally, "He did not know with him anything except the food that he was eating." The above translation assumes that it is the Egyptian who does not know and who does not need to know about anything that Joseph is doing with his possessions except when it all came down to a personal level. This phrase is used again in v. 9.

44. The same phrase is used to describe Rachel in Gen 29:17 (see also 12:11; 24:16; and 26:7). The section that begins here (vv. 6b–23) has an interesting parallel in Egyptian literature—*The Story of Two Brothers* (ANET, 23–25; COS 1.40 [pp. 85–89]). In *The Instruction of the Vizier Ptah-Hotep* (ANET, 413) there is a warning against such a women—"One is made a fool by limbs of fayence." Also in Gaster, *Myth, Legend, and Custom*, 218, there is suggested a Canaanite parallel.

45. "Lifted up her eyes to Joseph" means that "she desired Joseph." This was left in its literal form for several reasons, but the main reason is that we have a parallel in the *Gilgamesh* text (VI, 6) of this idiom describing Ishtar's desire for Gilgamesh (see ANET, 83).

Genesis, a Royal Epic

you are his wife. How could I commit this great crime? [How could] I offend Elohim?"[46]

10 This was her word to Joseph day after day, but he did not listen to her [propositions] to lie beside her, to be with her. 11 One such day, he came into the house to do his work. There was no one from the household personnel there in the house.

12 She caught hold of him by his garment, saying, "Lie with me."

He left his garment in her hand; he fled; he went outside.[47]

13 When she saw that he had left his garment in her hand (he had fled outside), 14 she summoned the personnel of her house; she said to them the following: "See, he[48] had to bring us a Hebrew to have sex[49] with us; he came to me to lie with me. I called out with a terrible scream. 15 When he heard that I screamed and called out, he left his garment beside me; he fled; he went outside."

16 She kept his garment beside her until his master came home; 17 she told him about these events as follows: "The Hebrew slave, whom you brought to us, came to me to have sex with me. 18 When I screamed and called out, he left his garment beside me; he fled outside."

19 When his master heard the words of his wife that she spoke to him, namely, "about these things that your slave did to me," his anger flared up. 20 Joseph's master took him; he put him in prison[50] (the place where the royal prisoners were confined).

He was there in prison; 21 Yahweh was with Joseph; he extended kindness to him; he made clear his good qualities in the eyes of the warden.[51] 22 The warden put all the prisoners who were in the prison under the supervision of Joseph, and he was the one who did everything that was accomplished there. 23 The warden did not oversee anything that was under

---

46. The second question is usually translated, "How could I sin against Elohim?" The verb "sin" in Hebrew has the basic meaning "to miss/miss the mark." Most of the time it is used in the sense of "sin," but here Elohim is the object of the verb, and "offend" works well here and in Gen 40:1.

47. When Joseph leaves his garment trouble is just ahead (remember Gen 37:23).

48. This "he" = her husband.

49. For this meaning see Gen 26:8. For the more common meaning "to play" see Gen 21:9.

50. Literally, "the round house."

51. Literally, "the chief of the prison."

his supervision, because Yahweh was with him. Whatever he did, Yahweh made successful.[52]

40:1 It was after these events that the cupbearer and the baker of the king of Egypt offended their lord, the king of Egypt. 2 Pharaoh was angry with his two officers: the head of the cupbearers and the head of the bakers. 3 He put them in the jail on the estate of the head of the stewards[53]—in the same prison where Joseph was confined. 4 The head of the stewards assigned Joseph to them; he attended them.

They had been in jail [for many] days. 5 The two of them, the cupbearer and the baker of the king of Egypt, who were confined in the prison, had dreams; each one had his own dream during the same night; each one had its own meaning.[54] 6 Joseph came to them in the morning; he saw them; they were distraught.

7 He asked the officers of Pharaoh, who were with him in the jail on the estate of his master, saying, "Why are you vexed today?"

8 They said to him: "We had dreams, and there is no one to interpret them."

Joseph said to them: "Do not interpretations belong to Elohim? Please tell [the dreams] to me."

9 The head of the cupbearers recounted his dream to Joseph.

He said to him: "In my dream there was a vine in front of me, 10 and on the vine were three branches. As it budded, its blossoms came out; its clusters ripened; [there were] grapes. 11 Pharaoh's cup was in my hand; I took the grapes; I squeezed them into Pharaoh's cup; I placed the cup in Pharaoh's hand."[55]

12 Joseph said to him: "This is its interpretation: the three branches are three days. 13 In three days Pharaoh will summon you;[56] he will restore

---

52. See v. 3 for this same expression.
53. This is Potiphar.
54. Literally, "each according to the interpretation of his dream." For this difficult phrase see Gen 41:11 and 12.
55. Literally, "I placed the cup on the palm of the Pharaoh."
56. Literally "lift up your head." It can mean "to summon" or "to release" (from prison, as in 2 Kgs 25:27), and this meaning works well for this verse and v. 20. This idiom is also used in Akkadian. In v. 19 we have the same idiom, but it is complicated

you to your position; you will place Pharaoh's cup in his hand, as was [your] former practice when you were his cupbearer. 14 But when [all] is well with you, [and] you have remembered that I was with you, please do me a favor: mention me to Pharaoh; you will get me out of this house.[57] 15 For I was brutally kidnapped from the land of the Hebrews, and further, I have not done anything here that they should have thrown me in the 'pit.'"[58]

16 The head of the bakers saw that he had interpreted favorably; he said to Joseph: "Just like mine![59] In my dream there were three baskets of white baked goods on my head. 17 In the top basket were all kinds of food for Pharaoh that a baker makes. The birds were eating them from the basket on my head."

18 Joseph answered; he said: "This is its interpretation: the three baskets are three days. 19 In three days Pharaoh will summon you;[60] he will hang you on a tree; and the birds will eat your flesh from you."[61]

20 On the third day, which was Pharaoh's birthday, he gave a banquet for all his officials. He summoned[62] the head of the cupbearers and the head of the bakers into the presence of his officials. 21 He restored the head of the cupbearers over his cupbearer[s]; he placed the cup in Pharaoh's hand. 22 He hanged the head of the bakers, just as Joseph had interpreted to them. 23 But the head of the cupbearers did not remember Joseph; he forgot him.

41:1 After a time of two years, Pharaoh was the dreamer. In [his dream],[63] he was standing beside the Nile, 2 and there, from out of the Nile,

---

by a later addition.

57. "This house" refers to "the house of the prison" translated "prison" in v. 3.

58. The use of "pit" for prison is very interesting, and it takes the reader back to the time and place of the kidnapping, Gen 37:28. Joseph has moved from one pit to another! This is used again in Gen 41:14. Most recent translations use "dungeon."

59. Literally, "Also I!"

60. The MT literally reads: ". . .Pharaoh will lift up your head from you." Some think that this means that he was decapitated. The final "from you" is probably a late addition by someone who understood it that way, but there is a better way in Hebrew to describe decapitation. Note 1 Sam 17:46, "I will cut off your head from you." Also not all Hebrew mss have this addition. It is also important to note that in v. 22 and in Gen 41:13 there is no mention of beheading. "To lift up your head" just means "to summon you as in vv. 13 and 19.

61. This means that there is no burial for the baker. In Egypt this is bad news.

62. Literally, "He lifted up the head." See vv. 13 and 19 for the same expression.

63. "In [his dream]" stands for Hebrew, "there," i.e., in the dream of the dreamer."

came up seven good looking and fat cows; they grazed on the irrigated pasture.⁶⁴ 3 After them, there were seven other cows that came up out of the Nile; [these were] poor looking and thin. They stood beside the [first] cows on the bank of the Nile. 4 The poor looking and thin cows devoured the seven good looking and fat cows; Pharaoh woke up! 5 He went back to sleep; he dreamed a second time. There were seven heads⁶⁵ [of grain] that came up from one plant;⁶⁶ [they were] plump and good. 6 After them, there sprouted seven heads, thin and scorched by the east wind. 7 The thin heads swallowed up the seven plump and full heads. Pharaoh woke up; it was a dream.

8 The next morning he was very disturbed; he sent [messengers] and summoned all the magicians⁶⁷ of Egypt and all her wise men. Pharaoh recounted to them his dream[s]; there was not one who could interpret them for Pharaoh.

9 The head of the cupbearers spoke with Pharaoh saying: "Today, I have remembered my offenses. 10 Pharaoh was angry with his servants; he put me in the jail on the estate of the head of the stewards, me and the head of the bakers. 11 We had dreams during the same night, he and I; we had [dreams, and] each one had its own meaning.⁶⁸ 12 A Hebrew youth was there with us, a servant of the head of the stewards; we recounted [our dreams] to him; he interpreted our dreams for us—he interpreted [for] each according to his dream. 13 Then just as he had interpreted for us, so it was: I was restored⁶⁹ to my position, and [the other]⁷⁰ was hanged."

---

64. "Irrigated pasture" for "meadow." This is the pastureland along the Nile. The Hebrew word comes from Egyptian, and it is used in other Semitic languages. See *UT,* 355, #129. "Reeds" or "reed grass" that is used in most translations would not be very good for cows.

65. In English the traditional "ears" would only work for corn.

66. Literally "one stalk/stem" but if we are dealing with grain then "plant" makes more sense.

67. Here we are dealing with an Egyptian loan word. Everyone translates "magicians," but there might be a better term from the Egyptian point of view.

68. See Gen 40:5 for the same difficult phrase.

69. Literally, "he restored me."

70. Hebrew has only "he."

Genesis, a Royal Epic

14 Pharaoh sent [messengers]; he summoned Joseph; they rushed him from the "pit."[71] He shaved; he changed his clothes; he came before Pharaoh.

15 Pharaoh said to Joseph: "I had a dream, and there was no one who could interpret it. I have personally heard concerning you a saying: 'You [only have to] hear a dream to interpret it.'"

16 Joseph answered Pharaoh, saying: "Not I! Elohim will deal[72] with Pharaoh's welfare."

17 Pharaoh spoke to Joseph: "In my dream, there I was, standing by the bank of the Nile, 18 and there, from out of the Nile, came up seven fat and well formed cows; they grazed on the irrigated pasture. 19 After them, there were seven other cows that came up; [these were] weak, with very poor conformation and thin—I have never seen in the entire land of Egypt the likes of them; [they were] awful! 20 The thin and poor cows devoured the first seven fat cows; 21 they went into their bellies, and it could not be known that they had gone into their bellies; their appearance was just as bad as before! I awoke. 22 In my dream, I had a vision:[73] there were seven heads [of grain] that came up from one plant; [they were] full and good. 23 After them, there sprouted seven heads, hard, thin, and scorched by the east wind. 24 The thin heads swallowed up the seven good heads. I have spoken to the magicians, but there is none who can interpret for me."

25 Joseph said to Pharaoh: "Pharaoh's dream is one: that which this God[74] is about to do, he has made known to Pharaoh. 26 The seven good cows: they are seven years. The seven good heads: they are seven years. It is one dream. 27 The seven thin and poor cows, the ones that came up after them: they are seven years, and the seven empty heads, scorched by the east wind: they are seven years of famine. 28 This is the word that I have spoken to Pharaoh: this God has revealed to Pharaoh what he is about to do. 29 There are seven years of great abundance coming in the entire land of Egypt. 30 After them, seven years of famine will be in place; all the abundance in the land of Egypt will be forgotten. The famine will destroy the land. 31 The

71. See Gen 40:15 for the note. Joseph is finally out of the pit.

72. The literal meaning of the Hebrew verb is "answer." But this Hebrew root has at least two basic meanings: 1) "to answer/respond"; and 2) "to put down." What we have here is a double entendre. Elohim will respond with favor and he will bring down the welfare of Pharaoh.

73. In v. 5, this second part or "vision" was a second dream. Others (like NRSV) add "I fell asleep a second time." However this verse already anticipates v. 25.

74. "This God" refers back to v. 16 or to Elohim.

abundance will not be known in the land, because of that famine which will follow, for it will be very severe. 32 Concerning the dream being repeated twice to Pharaoh, [it means] that the matter has been determined by this God, and this God will soon accomplish it. 33 And now, let Pharaoh look for a man of understanding and wisdom and put him in charge of the land of Egypt. 34 Let Pharaoh proceed and appoint overseers over the land; he should organize[75] the land of Egypt during the seven years of plenty. 35 They shall gather all the food of these good years that are coming; by the authority of Pharaoh, they shall store grain [for] food in the cities;[76] they shall set up a guard. 36 That food shall become a "food-bank" for the land for the seven years of famine that will come upon the land of Egypt, and the land shall not be devastated during the famine."

37 This word seemed good in the eyes of Pharaoh and in the eyes of his officials.

38 Pharaoh said to his officials: "Can we find a man who has the spirit of Elohim in him like this one?"

39 Pharaoh said to Joseph: "Since Elohim informed you with all this, there is no one [with] understanding and wisdom like you. 40 You shall be in charge of my palace and on your order my troops will be armed.[77] Only [with respect to] the throne shall I be superior to you."

41 Pharaoh said to Joseph: "See, I have put you in charge of all the land of Egypt."

42 Pharaoh removed his signet ring[78] from his hand; he put it on the hand of Joseph. He dressed him in linen[79] robes and put the gold chain about his neck. 43 He had him ride in the chariot of his second-in-command;[80]

---

75. Here the Hebrew root can mean "five," and so many translate "he should take a fifth [of the produce] of the land . . . ," or one could just say, "take a fifth of the land.

76. See v. 48 for some help with this verse.

77. "Be armed" is difficult. The Hebrew root usually means "to kiss," but this does not make much sense so most translators see some mistake at this point. However, the same Hebrew root could go back to *ntq* in Ugaritic with the meaning of "weapon."

78. Here the Hebrew word is from the Egyptian *ḏbʿt*. Joseph is now the Seal-bearer.

79. "Linen" is the translation of yet another Egyptian word.

80. Instead of "second-in-command" it is tempting to translate "the chariot that was a copy of his" (for the same phrase see 2 Chr 35:24). Others translate: "the chariot of his second-in-command" (Tanakh) or in AAT, "the second of his chariots." The NRSV is not consistent. For Gen 41:43 they have, "the chariot of his second-in-command," but in 2 Chr 35:24 they have "his second chariot" with a note that it could be "the chariot of his deputy."

Genesis, a Royal Epic

they[81] called out before him, "Attention."[82] He put[83] him in charge of all the land of Egypt.

44 Pharaoh said to Joseph, "I am Pharaoh, but without your [approval] a person shall not raise hand or foot[84] in all the land of Egypt." 45 Pharaoh called forth Joseph's name, "Zaphenath-paneah."[85]

He gave him Asenath,[86] the daughter of Poti-phera (priest of On), for a wife. Joseph went out in charge of the land of Egypt.

46 Joseph was thirty years old when he was commissioned by Pharaoh,[87] king of Egypt. Joseph went out from the presence of Pharaoh; he made a survey throughout all the land of Egypt. 47 During the seven years of plenty the land produced more than enough;[88] 48 he gathered all the food of those seven years in the land of Egypt. He put the food in the cities (the food from the fields that were around each city, he put in that city).[89] 49 Joseph stored up grain like the sands of the sea, a tremendous amount, until he ceased counting; it was beyond numbering. 50 Before the years of the famine came, two sons were born to Joseph, whom Asenath, the daughter of Poti-phera (priest of On), bore to him.

---

81. "They" refers to heralds.

82. "Attention" is the translation of an Egyptian phrase, *ib.r.k*; it means, "heart/mind to you," and in Hebrew we are instructed to pronounce it, *abrek*, and most early translations thought that it was from *brk* in Hebrew and could mean, "bow the knee." But the form is not correct for Hebrew (one would have to go back to Ugaritic to have a imperative with a prothetic aleph).

83. Hebrew scholars note that this is an infinitive absolute.

84. Literally, "his hand or his foot, but what does this mean? Most suggest that no one makes a move unless Joseph approves. But since one lifts the hand to praise or take an oath and lifts the foot or heel in rebellion, perhaps this suggests that no one can praise or blame with any move without Joseph's consent.

85. Joseph's new name probably means (in Egyptian) "God speaks and lives."

86. "Asenath" probably means, "belonging to Neith (a goddess)."

87. Literally this phrase is "in his standing before Pharaoh." For the same phrase see 1 Sam 16:22. The usual translation of "when he entered the service of Pharaoh" might work in some situations, but for here it just does not carry the power that belongs to Joseph.

88. "More than enough" is literally "by handfuls."

89. In Hebrew "that city" is "her."

Genesis 37:2—50:26

51 Joseph called forth the name of the firstborn, "'Manasseh,' because [he continued],[90] Elohim has made me forget[91] all my troubles and all about my father's house." 52 He called forth the name of the second one, "'Ephraim,' because [he continued], Elohim has made me fruitful[92] in the land of my suffering."

53 The seven years of plenty that were in the land of Egypt were finished; 54 the seven years of the famine had started to come just as Joseph had said. There was famine in all the lands, but in all the land of Egypt there was food. 55 When all the land of Egypt was hungry, the people cried out to Pharaoh for food.

Pharaoh said to all Egypt: "Go to Joseph; whatever he tells you, you shall do."

56 The famine covered the entire land. Joseph opened up everything among them; he sold grain to Egyptians. The famine became severe in the land of Egypt. 57 The entire world came to Egypt to buy grain from Joseph, for the famine was severe in all the earth.

42:1 Jacob saw that there was grain in Egypt.

Jacob said to his sons: "Why do you look to yourselves?" 2 He said: "I have just heard that there is grain in Egypt. Go down there and buy grain for us; we will live and not die."

3 The ten brothers of Joseph went down to buy grain from Egypt. 4 Jacob did not send Benjamin, the brother of Joseph, with his brothers, for he said that a disaster might encompass him.[93] 5 The sons of Israel came to buy grain along with others,[94] for the famine was [also] in the land of Canaan.

6 Joseph was the ruler over the land. He was the one who sold grain to all the people of the land. The brothers of Joseph came; they bowed down to

---

90. For this form of the naming ritual see Gen 4:25 as well as 41:52.

91. "Has made me forget" is represented in Hebrew by *nashshani* which is something like Manasseh (in Hebrew *menashsheh*).

92. "Has made me fruitful" is represented in Hebrew by *hiphrani* which is connected with Ephraim.

93. Or to put it in very recent English, "for he said that he might be in harm's way."

94. "Along with others" (literally, "among the ones who were coming") refers to others who were also coming to buy grain.

Genesis, a Royal Epic

him [with] their faces to the earth. 7 Joseph saw his brothers; he recognized them. He acted as if he were a stranger to them; he spoke harshly with them.

He said to them: "Where do you come from?"

They said: "From the land of Canaan to buy food."

8 Joseph recognized his brothers, but they did not recognize him.

9 Joseph remembered the dreams[95] that he had dreamed about them; he said to them: "You are spies! You have come to see the nakedness[96] of the land."

10 They said to him: "No, my lord! Indeed, your servants have come to buy food. 11 We are—all of us—the sons of the same man; we are honest; your servants have never been spies!"

12 He said to them: "No! Indeed, you have come to see the nakedness of the land."

13 They said: "We, your servants, were twelve brothers, the sons of one man in the land of Canaan, but the youngest is at this time with our father, and the [other] one is no more.[97]

14 Joseph said to them: "It is just as I have told you: 'You are spies!' 15 By this you shall be tested: [by] the life of Pharaoh [I swear] that you shall not leave this [place] unless your youngest brother comes here. 16 Send one of you to bring back your brother, but [the rest of] you remain imprisoned. Your words shall be tested [if] the truth is with you. And if not, [by] the life of Pharaoh [I will swear] that you are spies!"

17 He confined them to the jail for three days.

18 On the third day Joseph said to them: "Do this and you shall live! I am one who fears the gods.[98] 19 If you are honest, one of your brothers will remain in the cell of your jail, and [the rest of] you go and take grain [for] your hungry households. 20 But you must bring your youngest brother to me, and your words will be verified, and you shall not die."

---

95. In v. 6 they bow down to Joseph as he dreamed early in this story (Gen 37:5–10).

96. See Isa 20:4 where "the nakedness of Egypt" is usually translated "the shame of Egypt." Joseph is saying that they have come to uncover Egypt's weakness.

97. "Is no more" = "does not exist."

98. The plural fits the context. Remember that Joseph is an Egyptian official, and also he is, according to this story, speaking in Egyptian, and his words are being translated (see v. 23). All of this means that Joseph uses his religion as an excuse to back off just a bit, because he does want to get food to his father.

They did so.[99]

21 They said to each other, "For sure, we are guilty on account of our brother in that we saw his personal distress when he pleaded with us for mercy, but we did not listen. Therefore this distress has come to us."

22 Reuben answered them saying: "Didn't I tell you so by saying, 'Don't sin[100] against the boy'? But you did not listen! It is here that his blood has been avenged."[101]

23 They did not know that Joseph understood, for the interpreter was between them. 24 He turned away from them and wept. When he returned to them, he could speak to them. He took Simeon from among them and bound him before their eyes. 25 Joseph gave orders ([after] they had filled their bags [with] grain) to return their silver, each one's to his pack, and to give to them provisions for the journey. So it was done for them. 26 They loaded their grain on their donkeys; they departed from there. 27 One [of them] opened his pack to give feed to his donkey at the campground; he saw his silver. There it was in the mouth of his sack.

28 He said to his brothers: "My silver has been returned! It is here in my sack!"

Their hearts raced; they trembled, saying to each other: "What is this that Elohim has done to us?"

29 They came to Jacob, their father, in the land of Canaan.

They told him everything that had happened to them, saying: 30 "The man who is the lord of the land spoke harshly with us. He arrested us as ones who were spying out the land. 31 We said to him, 'We are honest; we are not spies! 32 We were twelve brothers, sons of our father; one is no more and the youngest is at this time with our father in the land of Canaan.' 33 The man who is the lord of the land said to us, 'By this I shall know that you

---

99. They follow what Joseph said in v. 18 above.

100. Most modern translations avoid the word "sin" at this point. But given the theological view of this verse the word "sin" is needed, even though this does refer back to the concrete warnings in Gen 37:21 and 22.

101. See Gen 9:5 for another example of avenging or requiring blood. Reuben probably figures that at least one of them is as good as dead. For "it is here" see v. 28 below.

are honest:[102] leave one of your brothers with me, load up for your hungry households, and go. 34 Bring your youngest brother to me, and I will know that you are not spies but you are honest. I will restore your brother to you, and you may trade[103] in the land.'"

35 They were opening their packs; there in each one's pack was his pouch of silver. They and their father saw their pouches of silver; they were afraid.[104]

36 Jacob, their father, said to them: "You have bereaved me! Joseph is no more; Simeon is no more; and you would take Benjamin. Everything comes down on me!"

37 Reuben said to his father: "You may kill my two sons if I do not bring him back to you. Put him in my hands, and I will bring him back to you."

38 He said: "My son shall not go down with you, for his brother is dead, and he alone is left. Disaster would encompass him on the journey which you are taking; you will send my white head down to Sheol in sorrow."

43:1 The famine was oppressive in the land.

2 When they had finished eating the grain that they had brought from Egypt, their father said to them: "Return. Buy us a little food."

3 Judah said to him: "The man threatened us, saying, 'You shall not see my face[105] unless your brother is with you!' 4 If you are one who is able to send our brother with us, we will go down and buy food for you; 5 if you are not one who is able to send [him], we will not go down, for the man said to us, 'You shall not see my face unless your brother is with you!'"

6 Israel said: "Why did you betray me by telling the man that you had another brother?"

7 They said: "The man kept asking about us and our family, saying, 'Is your father still alive? Have you [another] brother?' We were forced to an-

---

102. The brothers are guilty until proven innocent.

103. Here "trade" makes good sense; they came to Egypt for this. Compare the discussion concerning Gen 34:10.

104. In this verse, the last two verbs ("saw" and "afraid") sound alike: *vayyir'u* and *vayyiyra'u*.

105. "You shall not see my face" really means, "You shall not come before me for the purpose of requesting the return of Simeon."

swer these questions. How could we possibly have known that he would say, 'Bring down your brother!'"

8 Judah said to Israel, his father: "Send the boy with me! We will get ready; we will go; we will live and not die—we, you, and even our toddlers. 9 I personally will be liable for him; you shall hold me responsible for him: if I do not bring him back to you and set him before you, I shall stand condemned before you all the days [of my life]. 10 If we had not wasted time, we could have made two return trips by now."

11 Israel, their father, said to them: "If this is the case, then do this: take some of the choice products of the land in your bags; take down a gift for the man: a little balm, a little honey, gum, resin, pistachios, and almonds.[106] 12 Take double the silver with you; you shall take back with you the silver that was returned in the mouths of your sacks; perhaps it was a mistake. 13 Take your brother! Get ready and return to the man. 14 May El Shaddai grant you mercy before the man; may he[107] set free your other brother for you along with Benjamin. As for me, when I am bereaved, I am bereaved!"

15 The men took this gift, and they took double the silver with them along with Benjamin. They got on their way; they went down to Egypt; they stood before Joseph. 16 Joseph saw Benjamin with them.

He said to the one who was in charge of his house: "Bring the men into the house. Butcher and prepare a dressed carcass, for the men will eat with me at noon."

17 The man did according to what Joseph had said; the man brought the men into Joseph's house.

18 The men were afraid when they were brought into Joseph's house; they said: "We were brought here because of the silver that was returned to our sacks that first time so that [he may] overpower us, bring us down,[108] and take us for slaves along with our donkeys."

19 They approached the man who was in charge of Joseph's house; they spoke to him [out at] the entrance to the villa.

20 They said: "Pardon, sir, we only came down here that first time to buy food. 21 When we reached the campground, we opened our sacks, and

---

106. For a comment on some of these products see Gen 37:25.
107. Is this El Shaddai or "the man" (i.e. Joseph)?
108. It means something like "bring us down to our knees."

there was each one's silver in the mouth of his sack—our silver in full. We have brought it back with us.[109] 22 We have brought down additional silver with us to buy food. We do not know who put our silver in our sacks."

23 He said, "Shalom to you![110] Don't be afraid. Your God and the God of your father gave you the treasure in your sacks. Your silver was brought to me."

He brought out Simeon to them. 24 The man brought the men [back] into Joseph's house.[111] He gave them water; they washed their feet. He gave some hay to their donkeys. 25 They prepared the gift while [waiting for] Joseph's arrival at noon, for they had heard that they would break bread there.

26 Joseph arrived at the house; they brought him the gift that was with them in the house. They bowed down to the ground before him. 27 He asked them about [their] health; he said, how is the health of your father, the elderly one of whom you spoke? Is he still alive?

28 "Your servant, our father, is well; he is still alive." They bowed and prostrated themselves.

29 He lifted his eyes; he saw Benjamin, his brother, the son of his mother. He said, "Is this your youngest brother of whom you spoke to me?"[112] He added, "May Elohim be kind to you my son."

30 Joseph hurried [out], because his feelings for his brother were exploding; he wanted to weep; he went into another room; he wept there.

31 He washed his face; he went out; he controlled himself; he said, "Serve the meal!"

32 They served him by himself, [the men][113] by themselves, and the Egyptians, the ones who were eating with him, by themselves, for the Egyptians could not eat a meal with the Hebrews, because that is abhorrent

---

109. Literally, "in our hands."

110. This means, "all is well."

111. This sentence is not in the LXX. Some say that v. 17b is repeated here in order to return to the narrative, but the men went out of the main house (v. 19) and now they are coming back into the house.

112. What we are missing in this context is the silent nod of the brothers.

113. The Hebrew text has only "them." Earlier the brothers are referred to as "the men."

to the Egyptians. 33 [The men]¹¹⁴ were seated before him: the firstborn according to his first place and the youngest according to his last place. The men looked at one another in amazement.¹¹⁵ 34 He sent portions from that which was before him to [the men];¹¹⁶ Benjamin's portion was greater than the portions of any of them, [like] five portions.¹¹⁷ They drank; they got drunk with him.

44:1 [Joseph]¹¹⁸ commanded the one who was in charge of his house as follows: "Fill the sacks of the men [with] food, as much as they can carry. Put each one's silver in the mouth of his sack. 2 You shall put my cup, the silver cup, in the mouth of the youngest one's sack along with the silver for his purchase."

He did exactly as Joseph had said.¹¹⁹

3 In the morning, at dawn, the men were sent [on their way], they and their donkeys.

4 They had left the city; they had not gone far, when Joseph said to the one who was in charge of his house, "Get going! Go after the men! You will overtake them; you shall say to them, 'Why have you returned evil for good? 5 Is not this the one¹²⁰ from which my lord drinks and in which he always practices divination?¹²¹ You have committed a crime in this that you have done.'"

6 He overtook them; he repeated these words to them.

---

114. The Hebrew text has "they."

115. Why? Because, how did Joseph know to seat them in order? Also, they could have been amazed that they were sitting before him, even though, according to v. 32 they were "served" separately.

116. The Hebrew text has "them."

117. The Hebrew literally means "hands," but as in Ugaritic (*yd*) and Akkadian (*qâtu*) the word for hand may mean portion.

118. The Hebrew text has "he."

119. This last sentence is literally, "He did according to the word of Joseph that which he had said."

120. "This the one" needs an antecedent. In the LXX, at the beginning of v. 5, there is the addition, "Why have you stolen my silver cup?" Something like this may be needed (but why "my"?). Others (e.g., AB) think that the MT is better and that Joseph's steward pretends that the brothers know what he means.

121. Or, "tells the future."

7 They said to him: "Why does [our][122] lord speak such words as these? Never would your servants do such a thing! 8 If the silver that we found in the mouth of our sacks, we brought back to you from the land of Canaan, why then would we steal from your lord's house silver or gold? 9 The one from among your servants with whom it is found shall die. Moreover we, we shall become slaves for [our][123] lord."

10 He said: "Even now it may be just as you have said, [but] the one with whom it is found shall be my slave, and you shall be free."

11 Each one of them quickly lowered his sack to the ground; each one of them opened his sack. 12 He searched, beginning with the oldest and ending with the youngest; the cup was found in Benjamin's sack. 13 They tore their clothes; each one reloaded his donkey; they returned to the city. 14 Judah and his brothers entered Joseph's villa; he was still there. They fell down to the ground before him.

15 Joseph said to them: "What is this deed that you have done? Did you not know that a man like me always practices divination?"

16 Judah said: "What can we say to my lord? How can we plead? How can we clear ourselves? The divine[124] has discovered the crime of your servants. Here we are, the slaves of my lord, both we and also the one with whom the cup has been found."

17 He said: "Never would I do this![125] The man with whom the cup has been found, he shall be my slave![126] [The rest of] you, go north with safe passage to your father."

18 Judah came closer to him; he said: "O my lord, please allow your servant to speak a word [only] for the ears of my lord; do not be angry with your servant, for you are equal to Pharaoh. 19 My lord asked his servants, 'Have you a father or [another] brother?' 20 We said to my lord, 'We have an elderly father and [there is] a child of [his] old age,[127] [the] youngest, and his

---

122. The Hebrew text has "my lord."

123. Again the Hebrew text has "my lord." If one person is speaking for the group "my lord" might work, but even so the meaning is "our lord." In v. 9 it is more important to note that "our lord" could refer to Joseph rather than Joseph's man, but in v. 10 Joseph's man speaks of the slave as his.

124. This refers to the divine power that makes possible Joseph's divination.

125. Joseph uses the same idiom as the brothers in v. 7 above.

126. This is certainly from a different point of view than that of v. 10.

127. Literally "child of aged" (m. pl.). This is like Gen 37:3.

brother is dead; he alone is left from his mother, and his father loves him.' 21 You said to your servants, 'Bring him down to me; I will look after him.'[128] 22 We said to my lord, 'The boy cannot leave his father; [if] he leaves his father, he[129] will die.' 23 You said to your servants, 'Unless your youngest brother comes down with you, never again shall you see my face.'[130] 24 Then we went north[131] to your servant, my father. We reported to him the words of my lord. 25 [Later] our father said, 'Return and buy for us a little food.' 26 We said, 'We cannot go down! If our youngest brother is with us, we can go down, for we cannot see the man's face if our youngest brother is not with us.' 27 Your servant, our father, said to us, 'You know that my wife[132] bore two [sons] for me. 28 The one left me, I said, he must have been torn up.[133] And I have not seen him since. 29 You would take this one from me as well? Disaster would encompass him. You will send my white head down to Sheol in grief.'[134] 30 And now, when I come to your servant, my father, and the boy is not with us (his life is bound with his life), 31 when he sees that the boy has vanished, he will die! Your servants will send the white head of your servant, our father, down to Sheol in sorrow, 32 for your servant has taken responsibility[135] for the boy from my father, saying, if I do not bring him back to you, I shall stand condemned before my father all the days [of my life]. 33 And now, please let your servant remain in the boy's place [as] the slave of my lord; let the boy go north with his brothers, 34 for how can I go to my father if the boy is not with me? In that case I would witness the woe that would seek out my father."

---

128. Literally, "I will set my eyes on him," but this can mean to look after or care for (see Jer 40:4).

129. In light of v. 31 most translations change "he" to "his father," but "he" could refer to "the boy."

130. For "see my face" note Gen 43:3 (here the word "face" is actually plural). It is interesting that the Hebrew behind "again" in this phrase is from the same root as the name "Joseph."

131. "Went north" is literally "went up." Also see v. 33.

132. Speiser in AB translates "that wife" for "my wife." This does not help, but it is tempting to add something in a situation where there is at least one other wife and the surrogates. The context does make "my wife" clear, but it is not an easy reading.

133. See Gen 37:33 for the complete statement. It means to be torn up by wild animals.

134. In Gen 42:4 and 38 we have the same thought. Also note v. 31.

135. In Gen 43:9 this word was translated "liable."

Genesis, a Royal Epic

45:1 And Joseph was not able to control himself before all his attendants, he cried out, "Everyone leave me!"

So no one was attending him when Joseph made himself known to his brothers.

2 He broke down with weeping;[136] [the] Egyptians heard; the house of Pharaoh heard.

3 Joseph said to his brothers, "I am Joseph. Is my father still alive?"

His brothers were not able to answer him,[137] for they were petrified before him.

4 Joseph said to his brothers, "Please come closer to me." They came closer; he said: "I am Joseph, your brother, whom you sold to Egypt. 5 Now, you should not be distressed, and let there be no anger in your eyes,[138] because you sold me here. Because it was for a savior [that] Elohim sent me ahead of you. 6 For it is two years now that the famine has been in the land, and there are still five years [to come] in which there will be no plowing or harvesting. 7 Elohim sent me ahead of you to make you a remnant in the land and to save you for [the] great escape.[139] 8 In sum: You did not send me here but rather this God;[140] he made me a counselor[141] of Pharaoh, lord of all his house, and ruler over all the land of Egypt. 9 Hurry! Go north to my father. You shall say to him: 'Thus your son Joseph has said: "Elohim made me lord of all Egypt; come down to me; you shall not delay. 10 You shall live in Goshen; you shall be close to me—you, your sons, your grandsons, your sheep, your cattle, and all that is yours. 11 There I will support you—for there are still five more years of famine—so that you, your house, and all that is yours will not be dispossessed."' 12 So your eyes have seen, and the eyes of my brother Benjamin, that my mouth is the one who speaks to you. 13 You shall make known to my father everything concerning my important posi-

---

136. "Broke down with weeping" is literally "He gave forth his voice in weeping." The word for "voice/sound" is used again in v. 16.

137. See Gen 37:4b where the brothers are not able to deal with Joseph's words.

138. See Gen 31:35 for this phrase.

139. This is a difficult verse. This translation is literal and assumes that "the land" refers to Egypt (not earth as in other translations). The "great escape" points to the future and the exodus from Egypt.

140. Here we have Elohim with the definite article.

141. Literally "father."

Genesis 37:2—50:26

tion in Egypt and everything that you have seen. You shall hurry! You shall bring my father down here."

14 [Joseph][142] fell on the shoulders of his brother, Benjamin; he wept; Benjamin wept on his shoulders. 15 He kissed all his brothers; he wept upon them. After that his brothers talked with him.

16 So the report[143] was issued[144] [from] the house of Pharaoh as follows: "Joseph's brothers have arrived! [This] has seemed good in the eyes of Pharaoh and in the eyes of his officials."[145]

17 Pharaoh said to Joseph: "Say to your brothers: 'Do this: Load up your animals and go; go into the land of Canaan. 18 Take your father and your households; come to me. I will give you the best of the land of Egypt; eat the fat of the land.' 19 You, [Joseph], are [also] commanded [to say]: 'Do this: Take wagons from the land of Egypt, for yourselves, for your toddlers, and for your wives. You shall bring your father. You shall return. 20 Your eyes should not look longingly upon your possessions, for the best of all the land of Egypt is yours.'"

21 The sons of Israel did so.

Joseph gave them wagons, as Pharaoh had ordered. He gave them provisions for the road. 22 To each of them he gave a change of clothing,[146] and to Benjamin he gave three hundred [shekels] of silver and five changes of clothing, 23 and to his father he sent the following: ten male donkeys who carried the best things of Egypt[147] and ten female donkeys who carried grain, bread, and food for his father for the road.

24 He sent his brothers away; they left; he said to them, "Do not get too excited on the road."

---

142. Hebrew = "he."

143. The Egyptians/the house of Pharaoh heard the "sound of weeping" in v. 2. But here the "sound/report" is coming from Pharaoh's house. This verse does not repeat v. 2.

144. "Issued" is literally "heard."

145. This statement of approval was used in Gen 41:37.

146. In Gen 37:23 the brothers took Joseph's royal robe. Here he gives them "a change of clothing" (probably very special clothes).

147. Note a list of such "good things" in *The Eloquent Peasant*, lines 5–35, in Lichtheim, *Ancient Egyptian Literature*, vol. 1, 170.

Genesis, a Royal Epic

25 They went north from Egypt; they entered the land of Canaan [and came] to their father Jacob.

26 They told him: "Joseph is still alive!" and that he is the one who rules in all the land of Egypt.

His mind[148] became numb, for he did not believe them. 27 They repeated to him all the words of Joseph that he had spoken to them. He saw the wagons that Joseph sent to transport him. The spirit of Jacob, their father, revived.

28 Israel said, "Enough! Joseph, my son, is still alive; I must go; I will see him before I die."

46:1 Israel departed with all that belonged to him. When he entered Beer-sheba, he offered sacrifices to the God of his father Isaac.

2 Elohim spoke to Israel in a vision of the night; he said: "Jacob, Jacob!" [Jacob][149] said: "Here am I."

3 He said: "I am the God, the God of your father. You shall not fear going down to Egypt, for I will make you into a great people there. 4 I, I will go down with you to Egypt; I, I will even bring you up again, and Joseph shall put his hand upon your eyes."[150]

5 Jacob left Beer-sheba. The sons of Israel put Jacob, their father, their toddlers, and their wives in the wagons that Pharaoh sent to carry them.[151] 6 They took their livestock and their possessions that they had acquired in the land of Canaan; Jacob and all his descendants with him entered into Egypt: 7 his sons and grandsons were with him, his daughters and granddaughters, and all his descendants, he brought with him to Egypt.

8 These are the names[152] of the Israelites, Jacob and his sons, who came into Egypt (Jacob's firstborn was Reuben):

    148. "Mind" is literally "heart."
    149. Hebrew = "he."
   150. Joseph will close Jacob's eyes at the time of his death. These first four verses in Genesis 46 are very important. At the beginning of an important journey, Jacob goes to a sanctuary as he does in Gen 28:10–22 and also in Gen 32:2–3.
    151. Here a singular suffix must be translated as plural. This happens many times in these texts.
    152. "These are the names" is a phrase that is used at the beginning of documents

9 **Reuben's** sons: Hanoch, Pallu, Hezron, and Carmi.

10 **Simeon's** sons: Jemuel, Jamin, Ohad, Jachin, Zohar, and Shaul (the son of a Canaanite woman).

11 **Levi's** sons: Gershon, Kohath, and Merari.

12 **Judah's** sons: Er, Onan, Shelah, Perez, and Zerah (Er and Onan had died in the land of Canaan; Perez' sons were Hezron and Hamul).

13 **Issachar's** sons: Tola, Puvah, Iob,[153] and Shimron.

14 **Zebulun's** sons: Sered, Elon, and Jahleel. 15 (These are the sons of Leah whom she bore to Jacob in Paddan-aram along with his daughter, Dinah. Persons in all, his sons and his daughters, equaled thirty-three.)

16 **Gad's** sons: Ziphion, Haggi, Shuni, Ezbon, Eri, Arodi, and Areli.

17 **Asher's** sons: Imnah, Ishvah, Ishvi, Beriah, and their sister Serah (Beriah's sons were Heber and Malchiel). 18 (These are the children of Zilpah whom Laban gave to his daughter Leah. These she bore to Jacob, sixteen persons.) 19 (The sons of Rachel, Jacob's wife, were Joseph and Benjamin.)

20 To **Joseph** in the land of Egypt were born Manasseh and Ephraim, whom Asenath, the daughter of Poti-phera (priest of On), bore to him.

21 **Benjamin's** sons: Bela, Becher, Ashbel, Gera, Naaman, Ehi, Rosh, Muppin, Huppim, and Ard. 22 (These are the sons of Rachel who were born to Jacob; persons in all equaled fourteen.)

23 **Dan's** son: Hushim.

24 **Naphtali's** sons: Jazeel, Guni, Jezer, and Shillem. 25 (These are the sons Bilhah, whom Laban gave to his daughter Rachel. These she bore to Jacob; persons in all equaled seven.)

26 All the persons belonging to Jacob who came to Egypt—the ones who came from his loins,[154] not including the wives of the sons of Jacob—all these persons totaled sixty-six. 27 Joseph's sons, who were born to him in Egypt, were two persons. The persons belonging to the house of Jacob who came to Egypt were seventy in all.

(note Exod 1:1). The following list is from another source, and it is used here. Most scholars say that this source is P. This seems impossible, because it is not like other parts of "P."

153. This is the MT reading, but others read "Jashub."

154. See the note on Gen 24:2 where we have translated 46:26, "those who came out of his thigh (or genital organ)." Also note of thigh/loins in 47:29.

28 [Israel][155] sent Judah ahead of him to Joseph to give directions before his [arrival] in Goshen. They arrived in the land of Goshen. 29 Joseph hitched up his chariot; he went up to meet his father, Israel, in Goshen. He saw him; he fell upon his shoulders; he wept on his shoulders incessantly.

30 Israel said to Joseph, "Now let me die since I have seen your face; [I have seen] that you are still alive."

31 Joseph said to his brothers and to the house of his father: "I will go and tell Pharaoh; I will say to him, 'My brothers and the house of my father, who were in the land of Canaan, have come to me. 32 The men are shepherds[156]—yes, they have always been stockmen.[157] They have brought their flocks, their herds, and all that is theirs.' 33 When Pharaoh summons you and asks, 'What is your occupation?' 34 You shall answer, 'Your servants have been stockmen from our youth until now, even as our fathers,'[158] in order that you may settle in the land of Goshen, for every shepherd is abhorrent to Egyptians."

47:1 Joseph came; he told Pharaoh; he said: "My father, my brothers, their flocks, their herds, and all that is theirs have come from the land of Canaan, and they are here in the land of Goshen."

2 From all his brothers, he took five men; he presented them to Pharaoh.

3 Pharaoh said to his brothers: "What is your occupation?"

They said to Pharaoh: "Your servants are shepherds, even as our fathers."

4 They said to Pharaoh: "We have come to sojourn in the land, for there is no pasture for the flocks that belong to your servants in the land of Canaan, because the famine has been severe in the land of Canaan. Now, please allow your servants to settle in the land of Goshen."

---

155. Hebrew = "he."
156. "Shepherds" = "keepers of flocks."
157. Stockmen/cowboys" is "men of cattle/herds." Or as in other places perhaps the word "men" is an indication that what follows is to be taken as a occupation. See the note for Gen 9:20.
158. Verse 32-34 are very difficult to understand. Are "shepherds" and "stockmen" the same or different? Are "stockmen/cattlemen" better? The instructions in v. 34 are not followed in 47:3. It is difficult to give a translation when one does not understand.

Genesis 37:2—50:26

5 Pharaoh said to Joseph as follows: "Your father and your brothers have come to you. 6 The land of Egypt is before you; in the best part of the land, settle your father and your brothers; they shall settle in the land of Goshen. And if you know that there are soldiers among them, you shall appoint them cattle foremen over my herds."

7 Joseph brought Jacob, his father, and presented him to Pharaoh. Jacob blessed Pharaoh.[159]

8 Pharaoh said to Jacob: "How many are the days of the years of your life?"[160]

9 Jacob said to Pharaoh: "The days of years of my sojourn are one hundred thirty years. Few and hard have been the days of the years of my life, and they have not added up to the days of the years of the lives of my fathers in the days of their sojourns."

10 Jacob blessed Pharaoh. He went out from the presence of Pharaoh.

11 Joseph settled his father and his brothers; he granted them property in the land of Egypt—in the best part of the land, in the land of Rameses, as Pharaoh had commanded. 12 Joseph sustained his father, his brothers, and all the house of his father [with] food, even for the mouths[161] of the toddlers.

13 There was no food in the entire land, for the famine was very severe. The land of Egypt and the land of Canaan languished before the famine. 14 Joseph had received all the silver to be found in the land of Egypt and the land of Canaan for the grain that they were buying. Joseph brought the silver to the house of Pharaoh. 15 The silver was gone from the land of Egypt and from the land of Canaan.

All the Egyptians came to Joseph saying: "Give us food! Why should we die, since you are here,[162] [just] because [the] silver is gone?"

---

159. This is a literal translation. If one translates this as "greeted" or the like, one must say just the opposite in v. 10.

160. This idiom is used in Gen 25:7 in giving the age of Abraham, and again in 2 Sam 19:35. I could go along with AAT ("How old are you?"), but since it is used several times in Genesis 47, it is best to keep the literal form. Perhaps the fuller form in v. 28 contains important clues.

161. "Mouth" can mean "portion," or with "to/for" it can mean "according to." Our translation is influenced by v. 24 below.

162. "Since you are here" is literally "in your presence." In other words, they know

16 Joseph said: "Give your livestock, and I will give[163] [food] to you in exchange for your livestock, since [the] silver is gone."

17 They brought their livestock to Joseph. Joseph gave food to them in exchange for the horses, for the flocks of sheep, for the herds of cattle, and for the donkeys. During that year he provided them with the food that was exchanged for all their livestock. 18 That year was complete.

They came to him in the second year; they said to him: "We can not hide from my lord that, since the silver is spent, and the herds of animals belong to my lord, nothing is left for my lord except our bodies and our farms. 19 Why should we be destroyed before your eyes, both we and our farms? Buy us and our farms in exchange for food. We and our farms shall become the servants of Pharaoh. Give us seed! We shall live! We shall not die, and the farms shall not become a wasteland."

20 Joseph purchased all the farms of Egypt for Pharaoh, for every Egyptian sold his field, because the famine was so severe on them. The land became Pharaoh's. 21 He moved the people to the cities from one border of Egypt to the other. 22 Only the farms of the priests he did not purchase, because of the entitlement of the priests [issued] by Pharaoh.[164] They lived from their fixed income that Pharaoh gave to them. Therefore they did not sell their farms.

23 Joseph said to the people: "Now [from] this day, I have purchased you and your farms for Pharaoh. Here is seed for you. You shall sow the farms. 24 When harvest comes, you shall give one-fifth to Pharaoh. Four of the parts shall be for you: the seed for the fields, food for you, for those in your house, and for feeding your toddlers."

25 They said: "You have kept us alive. May we find favor in the eyes of our[165] lord. We shall become the servants of Pharaoh."

26 Joseph made it a statute until this day concerning the farms of Egypt; a fifth belongs to Pharaoh. Only the farms of the priests did not become Pharaoh's. 27 Israel settled in the land of Egypt, in the land of Goshen. They acquired property in it. They were fruitful; they multiplied greatly.

---

that Joseph can do something. Also note v. 19.

163. "Give" means "sell" here. Also the MT does not give the object ("food/bread"), because it is understood and is given in v. 15.

164. The priests (also see v. 26) did not have to sell their farms. They did not have to worry because of their fixed income.

165. Hebrew has "my lord."

28 Jacob lived in the land of Egypt seventeen years. The days of Jacob, the years of his life were one hundred forty-seven years. 29 The days of Israel came close to death. He summoned his son Joseph.

He said to him: "If I have found favor in your eyes, please place your hand under my thigh.[166] You shall treat me with kindness and truth.[167] Please do not bury me in Egypt. 30 I will lie down with my fathers. You shall take me up from Egypt; you shall bury me in their sepulchre."[168]

[Joseph][169] said: "I will certainly do according to your word."

31 He said: "Swear to me."

[Joseph][170] swore to him. Israel bowed low at the head of the bed.

48:1 It was after these events that [a messenger] said to Joseph, "Your father is ill."

He took with him his two sons, Manasseh and Ephraim.

2 [A messenger] informed Jacob; he said, "Here he is! Your son Joseph has come to you."

Israel strengthened himself and sat up in bed.

3 Jacob said to Joseph:

"El Shaddai appeared to me at Luz[171] in the land of Canaan. He blessed me. 4 He said to me:[172]

'Yes, I am the one Who will make you fruitful.[173]

I will make you many;

I will make you a community of peoples.

I will grant this land to your descendants,

[The ones who] follow you,

[as] an everlasting possession.'

---

166. For a discussion of "thigh" see the note for Gen 24:2.
167. "Kindness and truth" has to do with keeping an oath. See Gen 24:27.
168. Jacob must be buried in the correct place.
169. MT has "he."
170. MT has "he."
171. The ancient name of Bethel, Gen 28:19.
172. The following blessing needs to be compared to Gen 28:1-4 and 35:11-12.
173. The usual translation of "I will make you fruitful" pays no attention to this text.

Genesis, a Royal Epic

5 Now your two sons, the ones who were born to you in the land of Egypt before the time of my coming to you in Egypt, they are mine; Ephraim and Manasseh just as Reuben and Simeon, they are mine.

6 Your children whom you fathered after them, they are yours; instead[174] of the names of their brothers, they will be called in their inheritance.[175]

7 And I,[176] when I was returning from Paddan, Rachel died on me in the land of Canaan, on the road to Ephrath, with still some distance to go. I buried her there on the road to Ephrath (that is, Bethlehem)."[177]

8 Israel saw Joseph's sons; he said: "Who are these?"

9 Joseph said to his father: "They are my sons whom Elohim has given me here."

He said: "Please bring them to me. I will bless them. 10 Israel's eyes were dim from old age; he was not able to see. [Joseph][178] brought them close to him. He kissed them; he embraced them.

11 Israel said to Joseph: "I never expected to see your face again, and here Elohim has allowed me to see your descendants as well."

12 Joseph took them from his knees.[179] He bowed low before him[180] to the earth. 13 Joseph took the two of them, Ephraim in his right [hand] opposite Israel's left and Manasseh in his left [hand] opposite Israel's right. He brought [them] close to him. 14 Israel put forth his right [hand]; he laid [it] on the head Ephraim, who was the younger, and his left [hand] on the head

---

174. "Instead of" or "above" as in v. 22.

175. "They will be called in their inheritance" is difficult. Their names will be called at the grave. See the discussion under v. 16 below.

176. This is for emphasis (Hebrew *'ani*). "It was me; she left me, and I buried her there."

177. Most scholars see v. 7 as a misplaced fragment. It is a very difficult note, but it is probably not misplaced. This account follows Genesis 35, and this note is a reminder by Jacob of the place of Rachel's burial.

178. Hebrew = "he."

179. This is an adoption ritual. See Gen 30:3 and 50:23.

180. "Before him" as in 1 Sam 25:23. It is literally "to his nose" which is used in many places as part of the idiom "to bow his nose/face to the earth."

of Manasseh, although[181] Manasseh was the firstborn (he crossed his hands). 15 He[182] blessed Joseph.[183]

He said:[184] "The God before whom my fathers, Abraham and Isaac, walked, the God who has been my shepherd from my birth until this day,[185] 16 the Messenger who has delivered me from all harm, may he bless these young men. My name and the names of my fathers, Abraham and Isaac, shall be called forth by them.[186] They will become a multitude in the land."

17 Joseph saw that his father was laying his right hand on the head of Ephraim. This was wrong in his eyes. He took hold of his father's hand to move it from the head of Ephraim to the head of Manasseh.

18 Joseph said to his father: "Not so, my father, for this one is the firstborn. Lay your right [hand] on his head."

19 His father refused. He said: "I know, my son, I know. He too shall become a people; He too shall become great, but his younger brother shall be greater than he,[187] and his descendants shall become the masses of the peoples."

20 He blessed them on that day as follows: "By you shall Israel bless itself saying, 'May Elohim make you like Ephraim and like Manasseh.'"

He put Ephraim before Manasseh.

21 Israel said to Joseph: "I am about to die. Elohim will be with you and return you to the land of your fathers. 22 And I, I grant to you, as one above your brothers, Shechem, which I captured from the power of the Amorites with my sword and with my bow."[188]

---

181. Buber and Rosenzweig have *obschon*.

182. This is Jacob/Israel.

183. The LXX replaces "Joseph" with "them," referring to Joseph's sons. This seems to make more sense, but it is difficult to account for such a mistake in the MT. It is much easier to have Jacob doing two things: he is blessing Joseph by blessing his sons, and by giving Joseph Shechem.

184. This is the blessing on the sons. Also note v. 20 which shows how all of this is continued.

185. "from my birth until this day" is literally "from my beginning to this day." This phrase also appears in Num 22:30.

186. Also see Gen 21:12. The names of the fathers are called forth or summoned during a ritual for the dead, and when this is done, one is blessed with heirs.

187. This is one of the main themes in royal epic.

188. This is why Joseph is buried in Shechem (see Gen 50:25; Exod 13:19; and Josh 24:32).

Genesis, a Royal Epic

49:1 Jacob summoned his sons; he said:
"Gather round; I will tell you what will happen to you in days to come.

2   Assemble and listen, sons of Jacob;
Listen to Israel, your father.

3   Reuben, my firstborn,
You are my power,
The best of my prime,
Excelling in rank,
Excelling in strength.

4   [But] unruly like a flood,
You shall excel no more,
For you mounted your father's bed;
Then you defiled my couch—
My couch he mounted![189]

5   Simeon and Levi are partners.[190]
Tools of injustice are their wares.[191]

6   My being shall not enter their council;
My person shall not join their assembly.
For when angry they killed men;
When pleased they hamstrung oxen.

7   Cursed be their anger for it is strong,
And their fury for it is relentless.
I will divide them in Jacob;
I will scatter them in Israel.

8   Judah, you really are![192]

---

189. The word "couch" appears once in the Hebrew text. This translation follows the suggestion of Sarna in TC Genesis. See Gen 35:22 and 1 Chr 5:1 for this act of Reuben.

190. "Partners" is from the Hebrew for "brothers." Since we already know that they are brothers this takes us to another point with another use of the word.

191. In Gen 34:10 there is the offer by Hamor of "free trade." Of course Simeon and Levi say, "no," and then they killed every male (Gen 34:25). They were some "traders." The word "wares" is a possible translation, but it remains difficult.

192. This means "You really are Judah"; you are living up to your name which

	Your brothers shall praise you—

       Your brothers shall praise you—
       Your hand is on the neck of your foes;
       The sons of your father shall bow down to you.
9   A lion's cub was Judah;
       On prey, my son, you have grown up.[193]
       He lay down; like a lion he crouched,
       And as an old lion, who will rouse him?
10   The scepter shall not pass from Judah,
       Nor the staff from between his feet.
       So tribute shall be brought to him;
       His shall be [the] homage of peoples.
11   He is the one who ties his colt to the vine,
       His donkey's colt to the choicest vine.
       He washes his garment in the wine,
       In blood of grapes his robe.
12   [His] eyes are darker than wine;
       [His] teeth are whiter than milk.

13   Zebulun shall dwell by [the] seashore,
       And he shall be a port for ships.
       His flank, on the north, is Sidon.

14   Issachar is a strong ass,
       Waiting among the sheep pens.
15   He saw a resting place—that it was good,
       And the land—that it was pleasant.
       He bent his shoulder to bear burdens;
       He became a corvée slave.

16   Dan shall govern[194] his people,
       As one of the tribes of Israel.
17   Dan shall be a serpent on [the] road,
       A viper on [the] path.

---

means "to be praised," and note that your brothers shall praise you.

    193. For another treatment of this image see Ezek 19:1–9. This verse is usually seen as an independent saying (note Num 24:9).

    194. "Govern" or "judge" is a play on Dan (*yadin*).

Genesis, a Royal Epic

	The one who bites [the] heels of a horse,
	Whose rider is thrown backward.
18	For your salvation, I wait, O Yahweh.[195]
19	Gad shall be raided by raiders;
	He shall raid at their heels.[196]
20	Asher's food shall be rich;
	He shall furnish royal delicacies.
21	Naphtali is a doe set free;
	The one who inspires words of beauty.
22	Joseph is a colt of a wild ass,
	A colt of a wild ass by a spring—
	Wild colts by Shur.[197]
23	Archers bitterly attacked him;
	They shot and assaulted him.
24	His bow was always steady;
	His arms were quickened,
	From the power[198] of the Abir[199] of Jacob,
	From that of[200] the Shepherd, the Rock of Israel,
25	From the God of your father, he helps you,
	And from Shaddai, he blesses you:
	Blessings of heaven above,
	Blessings of the deep who crouches below,
	Blessings of breasts and womb,
26	Blessings of your father, they are mighty.
	In addition, blessings of ancient mountains,
	Delights of eternal hills.

195. This prayer stands alone. The speaker is not indicated.
196. The word "raid/ed/ers" in both lines is related to "Gad."
197. This is very much like Gen 16:7 and 12: "by the spring on the way to Shur," and "He shall be a wild ass of the steppe." This is discussed in the note on Gen 16:12.
198. "The power" or "the hands."
199. "Abir" is usually translated as "the mighty one."
200. Literally "from there," i.e., "from the power."

>   May these be on the head of Joseph,
>   On the pate of the leader of his brothers.[201]

27   Benjamin is a wolf on the hunt.
>   In the morning he devours [the] prey;
>   In the evening he divides the spoil."

28 All these were the twelve tribes of Israel, and this is what their father said to them. He blessed them; each one he blessed with his own blessing.

29 He charged them; he said to them:
>   "I am about to be gathered to my people.
>   Bury me with my fathers,
>   at the cave that is in the field of Ephron the Hittite,
30   in the cave that is in the field of the Machpelah,[202]
>   that is before Mamre in the land of Canaan,
>   that Abraham purchased with the field from Ephron
>   the Hittite for [his] own sepulchre.[203]
31   There they buried Abraham and Sarah, his wife;
>   there they buried Isaac and Rebekah, his wife;
>   and there I buried Leah."[204]

32 The purchase: the field and the cave that is in it from the sons of the Hittites.[205] 33 Jacob finished charging his sons. He drew his feet into the bed. He expired. He was gathered to his people.

---

201. Also see Gen 48:22.

202. "The Machpelah" means "the double."

203. It is extremely important in these traditions for the father to have the legal possession of the burial place. Literally, this means "for a possession of a sepulchre." For the sale of the cave see Gen 23:1–20.

204. See 35:16–21 for the burial of Rachel.

205. This verse is unrelated and stands alone. It may be some kind of a title or colophon. To translate "purchase " the Hebrew pointing was changed.

50:1 Joseph fell down before his father;[206] he wept over him; he kissed him. 2 Joseph ordered his servants,[207] the physicians, to embalm his father. The physicians embalmed Israel. 3 Forty days were filled with it, for such are the days of embalming that are required. The Egyptians wept for him seventy days; 4 the days of weeping for him were over.

Joseph spoke to the house[208] of Pharaoh saying: 5 "If I have found favor in your eyes, please speak in the ears of Pharaoh, saying: 'My father made me swear, saying: "Behold, I am about to die. In my sepulcher that I prepared for myself in the land of Canaan, there, you shall bury me." And now, please let me go up, and I will bury my father, and I will return.'"

6 Pharaoh said: "Go up and bury your father as he made you swear."

7 Joseph went up to bury his father. They went up with him all the servants of Pharaoh, the elders of his house, all the the elders of the land[209] of Egypt, 8 all the house of Joseph, his brothers, and the house of his father; only their children, their sheep, and their cattle were left in the land of Goshen. 9 Even chariots and horsemen went up with him. The encampment was very large. 10 They arrived at the threshing floor of the Atad that is beyond the Jordan. They lamented there with a great and very solemn lamentation; he observed for his father a seven day mourning.[210]

11 The inhabitants of the land, the Canaanites, saw the mourning on the threshing floor of the Atad.

They said: "This is a solemn mourning (Gebel) for Egyptians."

Therefore its name was called Abel-mizraim;[211] it is beyond the Jordan. 12 His sons did for him as he had charged them. 13 His sons carried him to the land of Canaan. They buried him in the cave of the field of the Machpelah, that Abraham purchased with the field for [his] own sepulchre

---

206. Most translations read "Joseph fell down upon his father's face." Such is the literal sense, but it does not really work. It is interesting to relate this verse to 46:4, "when Joseph puts his hand upon your eyes."

207. "Servants" here really means "ministers" or "officials," as v. 7.

208. Or "court" as in Tanakh; and see v. 7.

209. This could be another example of a determinative in Hebrew (see the note for 9:20a). If so we should read "the elders of Egypt."

210. See 1 Sam 31:13; and for a lament of this type see 2 Sam 1:17–26.

211. "Abel mizraim" means "the meadow of Egypt," but it sounds like "the mourning of the Egyptians."

from Ephron the Hittite, before Mamre. 14 After burying his father,[212] Joseph returned to Egypt, he and his brothers, and all who had gone up with him to bury his father.

15 Joseph's brothers saw that their father was dead; they said: "Suppose Joseph hates us? He shall surely pay us back for all the evil that we dealt him."

16 They sent [a message][213] to Joseph, saying: "Your father, before his death, gave a command, as follows: 17 'Thus shall you say to Joseph: "Please forgive the crime of your brothers and their sin, for the evil that they dealt you."' And now, please forgive the crime of the servants of the God of your father."

Joseph wept from their words to him.

18 His brothers came; they fell down before him; they said: "Here we are; we are your slaves."

19 Joseph said to them: "Do not fear! For am I in the place of Elohim? 20 You planned evil against me. Elohim planned it for good, in order to accomplish today the survival of many people. 21 And now, do not fear! I will provide for you and your toddlers."

He reassured them; he spoke to their hearts.

22 Joseph settled in Egypt, he and the house of his father. Joseph lived a hundred and ten years.[214] 23 Joseph saw the sons of the third [generation] of Ephraim; also the sons of Machir-ben-Manasseh were born on the knees of Joseph.[215]

24 Joseph said to his brothers: "I am about to die. Elohim will surely visit[216] you. He will bring you up from this land to the land that he swore to Abraham, to Isaac, and to Jacob." 25 Joseph made the sons of Israel swear,

---

212. This phrase appears at the end in the Hebrew text.

213. "Sent [a message]" is literally "they commanded" with no object.

214. In Egyptian literature "a hundred and ten" is the "ripe old age." Also Joshua's age is described with this formula, see Josh 24:29.

215. See Gen 30:3.

216. "Visit" can mean "to punish," but here (and in v. 25 as well as Gen 21:1; Exod 13:19, etc.) it is a gracious visit. "Elohim will care for you."

saying: "Surely Elohim will visit you. Then you shall bring up my bones from here."[217]

26 Joseph died, being a hundred and ten years. They embalmed him. He was placed[218] in the sarcophagus[219] in Egypt.

---

217. See Exod 13:19 and Josh 24:32.
218. This follows the Sam reading.
219. Buber and Rosenzweig have *Schrein*; but see the examples in *KAI* 1:1, 2; 9:A2, B4; 11; 13:2, 3, 5; 29:1

APPENDIX I
You Can't Tell a Book by Its Cover

NIELS PETER LEMCHE, PROFESSOR of Old Testament studies at the University of Copenhagen, has produced a book with a beautiful cover.[1] In fact, I bought the book for the cover. On the cover is a beautiful colored digital image by Bruce and Kenneth Zuckerman of the *marzeaḥ* tablet from Ugarit. In 1970, I arranged for the purchase of this tablet by other universities and the Institute for Antiquity and Christianity in Claremont, California. Also, in that year, I cleaned this tablet with care and prepared it and the others for publication in *The Claremont Ras Shamra Tablets*.[2] So, I was disappointed to find out that the cover, as in some romance novels, was just an erotic come-on. It has nothing to do with the contents of the book. If Lemche had understood the importance of this tablet, he would have written a different book.

The picture on the cover is really beautiful. It is much better than the hurried-up photographs that we took when we published the tablet. On the back flap of the dust jacket, the picture appears again. This is where I would have expected to see Lemche's picture, because the biographical comments on Lemche are under the picture of the tablet. I think this is the first time that I have ever reviewed a dust jacket, but since I seem to be doing that, I will add one more note. Norman K. Gottwald's insightful comments on the back of the jacket are too kind. At one point he says, "Happily, Lemche's argument is free of the scornful polemics that have unfortunately characterized much of the scholarly debate on these issues in recent years, allowing the reader to consider

---

1. Lemche, *Prelude to Israel's Past*.
2. Fisher, ed., *The Claremont Ras Shamra Tablets*.

Appendix I

his claims on their own terms." My question is simple: How can the reader consider Lemche's claims "on their own terms" when the hidden text is not printed and the hidden agenda appears in another book?

The Debate

What is this "scornful" debate all about? A good review can be found in an article by Gary N. Knoppers.[3] I will not go into all of the details of the debate, because I want to confine most of my remarks to Lemche's book. So, briefly, Lemche and some of his colleagues (e.g., Philip R. Davies, Thomas L. Thompson, Keith W. Whitelam, and others) think that most of the traditions in the Hebrew Bible are late (i.e., from Persian or Hellenistic times, as late as 300 BCE). If this were true, it would mean that these traditions would not be helpful for the historian who wants to deal with early Israel. Not only do they say that the texts are late, but they also contend that the material remains of an early Israel do not exist. Earlier archaeologists were in error in their dating of such remains, so they say. Likewise, the patriarchs, David, Solomon, and the United Monarchy are all fiction. In fact, Lemche says in this new book, . . . "that the world of the patriarchs is a fiction, not reality."[4] Or note, "The narratives in the Pentateuch will not and cannot pretend to be historical documents pertaining to Israel's past."[5] In short, all of this has created a debate in the study of early Israel. As I said, I am not going to go into all the points of this debate.

Prelude to Israel's Past

Lemche's *Prelude* is filled with questionable scholarship. I cannot mention all of his mistakes and half-truths, because I would have to quote his entire book (245 pages). Before I give you some samples of his errors, I want to say something concerning his style. Lemche makes categorical and dogmatic statements on almost every page of his work. In his preface he says, "It will be shown beyond question that there is very little correlation between the biblical portrait of the past and the

---

3. Knoppers, "The Vanishing Solomon."
4. Lemche, *Prelude to Israel's Past*, 39.
5. Ibid., 65.

nonbiblical evidence from actual Bronze Age cultures."[6] But for others, he usually suggests great caution. When he discusses the use of Ugaritic texts to help explain Syro-Palestinian religion, he says, "Such connections must be made with great caution."[7] I call this type of writing, "I-can-you-can't." It helps to win debates. Another real master of this is John Van Seters. His categorical statements are on every page, and yet he can scold Hubert Cancik for making "categorical statements."[8] But back to Lemche's errors and confusing statements of which I will mention four.

1. It is difficult to decide if Lemche only has a "Sunday School knowledge" of the biblical story, or if he tells the story in literal and conservative fashion in order to make it seem ridiculous and of course unhistorical. His straw men are always clothed in conservative garb, all the better to run them through. For example, he never tires of putting the patriarchs as far back in the past as is possible according to biblical chronology (i.e., at the end of the third millennium BCE).[9] Or, he will put Israel in Egypt for "four hundred years,"[10] because the Bible says this. He has to acknowledge that others would place the patriarchs much later, but that does not change things for him.[11] It is not honest for him to keep from his readers the fact that in the Joseph story, the people of Israel are only in Egypt for, at the most three generations, and this could be during the lifetime of one person. Lemche keeps the patriarchs in the distant past in order to increase the gap between them and their stories.

2. This next set of errors is surely not part of his plan. Either his Sunday School teacher told a sanitized version of the stories of Sarai and Rebekah or Lemche has a poor memory. Lemche says, "Only God's intervention prevents Sarai from becoming Pharaoh's wife."[12] Did Lemche forget his bible? In Gen 12:19 the Pharaoh says to Abram, who had said that beautiful Sarai was his sister, hoping to save himself, "Why did you

---

6. Ibid., xv.
7. Ibid., 151.
8. Van Seters, *In Search of History*, 104.
9. Lemche, *Prelude to Israel's Past*, 31.
10. Ibid., 5.
11. Ibid., 21, 21 n. 1, and 29.
12. Ibid., 4.

Appendix I

say, 'She is my sister,' so that I took her for my wife?" It is the case, that in Genesis 20, God's intervention does save her from King Abimelech of Gerar, but Lemche is careless again with the Rebekah story. He says, "Rebekah almost marries the Philistine king, Abimelech of Gerar."[13] This is not the case at all. The stories are about the same, because Isaac also went to Gerar, and he did say that Rebekah was his sister.

But then one reads:

> Now after he had been there for many days,
> Abimelech, king of the Philistines, looked down from the window;
> he saw Isaac making love with Rebekah, his wife.
> Abimelech summoned Isaac; he said:
>
> "So she really is your wife!
> How could you have said, 'She is my sister?'"
>
> Isaac said to him:
>
> "Because I thought that I might die on account of her."
>
> Abimelech said:
>
> "What is this you have done to us?
> Just a little longer and someone might have laid your wife;
> you would bring guilt upon us." (Gen 26:8–10)

There is no mention of Abimelech wanting to marry Rebekah. I do not consider such mistakes of great importance, but it demonstrates Lemche's carelessness.

3. He does not do much better when he is discussing Syrian and Palestinian religion and culture. However, I should say that Lemche's translator might have caused some of these problems. For example, he seems to know something about how Akkadian/Babylonian was written with syllabic signs, and compares that to Ugaritic, which was written with an alphabet.[14] But Lemche writes about Grotefend's work on Old Persian (he says that Grotefend was an orientalist, but that is not the case), and then he talks about Rawlinson's work on the "cuneiform alphabet."[15] If he is still talking about Old Persian then he is half right (the Old Persian system is somewhere between an alphabet and a syllabary), but if he is referring to Rawlinson's work on Babylonian,

---

13. Ibid., 6.
14. Ibid., 173.
15. Ibid., 78–79.

"cuneiform alphabet" does not make sense. Later, he seems to credit the "people of the Hellenistic-Roman period" with a "fully developed alphabet—that greatly enhanced literary activity."[16] But, this was also true at Ugarit at a much earlier period.

4. He overstates his case when he says, "In Syria and Palestine, nothing like the urban cultural milieu of Mesopotamia developed."[17] One might say such a thing if the culture of Ugarit was unknown, but later, after dealing with Homeric Epic, he says, "From Bronze Age Syria, three such epics have survived: the Ugaritic poetry concerning Aqhat, Kirta, and Baal . . . Here we only mention them to emphasize that such literature existed in ancient Syria and probably also in Palestine. It was most likely not something unique to Ugarit."[18] He cannot have it both ways. I guess that he agrees, because later he takes the second statement back. "We cannot identify concretely the circumstances within which these Ugaritic poems developed. Nonetheless, we must consider them unique compositions. A comparable literary tradition developed only in the large Mesopotamian cities and later in Greek city-states . . ."[19] The structure of this argument follows a strange pattern: They do not have it; they have it; they do not have it. Also, he does not recognize a creation myth at Ugarit,[20] and his treatment of Ugaritic ritual is abysmal.[21]

Good Points

Now, I want to reverse the field. I found several points for which I want to give him credit: 1) There is "a common tradition among the peoples of the ancient Near East of telling stories . . ."[22] 2) He says of the patriarchs, "their background was urban rather than nomadic."[23] 3) In his discussion of the Kirta epic and Aqhat he says, "Their primary concern is to show that every human dies—even humans like Kirta, who would

---

16. Ibid., 171.
17. Ibid., 154.
18. Ibid., 167.
19. Ibid., 177.
20. Ibid., 193, 194.
21. Ibid., 185–86.
22. Ibid., 15.
23. Ibid., 31.

claim partial divine origins."[24] This is almost correct. 4) He notes, "In its present form, the Baal text could not possibly reflect a simple one-year fertility cycle."[25] 5) Once again, "they have it" (referring to the above structure). "The Ugaritic epics confirm our earlier suspicions, namely, that folk literature blossomed in Bronze Age Syria and Palestine, though only a small fraction of it has survived for archaeologists to uncover."[26] 6) I like his interpretation of RS 34.126, an Ugaritic funeral liturgy. "The invocation is a benediction for Ugaritic royalty . . . it shows that the deceased might intervene on behalf of the living."[27] At this point he could have mentioned the tablet on the dust jacket! 7) In his discussion of creation he says, "Chaos became cosmos."[28] These seven points remind me of Thomas Jefferson's collection of the true sayings of Jesus. He said that the true ones were "as easily distinguishable as diamonds in a dunghill."[29]

Major Problems

So, there are some good points, but one must underline some major problems. These are more serious than the above lists of simple mistakes. First, again and again, Lemche sets up a conflict between art/literature and history. But, first I need to clarify a problem; Lemche never tells us what he means by history. When I use the word history, I am referring to the past (Lemche does this a few times) and not to that which historians write, but with Lemche, his "history in the modern sense" is the writing that good historians produce. It goes without saying that an ancient could not write "history in the modern sense."[30] Therefore, it is easy for him to say that something is not historical. Now for some examples: 1) Lemche says, "This study demonstrates that the biblical portrayals of Israel's earliest history [here 'history' does refer to the past] . . . are literary compositions rather than historical sources

---

24. Ibid., 181.
25. Ibid., 183.
26. Ibid., 184.
27. Ibid., 203.
28. Ibid., 211–13.
29. See Fisher, "Pat Robertson's Founding Fathers," 7.
30. Lemche, *Prelude to Israel's Past*, 12, 225.

... A literary analysis of the Pentateuch proves incontrovertibly that its narratives are not reliable sources for the study of antiquity; rather, they are works of art."[31] I must say that he is consistent in this antagonism, i.e., between art and history. Notice what he says about the Greeks: "Greek literary tradition (including Homeric poetry) may in places focus on previous times; however, those texts are so colored by artistic storytelling that they are virtually useless for historical reconstruction of the times and places they describe."[32] The last example: "In our analysis of the biblical narratives concerning Israel's ancestors, we concluded that the Old Testament represents a purely or at least primarily literary product with its own distinctive understanding of antiquity."[33] Lemche is the kind of historian who makes things dull. He is only interested in observable events (i.e., what a neutral observer would have seen if he had been there). He does not understand that since there are no neutral observers his task is hypothetical. Historians like Lemche usually disdain the attempts of other historians to deal with the actual occasions of experience, which were lived by the participants in past events. Granted, it is difficult to know how people experienced certain events, but it is important if one wants to know anything substantial about the past. For these kinds of events we need sources of all kinds, including what Lemche calls literature and art. His treatment of this is insensitive at best. I should add that this does not mean that we have to accept everything uncritically.

Another serious matter that needs to be addressed is his use of "epic." For him an epic must be composed in what he identifies as "poetry."[34] My reading of Genesis is based on the presupposition that Genesis is the Royal Epic of the Davidic Monarchy. Lemche would oppose this on two counts. He would say that there was no Davidic Monarchy (these traditions are only late fiction), and Genesis is not an epic, because it is not poetry. Genesis, however, does contain much poetry, epic themes, and what I call "high prose" or "intermediate style," a term that I borrow from Miriam Lichtheim, who says, "If prose is to poetry as walking is to dancing, the intermediate style may be compared

---

31. Ibid., 61.
32. Ibid., 76.
33. Ibid., 214.
34. Ibid., 15.

Appendix I

to the formal parade step."[35] Also, Genesis functions as a Royal Epic in that it attempts to unite Israel and Judah under David, the legitimate king.

The next serious problem with Lemche is his late date for these traditions, which contain fictive accounts and are "far removed from the period to which they refer."[36] His defense of this position is strange and weak. He brings up some old arguments concerning Abraham's home in "Ur of the Chaldeans"[37] and about the use of camels in the stories of the patriarchs. The old charge is that these items are anachronisms. The domestication of the camel was later than Abraham and so were the Chaldeans. On this matter Lemche is out of touch. Years ago Cyrus H. Gordon pointed to the evidence on these matters. Camels were used much earlier, and there was a northern Ur of Chaldea.[38] Lemche further informs us that since the Old Testament traditions have a "fully developed" monotheism, this means that all is from Jewish-Hellenistic times. He says, "The patriarchal narratives, like the rest of the Old Testament, speak of a single God: even Israel's earliest ancestors are made out to be monotheists."[39] This is simply not true. It is true that most translations cover up any reference to "gods" in the stories of the fathers, but Lemche should know that. There is no doubt that in Gen 35:7 we have more than one god. In this passage, Jacob "built there an altar; he called the sanctuary El-Bethel, for there the gods were revealed to him when he was fleeing from his brother." Here we have not only the definite article with *ĕlohim* (a plural form "gods"), but even the verb ("were revealed") is plural. Genesis 35:7 refers back to 28:20–22 where Jacob deals with two gods, one designated "Elohim" and the other designated "Yahweh." Here is the translation:

> 20   Jacob vowed a vow saying:
>   "If Elohim will be with me,
>   if he will guard me on this journey that I am making,
>   if he will give me food to eat and clothing to wear,
> 21   if I return in health to the house of my father,

---

35. Lichtheim, *Ancient Egyptian Literature*, 11.
36. Lemche, *Prelude to Israel's Past*, 218.
37. Ibid., 39, 62.
38. Gordon, "Hebrew Origins in the Light of Recent Discovery," 10.
39. Lemche, *Prelude to Israel's Past*, 217.

> and if Yahweh will be for me, O Elohim,
> 22 then, this stone that I have set up [as] a sacred pillar
> shall be the house of Elohim,
> and of all that you give to me, a tenth I will give to you."

This is a strong case for the use of the plural, but most translators avoid the issue. Other places where we have more than one god in stories are: Gen 20:13, 17, 18; and 31:53. Again the translations either cover this up or explain it away. I did not translate "gods" in these stories to get at Lemche. I did it, because the term "gods" was there.

My translation of the book of Genesis was not undertaken to argue with Lemche. In fact, Lemche's name only appears in my notes to the Introduction that I have added in light of the present debate. Since I am a historian, I know that we never have enough information; at times we have to say, "I do not know." However you should know that I do attempt this new translation with a hypothesis in mind. As I said above, the Davidic Monarchy needed the book of Genesis in order to unify Israel and Judah. Also, stories of the patriarchs and the patriarchs themselves are not much older than the monarchy. I think these stories took their form at the tomb of the patriarchs. Now, this is where the picture on the cover of Lemche's book becomes important. A text from Ugarit tells us about the forming of an association (called a *marzeaḥ*). Most scholars understand this as not limited to but including a funeral association (you can read about this institution in Jer 16:1–13). The funeral text explains how important it was to care for the dead. At the tomb the names of the dead were "called forth." Sacrifices were offered, and the one who called forth the names was blessed. There are reasons to think that the stories of the great heroes were repeated in this setting. Now these stories may not give us as much information as we would like concerning the patriarchs, but these people standing at the tomb(s) knew their names. No one could change those names. These stories may be fictive in many ways, but they are not "pure fiction" from Hellenistic times. I should point out that my notion about these matters is really not new in our studies of ancient literature. Miriam Lichtheim has an interesting discussion of how in Egypt, "it was in the context of the private tomb that writing took its first steps toward literature." Here "the autobiography was born," and it "became a truly literary

Appendix I

product."⁴⁰ Also in her introduction to "Prose Tales," she relates that *The Story of Sinuhe* "is told in the form of the autobiography composed for the tomb."⁴¹

In Genesis, you can find a good example of how the people are to "call forth" the names of the fathers at the tomb. Consider Gen 48:15–16:

> 15 He blessed Joseph.
> He said:
>> "The God before whom my fathers, Abraham and Isaac, walked,
>> the God who has been my shepherd from my birth until this day,
> 16 the Messenger who has delivered me from all harm,
>> may he bless these young men.
>> My name and the names of my fathers, Abraham and Isaac,
>> shall be called forth by them.
>> They will become a multitude in the land."

No one that I know of translates "shall be called forth," because they do not know what it means. Joseph's sons will "call forth" the names at the tomb (as in the Ugaritic funeral ritual), and they will be blessed; "they will become a multitude."

I wanted to make an honest translation of Genesis. I knew my translation and my approach would be important to historians and their work with the early History of Israel. However, I started my work a long time ago, and I did not know that it would address this present debate. This is serious business, and Lemche has a hidden agenda that does not appear in *Prelude*. This agenda calls into question a great deal of his work, but perhaps I should not call it "hidden." In one article Lemche has shown his real agenda. He intends to discount any history of ancient Israel (which, after all according to him, is only a creation of the minds of scholars) that in some way might increase the nationalism of the modern state of Israel. He says, "And it is certainly tragic that this Western myth (i.e., the Nazi '*Blut und Boden*' ideology) can also be seen to form a part of the ideological back-up for the modern state of Israel."⁴² The word "tragic" should be used to modify Lemche's statement.

40. Lichtheim, *Ancient Egyptian Literature*, vol. 1, 3–4.
41. Ibid., 211.
42. Lemche, "Clio Is also among the Muses," 128.

APPENDIX II
"Let There Be Light": A Scientific Approach to Genesis

"The history of thought is a tragic mixture of vibrant disclosure and of deadening closure. The sense of penetration is lost in the certainty of completed knowledge. This dogmatism is the antichrist of learning."[1]

Introduction

ALABAMA, ARKANSAS, LOUISIANA, TENNESSEE, New Mexico, Nebraska, and now Kansas have been plagued with the irrationalism of the Christian creationists. This plague is spreading; some states have survived it, but who will be next? In the past, the creationists have tried to include their teachings in public school programs, but this time, in the case of Kansas, they have come up with a new strategy. Instead of trying to add "creation science" to the curriculum, the Kansas Board of Education has deleted evolution and the Big Bang theory from the state-testing program. In effect, this deletes such theories from their curriculum in the biological and physical sciences. This is tragic. Stephen Jay Gould has written an interesting comment on the Kansas affair in "Dorothy, It's Really Oz."[2] The news of this outbreak has been sweeping the nation in newspapers, in publications like *Science*,[3] and

---

1. Whitehead, *Modes of Thought*, 58.
2. Gould, "Dorothy, It's Really Oz."
3. Holden, "Kansas Dumps Darwin, Raises Alarm across the United States."

Appendix II

on the World Wide Web.[4] The presidential candidates are even talking about it, mostly voicing opinions that fail to catch either the subtlety or the immensity of the issues.[5] At times, we can be amused by the irrationality and the dogmatic claims of the creationists. But, there is no humor to be found in what they try to take away from our next generation. They deny young people a vision of the universe that most of us value as one of the most exciting accomplishments of the human mind; they deny students the adventure of searching the unknown; they deny our children the thrill of *The Immense Journey*, as Loren Eisely put it.[6]

What are we to do? We need to appreciate what has been done to deal with the irrationalities of the past and present. However, it is time to do more. It is important to know that the creationists know very little about Genesis, and we need to make known, that is, make public, some of the interesting results of recent scholarship on Genesis.

Creation Science is not Science

These kinds of debates and tactics have been going on for many years. They really go all the way back to early discussions on the separation of church and state. In 1785, James Madison wrote his *A Memorial and Remonstrance*; he was writing against the state's support of the teaching of religion. A bill establishing "a provision for Teachers of the Christian Religion" had been presented to the General Assembly of the Commonwealth of Virginia, and Madison argued "it degrades from the equal rank of Citizen all those whose opinions in Religion do not bend to those of the Legislative authority."[7]

In 1999, the irrationalism of the Christian creationists continues to make headlines. They keep turning things upside down. This is not a sign of a great reformation, but rather a sign of irrationalism and not a little dishonesty. Some years ago, in Mobile, Alabama, these creationists charged that secular humanists were "religious," and in Greenville, Tennessee, they waged a textbook war in which they called their religious demands an exercise in "religious freedom." As creation science

4. Belluck, "Evolution May Die Out in Kansas Classrooms."
5. Elsner, "Gore Shocks Scientists With Creationism Statement."
6. Eiseley, *The Immense Journey*.
7. Madison, "A Memorial and Remonstrance."

teachers they claim that their teachings are science, but on this the courts have said, "no."

In 1987, the U. S. Supreme Court heard an appeal from the State of Louisiana concerning their law entitled "Balanced Treatment for Creation-Science and Evolution-Science in Public School Instruction." This act had gone through the lower courts, and each time it had been declared unconstitutional (though the Louisiana Supreme Court did rule that it was not in violation of their state constitution). It was unexpected when the U.S. Supreme Court agreed to hear their case, because on 8 July 1985, in the case of *Aguillard v. Edwards*, U. S. Court of Appeals, Fifth Circuit, the act was declared unconstitutional, and Judge E. Grady Jolly wrote a very clear and interesting *Opinion*.[8] He said that it was a simple issue: "the act violates the establishment clause of the First Amendment, because the purpose of the statute is to promote a religious belief." Judge Jolly was very persuasive, and the decision was valid. But, the U.S. Supreme Court had to cover all of this again. To its credit it upheld the decisions of the lower courts. On 19 June 1987 the Louisiana Act was declared unconstitutional by a 7 to 2 majority (with Scalia and Rehnquist forming the minority).

In 1982, there was a case that should have made the Louisiana Act dead from the start. *The McLean v. the Arkansas Board of Education* case involved "The Arkansas Creation Science Statute" (Act 590) of 1981, and it was struck down on 5 January 1982. The court's *Opinion*, over the signature of William R. Overton, is one of the best statements on "creation-science." It is available as "Appendix B" in *Science and Creation*, a very useful book edited by Robert W. Hanson.[9] Judge Overton gives us a history of the Fundamentalists and their beliefs concerning "creation-science." He also points out the inconsistencies in the Arkansas Statute/Act 590 as well as in the statements of the creationists. The leaders of this movement claim that what they teach on creation is science and not religion. The court clearly ruled that they were not teaching science but rather religion. The court only had to point to Act 590 where it said, "Creation-Science includes the scientific evidences and related inferences that indicate: 1) Sudden creation of the Universe, energy, and life from nothing . . ." This one item was enough

8. Jolly, *Opinion*.
9. Robert W. Hanson, editor. *Science and Creation*.

to show that "creation-science" is religious and not scientific. In theology the corresponding Christian doctrine is called *creatio ex nihilo*, "creation out of nothing," and it has been a very important doctrine for Christians. Hence Overton said, "Every theologian who testified, including the defense witnesses, expressed the opinion that the statement referred to a supernatural creation which was performed by God." This is a religious concept and therefore a religious teaching.

Another problem with Act 590, according to Judge Overton, was its irrationalism as seen in its two-model approach. The creationists wanted equal time for "creation-science" and evolution-science as if these were the only two approaches. The court said that this "is a contrived dualism . . . which has no scientific factual basis or legitimate educational purpose." Also, the creationists tried to claim that since there were only two models of the origin of life that "all scientific evidence which fails to support the theory of evolution" is scientific evidence for "creation-science." The court could see that this was nonsense.

After reading Judge Overton's splendid work, I read Stephen Jay Gould's essay, "William Jennings Bryan's Last Campaign." His "Postscript" to this essay is thoughtful; in it he informs us of Judge William R. Overton's death from cancer. He also notes that "Judge Overton's brilliant and beautifully crafted decision is the finest legal document ever written about this question . . ."[10] Gould was correct, and it should be added that Judge Overton understood the meaning of science, and he was an excellent historian. We need more judges like William Overton, and of course the court room is an ideal place to use a scientific approach to history and a perfect stage for a narrative of the results of such study.

It is helpful to know that according to the courts, creation science is not science. But, creation science is also intrinsically non-scientific; it lacks a basic requirement of any scientific inquiry. Its central hypothesis (in this case supernatural creation) is not open to falsification.

These things we know, and the judges, scientists and theologians who have been active in clarifying these issues deserve our gratitude and praise. In spite of all the victories, however, the creationists are still invading our schools with their aggressive attacks on learning. We must turn things around and bring the battle to the creationists' own turf.

10. Gould, "William Jennings Bryan's Last Campaign."

"Let There Be Light": A Scientific Approach to Genesis

Creation Science Is not Based upon Genesis

Creation science is not based upon Genesis (and certainly not on a scientific approach to Genesis). To be sure, the readers of *Reports of the National Center for Scientific Education,* and of its earlier form, *Creation / Evolution,* have heard similar claims before.[11] But it is time to say it again, and to say it with greater firepower. Recent discovery and research can help us at this point. I say this, because it is still assumed by most reports (from friend or foe) of the court's decisions that these creationists know what Genesis says and means. Again and again, reporters, judges, and scientists credit them with knowing Genesis. (Today, Conrad Hyers' title could be reversed, "Scientific Creationism Knows Nothing of Genesis.") The reports usually state that the creationists take the Genesis story in a literal way, and that others see the Genesis story in a more symbolic way. But, things are not so simple. It is necessary to know what a passage says before talking about the literal or the symbolic meaning. For example, the creationists and some others translate Gen 1:1, "In the beginning . . . "; but is this correct? There was a time when scholars were about evenly divided on this question, but new evidence (grammatical advances and literary parallels) has convinced most translators that the above translation is not correct. As I translate Gen 1:1–3, one reads:

> When Elohim first began to form the heavens and the earth,
> The earth was devastation and desolation,
> Darkness was over [the] deep,
> The wind of Elohim was storming over the waters,
> Elohim said:
> "Let there be light."
> There was light.

We will never know enough to translate a text like Genesis without any errors, but we are in a position today to do much better than in the past. I use the word "form" in this story, because the Hebrew word *bara'* means "to form or fashion by cutting." Elohim / God is the great sculptor and his materials are chaotic. In addition, the word "create"

---

11. Hyers, "Genesis Knows Nothing of Scientific Creationism"; Hyers, "What Genesis Is Really About"; Greenspahn, "Biblical Views of Creation"; Rice, "Scientific Creationism."

Appendix II

is of doubtful use in our time, because it carries with it just too much theological baggage (for example, "creation out of nothing"). I hate to give up on words; I feel robbed, but the word "create" is no longer helpful in a translation of Genesis.

The story begins with "When." The first two verses describe the situation/circumstance. Nothing happens in the story until v. 3. Greenspahn understands this point.[12] In this story, nothing is mentioned concerning ultimate origins. Stephen Jay Gould in his essay, "Justice Scalia's Misunderstanding," underlines one point that is very interesting. He says, "Science does not deal with questions of ultimate origins."[13] This is the same point that I am making for Genesis. Genesis only says that when everything was chaotic, God said, "Let there be light." There is no answer or no interest, on the part of this text, in the question where did the chaotic earth come from? This text says nothing about "creation out of nothing," which is so important to the creationists. For the creationists to make an issue out of something that is not mentioned (*creatio ex nihilo*) in Genesis is nonsense, and it is far from a literal interpretation. I have previously written about creation in the ancient Mediterranean world,[14] and I have tried to explain that there were two basic types of creation stories in that world. The first was a theogony, showing the origin of things and especially the gods. The second was a cosmogony, showing how the chaos became a cosmos. Thorkild Jacobsen referred to these two aspects when they were put together as "a story of world origins and world ordering."[15] The Hebrew Bible is only interested in "world ordering." This has to do with stories about how Yahweh (or in other countries, Baal or Marduk) became king. This usually involves a battle between Yahweh and Yamm (the god of the sea and a symbol of chaos). The Hebrew psalms, prophets, and Job deal with ordering and kingship in this way.[16] Genesis 1 is different from the psalms, but there is still the interest in ordering chaos and not in "ultimate origins." Also one should remember that the story of the

---

12. Greenspahn, "Biblical Views of Creation," 34.
13. Gould, "Justice Scalia's Misunderstanding."
14. Fisher, "Creation at Ugarit and in the Old Testament."
15. Jacobsen, *Treasures of Darkness*, 191.
16. Greenspahn, "Biblical Views of Creation," 32.

"Let There Be Light": A Scientific Approach to Genesis

flood is a story concerning the return of chaos; once more there must be an ordering of chaos.

From this crucial example, it is obvious that the creationists do not base their creation science on Genesis; it is based on their theology. This is a clear illustration of how it is not the texts, but rather ignorance and old interpretations which determine the meanings of the texts for them. These meanings are assumed to be literal by most participants on both sides of the debate.

This business of literal meaning is full of problems. For example, at what stage of a tradition is the question of literal meaning aimed? The expression "Day One" in Gen 1:5 may indeed, in the final stage of the tradition, be understood as "the first day of creation," but my hypothesis is that in an earlier stage of the tradition "Day One" referred to the end of a "cultic day" on which the first act of creation was celebrated. This celebration lasted for seven days just like other ritual occasions in Jerusalem (for example, Passover) and other major centers such as Ugarit (Ugarit has given us many tablets from about 1400 to 1200 BCE and is located at modern Ras Shamra on the "Mediterranean" coast of Syria). In an essay, I have compared in detail the structure of a descriptive ritual text from Ugarit with Gen 1:1–5.[17] Both texts begin with a circumstantial clause and then the description of the action, but the most important point is that the final element in the structure of such texts was a time clause. In this case, both texts use *ym 'aḥd*, "day one," and this use of the cardinal as an ordinal is unusual. I should add that in the cultic calendars, where certain rituals are listed to be held on specific days, the time clause is at the beginning of the cultic day rather than at the end.

In the present text of Genesis 1, the ordering of the world is put into six days, but this was not always the case. In the first edition of the text, there might have been a time clause reading: "A sixth day" at the end of v. 25. Someone removed the time clause at the end of v. 25 as well as "A seventh day" from the end of v. 31. It was replaced with "The sixth day." Here is the text from Genesis 1 with my notes in brackets:

24   Elohim said:
    "Let the earth bring forth living beings with their kind:
    domestic animals, moving ones, and wild animals with their kind."

---

17. Fisher, "An Ugaritic Ritual and Genesis I, 1–5."

Appendix II

        So it was.
25   Elohim made the wild animals with their kind,
        the domestic animals with their kind,
        and all the moving ones of the ground with their kind.
        Elohim saw that it was good.

[*In an earlier edition of this text there was probably a time clause at this point:*
        There was evening.
        There was morning:
        A sixth day.]

26   Elohim said:
        "Let us make human beings in our image—after our likeness;
        they will supervise the fish of the sea,
        the birds of the heavens, the domestic animals,
        all of the earth, and all the ones who move upon the earth."

27   Elohim formed the human beings in his image;
        in the image of Elohim he formed them;
        male and female he formed them.

28   Elohim blessed them;
        Elohim said to them:
        "Be fruitful and multiply; fill the earth;
        make it a servant; and supervise the fish of the sea,
        the birds of the heavens, and all the living ones
        who move upon the earth."

29   Elohim said:
        "See, I give you every plant that scatters
        seed that is upon all the earth and every tree that scatters
        seed (that is in the fruit of the tree); it will be yours for food.

30   To all the wild animals, to all the birds of the heavens,
        and to all the ones who move upon the earth
        (that are living beings), [I give] all the green plants for food."
        So it was.

31   Elohim saw all that he had made, and behold, it was very good.
        There was evening.
        There was morning:
        The sixth day.

[*In an earlier edition, "The sixth day" was "A seventh day." When a priest-scribe deleted the sixth-day time clause at the end of v. 25 and moved it here, he should have kept the pattern with the indefinite article ("A sixth day"). Also, this change caused a major problem with 2:2a which was the end of this earlier edition, but it did allow this account to follow the tradition of Exod 20:11 ("For in six days Yahweh made the heavens and the earth . . ."). Deuteronomy 5:15 has another reason for observing the sabbath.*]

"Let There Be Light": A Scientific Approach to Genesis

2:1   The heavens and the earth were finished and all their entourage.
2   Elohim finished on the seventh day his work that he had been doing.
       [*Here we see that Elohim finished on the seventh day. The Greek translation of the Hebrew text (The Septuagint) changed "the seventh day" to "the sixth day" in 2:2a to avoid the contradiction.*]
       He rested on the seventh day from all his work that he had done.
3   Elohim blessed the seventh day; he hallowed it,
       because on it he rested from all his work that as Elohim,
       the maker, he had formed.
       [*This last part (2:2b–3) was added by the priest-scribe who was interested in the sabbath.*]

If the Hebrews praised Yahweh as the one who brought order out of chaos during a seven day celebration, it would have been in keeping with the way they worshiped on other occasions.

Genesis is not easy to understand, but it is certain that what the creationists want it to say is just not there. The same thing happens in Genesis 3. In Genesis 3, the human and his wife (after a conversation with the serpent) eat from the fruit of the tree in the midst of the garden. This fruit will give them all knowledge. Many theologians take Paul's interpretation of Genesis 3 (in Rom 5:12–14, dealing with sin) as the literal meaning of Genesis 3. In addition, they turn to Rev 20:2 for an interpretation of the serpent as Satan. This understanding of the serpent as Satan is then transferred to Genesis 3. If anyone wants to be literal, that person should be aware that the words "sin" and "Satan" do not appear in Genesis 3.

Creation science is based upon some old and well-organized interpretations of Genesis, but it rarely touches the Genesis story either in a literal or in a symbolic manner. Even when creation science comes close to the Genesis story, it only takes the ideas that fit into its worldview. Not many of them will want to make it known that human beings and the other animals are all classified by the same phrase in Hebrew, namely, *nephesh ḥayyah*, "living being" (Gen 2:7 and 19). This does not mean that the human (the Genesis text does not call the human by the name, "Adam." True, he names the other animals and Eve, but the human has no name.) could not make distinctions within those classified as "living beings" and give them separate names. It is also interesting that the human's mate is constructed from his own material. It is because they are of the same substance that the two can become one.

Appendix II

The creationists are usually blinded by their traditions so that they miss the important moments of these stories. For example, some great poet knew that humans could not be as the gods who possessed both knowledge and immortality. In Genesis 3, there is no fall into the grasp of Satan. In fact, there is no fall. However, there is the decision to give up life for knowledge. That is the basic trade-off. More than that, these humans give up a close relationship with their God. So, humans are mortal, God is not an everyday companion, and knowledge is precious. Also, knowledge enabled them to play an important role in the development of civilization. Knowledge is the gift of these mortals to subsequent generations. It is also a gift of freedom. This is the gift that puts fear into the hearts of the creationists.

Scientific Work on Genesis

To whom does scientific work on Genesis speak? Not to the creationists, because their belief system has already closed their ears to most of what such scholars would say. Nor does it speak directly to evolutionary biologists, at least as they act in that capacity. It is directed instead at the *onlookers* of this debate—the 'third parties' who are trying to make honest sense of this conflict. Most of us fall into this large category of onlookers, and whether we recognize it or not, the outcome of this debate is of vital interest to us all.

And what does scientific work on Genesis say? It says that the Bible of Christian fundamentalists is essentially an artifact of generations of mistranslation and misinterpretation of documents that meant something entirely different in the social and historical context in which they originated. It says that the issues that concerned the writers of Genesis were utterly unrelated to the ideas to which Christian fundamentalism clings to so tightly. What did motivate the writers of Genesis? Well, that's an exciting story, part of which can be deduced through careful scholarship and part of which can only be sketched in with informed speculation. But once we perceive the radical difference between the Genesis of the creationists and the Genesis that present scholarship is able to reconstruct, we see that the writers of Genesis had much more in common with evolutionists than we might have guessed. In any case, the terms of the debate on these subjects are profoundly altered. What is perhaps most ironic about such an outcome is that some evolutionists have been content to concede that creationists, if they knew nothing else, at least knew their Bibles. Yet even that gives them too much credit.

Scientific work on Genesis represents a voice that has up to now been backstage during the debates between creationists and evolutionists. And yet, it is a voice that I think the onlookers to this debate need to hear. In order to have a comprehensive understanding of this area of human thought and experience, we who are onlookers need to know, "If not a *creationist* interpretation of biblical traditions, how should we interpret them?" Although it may sound presumptuous of me to suggest, I believe that the creation-evolution conflict remains unresolved at least partly because of the absence of a perspective such as recent Genesis scholarship can offer. If this perspective becomes a part of the evolutionists' new direction, the storms of controversy will not immediately be calmed, but giving the onlookers a view of Genesis that grows out of a scientific approach to inquiry should be a large step forward.

Conclusion

"Let There Be Light" could be the title of a new song and the theme of new directions. Judges, scientists, and theologians have been too kind. They have been generous with their assumptions; they have assumed that the creationists know their Bibles. The creationists know their dogma, and they know how to use it as a cover. They have covered up the Genesis story, but this story cannot be concealed.

Three thousand years ago people loved this story and were entertained by it. They praised Elohim for ordering chaos, for bringing light to darkness and devastation. These humans thought of themselves and the other animals as "living beings." From out of the ground came "all flesh." Life was good in the garden, but immortality without knowledge was dull. In any case, the ones who listened to this story were more interested in another question. Why are humans mortal? Answer: because the human and Eve gave up life for knowledge. With all knowledge, they could participate in the building of civilization. They could build cities, work with copper and iron, and make musical instruments. This made life interesting. They paid a price for knowledge, and knowledge was their gift to these listeners.

Today, creationists do not tell this story, and they reject the gift of knowledge, a gift more valued than life. In addition, they reject

Appendix II

that which is so very real; they reject mortality, thus siding with most ancient Egyptians whose stance on immortality appears to be the dominant view in modern religious traditions. They are disrespectful of court orders, and education is curtailed. Vision and adventure are stymied. Creation science is a modern mythology, and its attempts to teach creationism as science have been declared unconstitutional. But, the leadership of this movement will keep trying, and they will attempt to carry along large numbers of conservative Christians into a regressive and intolerant past. Establishing a new front is not an easy task. But there is some good news. We have new directions and new views. All of this can help the onlookers, the parents, and those who will attack closure. Not closure but disclosure is the word for our time. Disclosure is the means of bringing light to dogma's dark chaos.

Bibliography

Alter, Robert. *The Five Books of Moses: A Translation with Commentary.* New York: Norton, 2004.

———. *Genesis: Translation and Commentary.* New York: Norton, 1996.

———. "Introduction to the Old Testament." In *The Literary Guide to the Bible*, edited by Robert Alter and Frank Kermode, 11–35. Cambridge: Harvard University Press, 1987.

An American Translation. Translated by J. M. Powis Smith and Edgar J. Goodspeed et al. Chicago: University of Chicago Press, 1939.

Astour, Michael C. "A North Mesopotamian Locale of the Keret Epic?" *UF* 5 (1973) 29–40.

Belluck, Pam. "Evolution May Die Out in Kansas Classrooms." *New York Times*, Aug 15, 1999. Online: www.spokane.net:80/news-story-body.asp?Date=081599&ID=s61929&cat=.

Bloch-Smith, Elizabeth. "The Cult of the Dead in Judah: Interpreting the Material Remains." *JBL* 111 (1992) 213–24.

———. *Judahite Burial Practices and Beliefs about the Dead.* JSOTSup 123. Sheffield, UK: JSOT Press, 1992.

———. Review of Lewis, *Cults of the Dead in Israel and Ugarit* in *JBL* 110 (1991) 327–30.

Bordreuil, Pierre, and Dennis Pardee. "Le funéraire ougaritique RS 34.126." *Syria* 59 (1982) 121–28.

Braudel, Fernand. *The Mediterranean.* Vol. 1. Translated by Sian Reynolds. New York: Harper & Row, 1972.

Brueggemann, Walter. "David and His Theologian." *Catholic Biblical Quarterly* 30 (1968) 156–81.

Buber, Martin, and Franz Rosenzweig. *Die Fünf Bücher der Weisung.* Berlin: Schneider, 1930.

———. *Scripture and Translation.* Translated by Lawrence Rosenwald with Everett Fox. Bloomington: Indiana University Press, 1994.

Cassuto, Umberto. *A Commentary on the Book of Genesis.* Part I, *From Adam to Noah.* Translated by Israel Abrahams. Jerusalem: Magnes, 1961.

———. *A Commentary on the Book of Genesis.* Part II, *From Noah to Abraham.* Translated by Israel Abrahams. Jerusalem: Magnes, 1964.

Bibliography

Dahood, Mitchell. "Additional Notes on the Mrzh Text." In *The Claremont Ras Shamra Texts*, edited by Loren R. Fisher, 51–54. Analecta Orientalia 48. Roma: Pontificium Institutum Biblicum, 1971.

de Moor, Johannes C. "Rapi'uma—Rephaim." *ZAW* 88 (1976) 323–45.

Donner, H., and W. Röllig, *Kanaanäische und Aramäische Insschriften*. 3 vols. Wiesbaden: Harrassowitz, 1966–1969.

Eiseley, Loren C. "Charles Darwin." *Scientific American* (Feb 1956) 62–72.

———. *The Immense Journey*. New York: Random House, 1957.

Elsner, Alan. "Gore Shocks Scientists with Creationism Statement." *Yahoo! News* (Reuters), 27 Aug 27, 1999. Online: dailynews.yahoo.com/h/19990827/pl/politics_creation_4.htr.

Finkelstein, J. J. "The Genealogy of the Hammurapi Dynasty." *JCS* 20 (1966) 95–118.

Fisher, Loren R. "An Amarna Age Prodigal." *JSS* 3 (1958) 113–22.

———, editor. *The Claremont Ras Shamra Texts*. Analecta Orientalia 48. Rome: Pontificium Institutum Biblicum, 1971.

———. "Creation at Ugarit and in the Old Testament." *VT* 15 (1965) 313–24.

——— (= Loren R. Mack-Fisher). "From Ugarit to Gades: Mediterranean Veterinary Medicine." *Maarav* 5 and 6 (1990) 207–20.

——— (= Loren R. Mack-Fisher). "Genesis Parallels." *The Fourth R*. 2,6 (1989) 7–9.

———. "An International Judgment." In *The Claremont Ras Shamra Texts*, edited by Loren R. Fisher, 11–21. Analecta Orientalia 48. Roma: Pontificium Institutum Biblicum, 1971.

———. *The Jerusalem Academy*. 2nd ed. Eugene, OR: Wipf & Stock, forthcoming.

———. "Literary Genres in the Ugaritic Texts." In *Ras Shamra Parallels*, vol. II, edited by Loren R. Fisher, 131–52. Analecta Orientalia 50. Roma: Pontificium Institutum Biblicum, 1975.

———. "A New Ritual Calendar From Ugarit." *HTR* 63 (1970) 485–501.

———. "Pat Robertson's Founding Fathers." *Westar Magazine* 1.2 (1987) 7.

———. "The Patriarchal Cycles." In *Orient and Occident: Essays presented to Cyrus H. Gordon*, edited by Harry A. Hoffner Jr., 59–65. Neukirchen-Vluyn: Neukirchener, 1973.

———. "An Ugaritic Ritual and Genesis I, 1–5." In *Ugaritica VI*, edited by Jacques-Claude Courtois, 197–205. Mission de Ras Shamra 17. Paris: Geuthner, 1969.

Fox, Everett. *The Five Books of Moses*. New York: Schocken, 1995.

Gaster, Theodor H. *Thespis*. Rev. ed. Garden City: Doubleday, 1961.

———. *Myth, Legend, and Custom in the Old Testament*. New York: Harper & Row, 1969.

Gesenius' Hebrew Grammar. Edited by E. Kautzsch. Second English edition by A. E. Cowley. Oxford: Clarendon, 1910.

Gilmour, David D. *Honor and Shame and the Unity of the Mediterranean*. Washington, DC: American Anthropological Association, 1987.

Goody, Jack, and Stanley Tambiah. *Bridewealth and Dowry*. Cambridge Papers in Social Anthropology 7. Cambridge: Cambridge Univ. Press, 1973.

Gordon, Cyrus H. "Abraham and the Merchants of Ura." *JNES* 17 (1958) 28–31.

———. "Asymmetric Janus Parallelism." *Eretz-Israel* 16 (1982) 80–81.

———. "Hebrew Origins in the Light of Recent Discovery." In *Biblical and Other Studies*, edited by Alexander Altmann, 3–14. Cambridge: Harvard University Press, 1963.

———. "Poetic Legends and Myths from Ugarit." *Berytus* 25 (1977) 5–133.

———. "'This Time' (Genesis 2:23)." In *"Sha'arei Talmon": Studies in the Bible, Qumran, and the Ancient Near East Presented to Shemaryahu Talmon*, edited by Michael Fishbane and Emanuel Tov, 47–51. Winona Lake, IN: Eisenbrauns, 1992.

———. *Ugarit and Minoan Crete*. New York: Norton, 1966.

———. *Ugaritic Textbook*. Analecta Orientalia 38. Rome: Pontificium Institutum Biblicum, 1965.

Gordon, Cyrus H., and Gary A. Rendsburg. *The Bible and the Ancient Near East*. 4th ed. New York: Norton, 1997.

Gould, Stephen Jay. "Justice Scalia's Misunderstanding." *Natural History* 96.10 (1987) 14–21.

———. "William Jennings Bryan's Last Campaign." *Natural History* 96.11 (1987) 16–27.

———. "Dorothy, It's Really Oz." *Time*, Aug 23, 1999, 59.

Greenspahn, Frederick E. "Biblical Views of Creation." *Creation/Evolution* 4.3 (1983) 30–38.

Hallo, William W. et al., editors. *The Context of Scripture*, vol. 1: *Canonical Compositions from the Biblical World*. Leiden: Brill, 1997.

———. *The Context of Scripture*, vol. 2: *Monumental Inscriptions from the Biblical World*. Leiden: Brill, 2000.

Hanson, K. C. "The Herodians and Mediterranean Kinship, Part III: Economics." *Biblical Theology Bulletin* 20 (1990) 10–21.

———. "'How Honorable!' 'How Shameful!': A Cultural Analysis of Matthew's Makarisms and Reproaches." *Semeia* 68 (1994[96]) 81–111.

Hanson, Robert W., editor. *Science and Creation: Geological, Theological and Educational Perspectives*. AAAS Issues in Science and Technology Series. New York: MacMillan, 1986.

Hendel, Ronald S. *The Epic of the Patriarch: The Jacob Cycle and the Narrative Traditions of Canaan and Israel*. Harvard Semitic Monographs 42. Decatur, GA: Scholars, 1987.

Holden, Constance. "Kansas Dumps Darwin, Raises Alarm across the United States." *Science* 285.5431 (Aug 20, 1999) 1186.

Horden, Peregrine, and Nicholas Purcell. *The Corrupting Sea: A Study of the Mediterranean*. Oxford: Blackwell, 2000.

Hyers, Conrad. "Genesis Knows Nothing of Scientific Creationism." *Creation/Evolution* 4.2 (1983) 1–21.

———. "What Genesis Is Really About." *Reports of the National Science Center for Science Education* 18.3 (1998) 15, 33.

Jacobsen, Thorkild. *The Treasures of Darkness: A History of Mesopotamian Religion*. New Haven: Yale University Press, 1976.

Jolly, E. G. Opinion. In 765 *Federal Reporter*. 2nd series. 1251–59. 1985.

Kilmer, Anne Draffkorn. "The Mesopotamian Counterparts of the Biblical Nepilim." In *Perspectives on Language and Text*, edited by Edgar W. Conrad and Edward G. Newing, 39–43. Winona Lake, IN: Eisenbrauns, 1987.

Kitchen, K. A. "The King List of Ugarit." *UF* 9 (1977) 131–42.

Knoppers, Gary N. "The Vanishing Solomon: The Disappearance of the United Monarchy from Recent Histories of Ancient Israel." *JBL* 116 (1997) 19–44.

Lambert, W. G., "New Light on the Babylonian Flood." *JSS* 5 (1960): 113–23.

———. *Babylonian Wisdom Literature*. Oxford: Clarendon, 1967.

Bibliography

Lemche, Niels Peter. "Clio Is also among the Muses." In *Can A 'History' of Israel Be Written?* edited by Lester L. Grabbe, 123–55. JSOTSup 245. Sheffield, UK: Sheffield Academic, 1997.

———. "From Patronage Society to Patronage Society." In *The Origins of the Ancient Israelite States*, edited by Volkmar Fritz and Philip R. Davies, 106–20. JSOTSup 228. Sheffield, UK: Sheffield Academic, 1997.

———. *Prelude to Israel's Past: Background and Beginnings of Israelite History and Identity*. Translated by E. F. Maniscalco. Peabody, MA: Hendrickson, 1998.

Levine, Baruch A., and Jean-Michel de Tarragon, O.P. "Dead Kings and Rephaim: The Patrons of the Ugaritic Dynasty." *JAOS* 104 (1984) 649–59.

Lewis, Theodore J. *Cults of the Dead in Ancient Israel and Ugarit*. Harvard Semitic Monographs 39. Atlanta: Scholars, 1989.

———. "The Ancestral Estate in 2 Samuel 14:16." *JBL* 110 (1991) 597–612.

Lichtheim, Miriam. *Ancient Egyptian Literature: A Book of Reading*. Vol. 1. Berkeley: University of California Press, 1973.

Madison, James. "A Memorial and Remonstrance." In *The Complete Madison*. New York: Harper, 1953.

Mazar, Benjamin. "The Historical Background of the Book of Genesis." *JNES* 28 (1969) 73–83.

Mazar, Eilat, Wayne Horowitz, Takayoshi Oshima, and Yuval Goren. "A Cuneiform Tablet from the Ophel in Jerusalem." *Israel Exploration Journal* 60 (2010) 4–21.

Miller, Patrick D., Jr., "The Mrzh Text." In *The Claremont Ras Shamra Texts*, edited by Loren R. Fisher, 37–49. Analecta Orientalia 48. Roma: Pontificium Institutum Biblicum, 1971.

Moran, William L., editor and translator. *The Amarna Letters*. Baltimore: Johns Hopkins University Press, 1987.

———. "The Scandal of the 'Great Sin' at Ugarit." *JNES* 18 (1959) 180–81.

Murphy, Joanne M. "Ideologies, Rites and Rituals: A View of Prepalatial Minoan Tholoi." In *Cemetery and Society in the Aegean Bronze Age*, edited by Keith Branigan, 27–40. Sheffield Studies in Aegean Archaeology 1. Sheffield, UK: Sheffield Academic, 1998.

Nielsen, Eduard. *Oral Tradition*. Studies in Biblical Theology 1/11. Chicago: Allenson, 1954.

Nougayrol, Jean, Emmanuel Laroche, Charles Virolleaud, and Claude F. A. Schaeffer. *Ugaritica V*. Mission de Ras Shamra 16. Paris: Librairie Orientaliste Paul Geuthner, 1968.

———. *Le Palais royal d'Ugarit*. Vols. III and IV. Paris: Librairie C. Klincksieck, 1955 and 1956.

Pope, Marvin H. *Job*. 3rd ed. AB 15. Garden City, NY: Doubleday, 1973.

Pritchard, James B., editor. *Ancient Near Eastern Texts*. 3rd ed. Princeton: Princeton University Press, 1969.

Rad, Gerhard von. *Genesis*. Translated by John H. Marks. Rev. ed. Old Testament Library. Philadelphia: Westminster, 1972.

Rendsburg, Gary A. "The Genesis of the Bible." Inaugural Lecture delivered at Rutgers University, New Brunswick, NJ, October 28, 2004. New Brunswick, NJ: Allen and Joan Bildner Center for the Study of Jewish Life, Rutgers University, 2005.

———. *The Redaction of Genesis*. Winona Lake, IN: Eisenbrauns, 1986.

Bibliography

Rice S. "Scientific Creationism: Adding Imagination to Scripture." *Creation/Evolution* 8.3 (1988) 25–36.
Rummel, Stan. "Narrative Structures in the Ugaritic Texts." In *Ras Shamra Parallels*, Vol. III, edited by Stan Rummel, 221–332. Analecta Orientalia 51. Rome: Pontificium Institutum Biblicum, 1981.
Sarna, Nahum M. *Genesis*. JPS Torah Commentary. Philadelphia: Jewish Publication Society, 1989.
Schmidt, Brian B. *Israel's Beneficent Dead: Ancestor Cult and Necromancy*. Winona Lake, IN: Eisenbrauns, 1996.
Skinner, John. *Genesis*. 2nd ed. International Critical Commentary. Edinburgh: T. & T. Clark, 1930.
Smith, Mark S. "The Invocation of Deceased Ancestors in Psalm 49:12c." *JBL* 112 (1993) 105–7.
Streck, Maximilian. *Assurbanipal und die letzten assyrichen Könige bis zum Untergang Ninivehs*. VAB 7. Leipzig, 1916.
Tanakh, The Holy Scriptures. Philadelphia: Jewish Publication Society, 1985.
Van Seters, John. *Abraham in History and Tradition*. New Haven: Yale University Press, 1975.
———. *In Search of History*. New Haven: Yale University Press, 1983.
Varro, Marcus Terentius. *De Lingua Latina*. Vol. I, II. Trans. by R. G. Kent. LCL 333, 334. Cambridge: Harvard University Press.
Wellhausen, Julius. *Prolegomena to the History of Ancient Israel*. Meridian Books. Cleveland: World, 1957 (German ed., 1878).
Westermann, Claus. *Genesis 1–11*. Translated by John J. Scullion. Minneapolis: Augsburg, 1984.
———. *Genesis 12–36*. Translated by John J. Scullion. Minneapolis: Augsburg, 1985.
———. *Genesis 37–50*. Translated by John J. Scullion. Minneapolis: Augsburg, 1986.
Whitehead, Alfred North. *Modes of Thought*. 1938. Reprinted, New York: Free Press, 1968.

Index of Ancient Documents

Ancient Near Eastern Documents

Akkadian

Adapa   48

Amarna Tablets
285–290   xii, 6
285–291   xi–xii

Assurbanipal
IV 65–82,38–39   15
VI 70–76   15

Code of Hammurabi
§266   148

Enuma elish   8, 37

Genealogy of the Hammurapi Dynasty   13

Gilgamesh Epic
VI, 6   177
VIII,ii,8–9   80

Jerusalem 1   xi–xii

Aramaic

KAI
1:1   210
1:2   210
9:A2   210
9:B4   210
11   210
13:2   210
13:3   210
13:5   210
29:1   210

Egyptian

The Eloquent Peasant
5–35   195
Instruction for King Meri-Ka-Re   xii, 168
Instruction of the Vizier Ptah-Hotep   177
Story of Sinuhe   9, 220
Story of Two Brothers   177

Ugaritic

Anat
   19–20
II:39–40   128
III:29–32   129

Index of Ancient Documents

Epic of Aqhat	19–20	1:2	58
		1:5	227
Epic of Keret		1:6–8	31
	146	1:6	38
195	101	1:9–13	31
199b–206	134	1:9	38
		1:11	38
PRU		1:12	38
IV, p. 139	106	1:14–19	31
		1:20–23	31
RS		1:24–31	31
16.129	110	1:25	41
16.239:79	144	1:26–27	52
34.126	11–14, 216	1:26	48
34.126:2–12	13	1:27	40
34.126:3	13	1:31	41
34.126:10	13	2:1–3	31
1957.1	146	2:1–2	42
		2:1	41
Ugaritica V, 499–504	22	2:2	41, 42
		2:2b–3	229
UT		2:4—4:26	16, 31
62:15	98	2:4—3:24	5
76:II:14	73	2:4	164
121–124	20	2:4a	30, 31, 41
128:III:13–15	13	2:4b–7	31
147:4	122	2:4b–6	41
		2:4b	28, 37, 41, 92
		2:6	26
		2:7	26, 46, 47, 70, 121, 229
		2:8–17	31
		2:8–9	31
Hebrew Bible		2:10–14	31
		2:15–17	31
Genesis		2:16	47
1–11	15	2:17	45, 48, 146
1–10	16	2:18–24	31
1:1—11:26	xi, 16,	2:19	42, 229
1:1—2:3	5, 16, 31, 41	2:23	136
1:1–31	31	2:24	157
1:1–5	31, 227	2:25—3:7	31
1:1–3	225	3	229
1:1	25, 28, 225	3:5	43, 146
1:1a	25		

3:8–21	31	6:9a	30, 32, 41
3:14	47	6:9b—8:22	32
3:16	47, 49, 55	6:10	64
3:17	53, 55, 120, 125	6:11	2, 55
3:19	42	7:9	58
3:22–24	31	7:21	55
3:22	40, 43, 45, 146	7:23	70
4	52	8:9	59
4:1–16	31	8:21	55, 59, 70
4:1	139	9:1–17	32
4:6	123	9:5	187
4:7	46	9:18–29	32
4:8	28	9:18	64
4:12	50	9:20	118, 172, 198
4:14	50	9:20a	208
4:17–24	31	9:21	64
4:22	50	10:1—11:26	16
4:23	47	10:1—11:9	32
4:24	51	10:1	32, 41, 64
4:25–26	31	10:1a	30
4:25	51, 52, 185	10:2–32	32
4:26	51, 66, 123	10:2	64
5	2	10:6	64
5:1—6:8	31	10:15	104
5:1—6:4	16	10:21	64
5:1	40	10:32	116
5:1a	30, 31, 41, 52	11:1–9	32, 133
5:1b–2	31, 52	11:10a	30, 41
5:1b	52	11:27—25:18	xi
5:2	40, 52	11:27—25:11	17, 20, 30, 32, 168
5:3–32	32		
5:3	52	11:27	117
5:11	55	11:27a	30, 32, 41
5:22	1, 25, 55	11:27b—12:4	32
5:24	1, 25, 52	11:28	106, 144
5:29	51	12–50	15
6	2	12	100
6:1–4	32	12:1–3	20
6:3	47	12:1	100, 106, 131, 144
6:5—9:29	16	12:2	82
6:5ff.	54	12:3	129
6:5–8	32	12:5–9	32
6:9—9:29	32	12:6	3, 100
6:9	2, 25	12:8	72, 123

241

Index of Ancient Documents

Reference	Pages
12:10—13:1	32
12:10–20	93
12:10	93
12:11	108, 120, 136, 177
12:13	120
12:19	213
13:2–18	32
13:4	123
13:8	72, 135
13:10	73, 84
13:12	172
13:18	73, 93, 172
14:1–24	32
15:1–21	32
15:2	106
15:3	77
15:18	79
15:19–21	79
16:1–16	32
16:2	47, 125, 139
16:3	114, 139
16:7	206
16:9	79
16:12	116, 206
17:1–27	32
17:1	162
17:3–8	7
17:6	83
17:6c	8, 162
17:16	8, 82, 162
17:17	86
17:19	83
17:20	83
17:21	119
17:23	89
18:1—19:38	32
18:1–16	32
18:1	93
18:3	85
18:8	87
18:10	90
18:14	85
18:16	92, 120
18:17–33	32
18:21	86
18:22b	87
19:1–29	32
19:2	100
19:4	84
19:8	108
19:11	90
19:17	91
19:19	91, 92
19:20	91
19:21	152
19:27	87, 88, 100
19:28	120
19:30–38	33, 64
19:31	92
19:32	92
19:38	96, 134
20:1–18	33
20:1	93, 120
20:2	120
20:6	83
20:7	94
20:8	100
20:13	26, 219
20:16	152
20:17	26, 219
20:18	26, 95, 219
21	20
21:1–21	33
21:1	124, 209
21:7	124
21:9	120, 178
21:11	124
21:12	10, 20, 47, 125, 203
21:12b	14, 97
21:14	88, 100
21:17	47
21:22–34	33
21:22	123
21:33	123
22	100
22:1–19	33
22:2	70, 119, 131
22:3	88

Index of Ancient Documents

22:4	100	24:62	114
22:8	100, 102	25:1–6	33
22:9	119	25:5	110, 115
22:12	100	25:6	114, 115
22:13	60, 100	25:7–11	17, 18, 33
22:14	100	25:7	199
22:17	113	25:9	21
22:18	47, 125	25:11	21, 69, 114
22:20–24	33	25:12–18	16, 33, 164
23	17, 20, 163	25:12	41, 164
23:1–20	17, 18, 33, 207	25:12a	30, 33
23:4	104	25:18	80
23:5	26, 104, 131	25:19—37:1	xi
23:6	105	25:19—35:29	17, 21, 30, 168, 172
23:9	104		
23:10	26, 159	25:19–34	17
23:11	104	25:19a	30, 41
23:13	104	25:19b–34	33
23:14	104	25:23	64
23:15	104	25:24	176
23:18	105	25:25	125
24	17, 117	25:26	153
24:1—25:6	17, 21, 33	25:27	125
24:1–67	33	25:29–34	129
24:2	197, 201	25:30	118
24:4	144	25:31	78
24:11	109	25:33	119
24:13	111	26	17, 117
24:14	70	26:1–33	33
24:15	70	26:5	47, 79, 97, 98, 100, 103, 125, 131, 139
24:16	71, 108, 120, 136, 177		
24:22	109	26:6	93
24:25	109	26:7	71, 108, 136, 177
24:26	109	26:8–10	214
24:27	112, 201	26:8	97, 178
24:29	110	26:9	120
24:30	109	26:13–14	143
24:42	111	26:19	165
24:43	111	26:25	51, 71, 72
24:45	108	26:27	124
24:47	109, 126	26:29	124
24:47b	109	26:32b	165
24:49	151	26:34—27:45	33
24:53	158	26:34–35	33

Index of Ancient Documents

26:34	131	31:20	146
26:35	131	31:24	43
27	131	31:26	146
27:8	47, 126	31:27	146
27:16	125	31:30	139, 146
27:19	125	31:32	146
27:24–29	127	31:35	194
27:25	125	31:36	157
27:27b	127	31:39	146
27:28	128	31:53	26, 219
27:31	125	32:2–21	33
27:35	155	32:2–3	196
27:42	130	32:4	144, 152
27:43	70, 100	32:8	150
27:46	26, 33, 124, 131	32:9	150
28	26	32:10	144
28:1–9	33, 131	32:11	150
28:1–4	162, 201	32:14	150
28:10–22	33, 196	32:17	150
28:12	161	32:18	150
28:15	144	32:19	150
28:18	148	32:21	91, 95, 150, 152
28:19	201	32:22–32	33
28:20–22	26	32:22	150, 152
28:20	28–29	32:23–33	150
28:21b	26	32:29	161
29:1–30	33	32:31	52, 155
29:17	71, 108, 120, 177	32:33	5
29:27	136	33:1–17	33
29:30	137	33:1	170
29:31—30:24	33	33:3	152
30:3	79, 202, 209	33:10	152
30:4	79, 139	33:18—34:31	33
30:6	138	33:18–20	17
30:22	140	33:19	156
30:25–43	33	34	141, 156
30:28	142	34:2	157, 163
30:37	142	34:3	157, 158, 160
30:42	143	34:6	157
31:1—32:1	33	34:7	157
31:3	151	34:10	188, 204
31:13	144	34:12	112
31:19	146	34:13	159

34:25	160, 204	37:5–10	186
35	202	37:7	28
35:1–15	34	37:8	169
35:3	29, 160	37:10	64
35:4	28	37:14	168
35:7	25–26, 29, 145, 218	37:21	187
35:8	113	37:22	187
35:11–12	132, 201	37:23	178, 195
35:11	8, 82, 118	37:25	189
35:16–21	21	37:28	171, 180
35:16–20	17, 34	37:33	193
35:18	47	37:36	28, 171, 176
35:19	169	38	18, 19, 30, 118, 168, 172
35:20a	21		
35:21–26	17, 34	38:1–30	34
35:22–26	114	38:1–9	26
35:22	204	38:2	93
35:27–29	17, 21, 34	38:3	173
35:29	18	38:14	114
36:1—37:1	34, 115, 164	38:19	114
36	124	38:27	118
36:1–8	16	38:29	64
36:1	30, 34, 41, 118, 164	39:1—41:57	34
36:2—36:43	34	39:1–23	34
36:2–8	34	39:1	171
36:2	124	39:3	179
36:3	124	39:4	155
36:7	72	39:5	155, 177
36:9–43	16	39:6	71, 108, 120, 136
36:9	34, 41, 164	39:6b–23	177
36:10–43	34	39:8	155
36:14	163	39:9	177
36:25	163	39:14	97, 120
36:31	3	39:17	97, 120
36:39	163	40:1–23	34
37:1	34	40:1	178
37:2—50:26	xi, 17, 22, 30, 34, 168	40:3	180
		40:5	181
37:2–36	17, 22	40:13	180
37:2a	30, 41	40:15	182
37:2b–36	34	40:19	179
37:3	192	40:22	179, 180
37:4b	194	41:1–57	34

Index of Ancient Documents

41:5	182	46:26	106, 197
41:11	179	46:28–34	34
41:12	179	46:32–34	198
41:13	180	46:34	198
41:14	180	47	115, 199
41:16	182	47:1–7	34
41:25	182	47:3	198
41:37	195	47:10	199
41:43	183	47:1–6	34
41:48	183	47:7–12	34
41:52	185	47:13–26	35
42:1—45:28	34	47:15	200
42:1–38	34	47:19	200
42:4	193	47:24	199
42:6	186	47:26	200
42:18	187	47:27–31	35
42:23	186	47:27	167
42:28	187	47:28–31	9
42:34	158	47:28	199
42:38	193	47:29	106, 197
43:1–34	34	48	22
43:3	193	48:1–20	35
43:9	193	48:1–7	9
43:11	170	48:3–4	132, 162
43:17b	190	48:7	202
43:19	190	48:8–20	9
43:32	191	48:15–16	9–10, 220
44:1–34	34	48:16	10, 14, 29, 97, 202
44:5	191	48:16b	10
44:7	192	48:19	64
44:9	192	48:20	10
44:10	192	48:21–22	9, 35
44:31	193	48:22	156, 202, 207
44:33	193	49:1–28	35
45:1–28	34	49:22	80
45:2	195	49:29—50:14	22, 35
45:3	169	49:29–33	22
45:16	194	49:29–31	18
46	196	50:1–14	17
46:1–7	34	50:1–11	22
46:4	208	50:7	208
46:8–27	5, 34	50:10	3
46:12	18	50:12	22

Index of Ancient Documents

50:13	18, 22	**Judges**	
50:14	22	5:7	71
50:15–21	17, 23, 35	5:9	76
50:22–26	17, 23, 35	8:30	106
50:23	202	9:2	136
50:25	203, 209	13:8	117
		13:9	117
Exodus		14	136
1:1	197	14:18	136
1:5	106	19	89
2:7	113	19:22	89
3:9	87		
3:18	101	**1 Samuel**	
13:19	23, 203, 209, 210	1:19b	96
22:11	148, 228	2:21	96
22:15	112	8:7	97
22:16	113	13:5	76
		16:12	118
Numbers		16:22	184
21:18	123	17:14	118
22:30	10, 203	17:46	180
24:9	205	20:6	24
24:9b	129	25:23	202
28	4, 5	31:13	22–23, 100, 208
29	4, 5		
31:9	160	**2 Samuel**	
		1:17–26	208
Deuteronomy		2:1–7	18
4:26	106	2:4	18
5:15	228	5:1	136
7:3	158	5:5	18
21:15–17	137	8:13	167
22:22	93	8:14	167
30:19	106	11:2	120
31:28	106	12:9	95
32:1	106	12:15	18, 173
		13:12	157
Joshua		13:15	137
24:29	209	13:18	168
24:32	23, 210	14:17	16, 43, 146
		14:20	16, 43, 146

Index of Ancient Documents

15:7–12	18
19:13	136
19:14	136
19:35	115, 199
21:1–13	152
21:3	152
21:10–14	15, 23
24:18–25	104

1 Kings

11:14–22	167
18:24–26	123
18:26	123
22:1–4	149

2 Kings

4:16	85
25:27	179

Isaiah

1:2	106
5:7	87
7:14	108
14:4–21	14
14:20	97
20:4	186

Jeremiah

4:23	37
16:1–13	219
16:1–9	23
16:5	23
40:4	193

Ezekiel

14:13–20	19
19:1–9	205
28	48
28:3	19

Amos

3:2	86
9:7	65

Psalms

45	136
68:4	128
78:67–68	19
133:1	72

Job

1:3	121
4:19	42, 54
10:9	42, 47
11:12	80
24:5	80
42:11	156
45	136

Proverbs

6:35	91, 95, 152
8	100
9	100
16:14	152
16:15	152

Ruth

	172
1:1	74
4:13–22	18
4:14	14, 97
4:18–22	30
4:18	18

1 Chronicles

1:32	114
1:43–51	167
5:1	204
16:3	89
21:22	104
21:24	104

Index of Ancient Documents

2 Chronicles
3:1 100
21:3 115
35:24 183

New Testament

Luke
1:59 47
2:21 47

Romans
5:12–14 229

Rabbinic Writings

Babylonian Talmud,
Baba bathra
14b–15a 3

Early Christian Writings

Origin, *Contra Celsum*
IV,42 3

Index of Names

Alter, Robert, xiii, 7, 27–29, 233
Altmann, Alexander, 234
Astour, Michael C., 13, 233
Astruc, Jean, 3
Belluck, Pam, 222, 233
Bloch-Smith, Elizabeth, 9, 233
Bordreuil, Pierre, 12, 233
Braudel, Fernand, 25, 233
Brueggemann, Walter, 233
Bryan, William Jennings, 224
Buber, Martin, 27, 51, 203, 210, 233
Cassuto, Umberto, 49, 54, 233
Celsus, 3
Courtois, Jacques-Claude, 234
Cowley, A. E., 234
Dahood, Mitchell, 23, 234
Darwin, Charles, ix
Davies, Philip R., xiii, 5
de Moor, Johannes C., 14, 234
Donner, Herbert, 234
Eiseley, Loren C., ix, 222, 234
Elsner, Alan, 222, 234
Ewald, Heinrich, 3
Finkelstein, J. J., 13, 234
Fishbane, Michael, 235
Fisher, Daniel C., x
Fisher, Judith P., x
Fisher, Loren R., 5, 7, 21, 28, 29, 38, 94, 110, 115, 121, 134, 211, 216, 226, 227, 234, 236
Fox, Everett, xiii, 27–29, 233, 234
Funk, Robert W., x
Gaster, Theodor H., 19, 20, 177, 234
Geddes, Alexander

Gesenius, Wilhelm, xv, 2, 53, 234
Gilmore, David D., 25, 234
Goody, Jack, 158, 234
Gordon, Cyrus H., ix, xvi, 8, 26, 42, 78, 121, 128, 129, 146, 158, 218, 234
Goren, Yuval, xi, 236
Gould, Stephen Jay, 221, 224, 226, 235
Graf, Karl Heinrich, 3
Greenspahn, Frederick E., 225–26, 235
Hallo, William W., xv, 235
Hanson, K. C., x, 140, 158, 235
Hanson, Robert W., 223, 235
Hendel, Ronald S., 235
Hoffner, Harry A., 234
Holden, Constance, 221, 235
Horden, Peregrine, 25, 235
Horowitz, Wayne, xi, 236
Hupfeld, Hermann, 3
Hyers, Conrad, 225, 235
Ibn Ezra, Abraham, 3
Jacobsen, Thorkild, 8, 37, 226, 235
Jolly, E. Grady, Judge, 223, 235
Kautzsch, Emil, xv, 234
Kermode, Frank, 233
Kuenen, Abraham, 4
Kilmer, Anne Draffkorn, 54, 235
Kitchen, K. A., 13, 235
Knoppers, Gary N., 5, 212, 235
Lambert, W. G., xv, 16, 235
Laroche, Emmanuel, 236

Index of Names

Lemche, Niels Peter, xii–xiv, 5, 6, 14, 211–20
Levine, Baruch A., 12, 236
Lewis, Theodore J., 9, 10, 233, 236
Lichtheim, Miriam, 9, 195, 217–20, 236
Madison, James, 222, 236
Mazar, Benjamin, 7, 236
Mazar, Eilat, xi–xii, 236
Miller, Patrick D., Jr., 23, 236
Moran, William L., xii, 94, 236
Murphy, Joanne M., 9, 236,
Origen, 3
Oshima, Takayoshi, xi–xii, 236
Overton, William R., 223–24
Pardee, Dennis, 12, 233
Pope, Marvin H., xv, 80, 236
Porphyry, 3
Pritchard, James B., 236
Purcell, Nicholas, 25, 235
Rad, Gerhard von, 236
Rendsburg, Gary A., 8, 235, 236
Reuss, Edouard, 3
Rice, S., 237
Röllig, Wolfgang, xvi, 234
Rosenwald, Lawrence, 233

Rosenzweig, Franz, xv, 27, 51, 203, 210, 233
Rummel, Stan, ix, xvi, 7, 21, 237
Sarna, Nahum M., xvi, 100, 113, 141, 204, 237
Schaeffer, Claude F. A., 236
Schmidt, Brian B., 9, 237
Sheldon, Jane, x
Skinner, John, 237
Smith, J. M. Powis, 233
Smith, Mark S., 9, 237
Streck, Maximilian, 15, 237
Tambiah, Stanley, 158, 234
Tarragon, Jean-Michel de, 12, 236
Thompson, Thomas L., xiii, 5
Tov, Emanuel, 235
Van Seters, John, 4, 8, 14, 213, 237
Varro, Marcus Terentius, 22, 237
Vater, Johann Severin, 3
Virolleaud, Charles, 78, 236
Wellhausen, Julisu, 4
Westermann, Claus, 10, 126, 127, 157, 237
Wette, W. M. L. de, 3
Whaley, Betty Lou, x
Whitehead, Alfred North, 221, 237

www.ingramcontent.com/pod-product-compliance
Lightning Source LLC
Chambersburg PA
CBHW031725230426
43669CB00007B/247